So present, so invisible

David Campany

So present, so invisible

Conversations on photography

Broomberg & Chanarin, Daniel Blaufuks, Robert Cumming,
LaToya Ruby Frazier, Lewis Baltz, John Stezaker, Paul Graham,
Rut Blees Luxemburg, Jeff Wall, Lucas Blalock, Susan Meiselas,
Victor Burgin, William Klein, Stephen Shore

contrasto

Contrasto®
is an editorial trademark of

Via Nizza, 56
00198 Roma
www.contrastobooks.com

ISBN: 978-88-6965-741-2

Front cover:
Stephen Shore, I-8, Yuma, Arizona, September 23, 1974.

Contents

David Campany
Introduction

Photography is the easiest thing to talk about, and for that reason it can be the most difficult. There is a lot of casual chat about it, just as there is a lot of casual photography. But there have always been articulate voices, able to see past the obvious, around the distracting, and through the trivial to say something about the more profound aspects of the medium.

Many of those voices have belonged to image makers. For one reason or another (it might have something to do with the close interplay of photography and words in modern culture), the world of serious photography has been noticeably blessed with articulate practitioners. This has been the case as far back as William Henry Fox Talbot, whose written insights into the implications of the medium that he was in the process of inventing remain as illuminating and readable now as they were in the 1840s.

As a twenty-year old student first encountering the range of thinking about photography and culture, I looked for books of conversations. Paul Hill & Thomas Cooper's *Dialogue with Photography* (1979), Barbaralee Diamonstein's *Visions and Images* (1982), and Pat Booth's *Master Photographers* (1983) introduced me to the thoughts of what seemed at the time like all the great photographers of the twentieth century. The format of the conversation had a special appeal. When "theory" seemed a little intimidating, particularly the French thought that really shaped me intellectually, I would search for published exchanges with the thinkers that mattered. Jacques Derrida, Julia Kristeva, Michel Foucault and Roland Barthes seemed much more approachable when they were talking freely to others, and not addressing *me*. Even if those conversations were just as challenging, there was something about the format that was freeing. I felt I was eavesdropping. Obviously, a published conversation is a rhetorical trick. It's still words on a page, after all. But if it works, it works.

I am often invited by artists and photographers to write about their practice, usually for an exhibition catalogue or book of their work. Every now and then I get the feeling that a conversation would be better. I never purposefully "research" in advance, the way a journalist might. Rather, the desire to converse emerges from the balance between already knowing enough, and wanting to discover more. I never prepare questions in advance either. I am not inclined to interrogate, although as you will see, the best moments come when both parties are really pushing and clarifying each other's thinking.

In a conversation, there is close connection between thought and speech. I think this is so whether it is happening face-to face in real time, via Skype, on the telephone or even via email. You will find examples of them all here, and I would like to think it is not so easy to tell the difference. The exchanges with Jeff Wall, Victor Burgin and Stephen Shore, for example, read as if those artists were committing highly considered thoughts directly to the page, when in fact this is how they speak about their work. My conversation with Lucas Blalock is quite flowing and spontaneous, like an easy verbal to and fro, but it was conducted by email, and intermittently over several weeks. The conversation with Rut Blees Luxemburg was recorded as we walked through the London night, from dusk to dawn.

Whether long or short, nearly all these conversations were open-ended. Neither party knew where we might go or where things would end up. For me, that is always the real value of a conversation, as opposed to an interview (or worse, a questionnaire). There is risk and excitement, a sense of mutual exploration and speculation. And somewhere in the back of my mind I guess I was trying to facilitate the kind of informative and provocative exchanges would have held the attention of my twenty-year old self.

For all the variety of voices here, each photographer has addressed the question of how they understand their medium. That understanding might be technical, philosophical, aesthetic, social, or a combination of these. Putting the voices together, you might get a good working definition of photography. At the same time, you might end up with a bunch of contradictions and paradoxes. Maybe that is all we can hope for from photography, because if it is a medium at all, it is one that has eluded any fixed or satisfying definition. And perhaps this is why photography remains so rewarding. Unlike so many other inventions of the nineteenth century, this one did not die. It has renewed itself constantly. Churning, transforming, mutating and reimagining itself. This is the source of its fascination.

Adam Broomberg and **Oliver Chanarin** have worked together for over two decades. The collaboration began with their pioneering editorial role at *Colors* magazine, and has since included work in photography, film, video, installation, performance and image appropriation. Always attuned to the political resonances of objects, people, places and moments in history, they have developed many new kinds of allegorical practice. Often weaving images and texts into complex dialogues, their ground-breaking book projects – including *War Primer II*, *The Holy Bible*, *Ghetto*, *fig.*, and *Chicago* – are among the most remarkable and influential artists' publications of recent years.

My conversation with Broomberg & Chanarin took place on the occasion of one of their richest and most playful projects. *Alias*, presented at Krakow Photomonth, Poland in 2011, was an exploration of creative identity. What is the relationship between an artist's sense of self and the art he or she might make? Operating as a duo, this is something they must consider all the time. They make work that is more than the sum of the two of them, and maybe it is made by a third, imaginary subject that is neither of them. Moreover, for this project they also acted as curators, inviting artists and writers to invent artistic personas that would then make the work for a series of exhibitions around the city of Krakow.

Broomberg & Chanarin

The starting point for your latest curatorial project, called *ALIAS*, is the Portuguese writer Fernando Pessoa's literary concept of the "heteronym" – a fictitious persona invented to enable writing or creation from a new perspective. For Pessoa it was a kind of "knight's move" to escape habit, even to mock the notion of "signature style". You have invited twenty-three writers to collaborate with artists, to invent heteronyms that then make art. Do you know what you're getting yourselves into?
Yes, trouble. But when we began our research we quickly discovered that the fictional persona was and still is a more common strategy in modern and contemporary art than we'd first imagined. We began with Pessoa as you've mentioned, and also the fictional anthology *Nazi Literatures of the Americas* by Roberto Bolano. Both of them showed us just how helpful the fictitious persona can be when exploring moral and political territory too terrifying to honestly explore in your own skin. That led us to the work of Brian O'Doherty, author of *Inside the White Cube*, who for over 30 years made work under the name of Patrick Ireland.

Brian invented Patrick Ireland after the Bloody Sunday massacres in 1972 and made a pledge to continue to inhabit this "heteronym" (or "non-existent acquaintances" as Pessoa described them) until the British withdrew from Northern Ireland. Patrick was finally buried in 2008, in a real grave under the lawn of the Irish Museum of Modern Art, Dublin, following the signing of the Good Friday Agreement. We'll be showing some of Patrick's work in Krakow.

We quickly began accumulating other examples of artists who have engaged this strategy – Marcel Duchamp (as Rrose Sélavy), Sophie Calle (as Paul Auster's Maria), Walid Raad (as The Atlas Group), Richard Prince (as John Dogg), Alec Soth (as Lester B. Morrison), Simon Fujiwara (as his father), William Kentridge (as Kentridge

vs Kentridge), Joe Scanlan (as Donnell Woolford) and Christian Jankowski (as a dove). To mention just a few. They will all be in a survey show at the remarkable brutalist Bunkier Sztuki Museum in the centre of Krakow.
"We never disembark from ourselves" complained Pessoa. And we wanted to give artists a chance to do exactly this... to disembark from themselves. So as you say we've asked writers and artists to collaborate. The writer's task was to invent a fictional character and the artist was required to inhabit this person and make their work. There are 23 commissions in all. They will be dotted around different spaces around Krakow including a church crypt, the town's central medieval tower and in a wing of the brand new Museum of Contemporary Art (MOCAK) built on the site of the Schindler factory. We didn't realize how difficult this task was going to be for the artists. Luckily! It would be rather depressing if an artist were able to effortlessly abandon their political, aesthetic or moral concerns.
Yet most of the people we approached jumped at the opportunity to be somebody else. To break from the exhausting task of being themselves. And to break from their own familiar artistic practice. We have the sense that artists are increasingly being forced to behave more and more like brands, and we wanted to offer some resistance to this tendency, to the tyranny of the professional curators!

Did you have a "hit-list" of artists to invite?
One of the first artists we approached was David Goldblatt, the South African photographer infamous for his rigorous and uncompromising conceptual approach to documenting South Africa in a career that now spans over 60 years. Although the country has gone through the most fundamental seismic changes to its DNA, David's theoretical, moral and aesthetic approach to documenting it has remained unnervingly consistent. Here was a chance, as in the case of all the artists we selected, to upset that consistency. David's first question in reply to our invitation was "how long do I have?" "Three months" we replied. "That's not enough time" he insisted. "But you don't know who you will be, David".

When the show is presented will it be declared who the "real" artists/writers are? Or will these heteronyms be given the op-

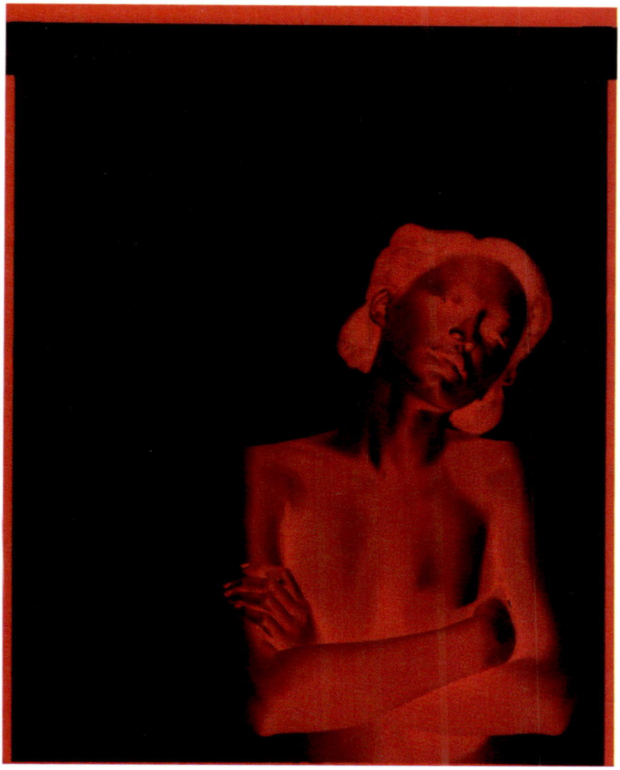

Dora Fobert, *Maria*, from the archive of Adela K, circa 1942

portunity to stand on their own two feet? In other words, are you interested in this as an exercise or as a potential for a genuine departure? I recall Michel Foucault once calling for all writing to be published anonymously for a year, so that readers would have to judge each text on its own merit, not in terms of a known quantity or a track record. Of course some texts are produced and consumed anonymously (advertising slogans and newspaper editorials) while other forms of writing (such as the novel) don't seem to be able to shake of what he called the "author function". Despite its history of pseudo-

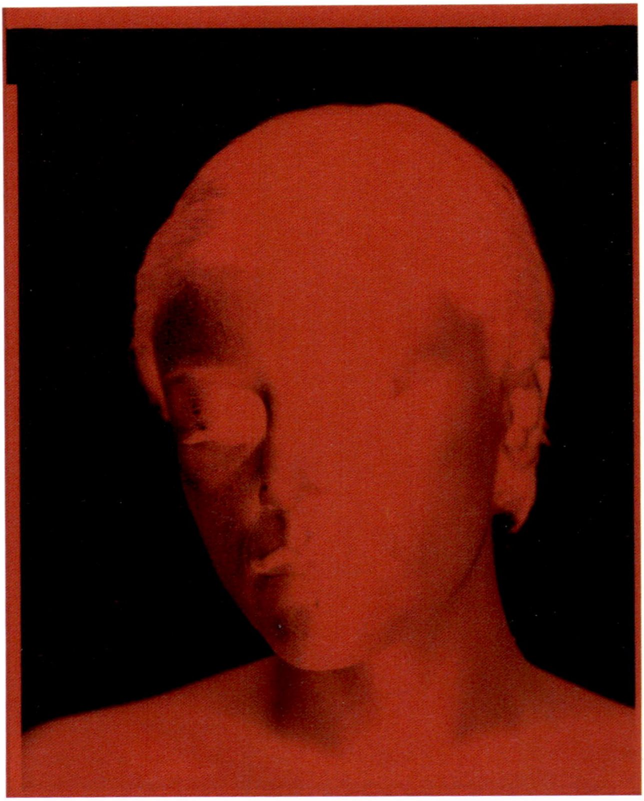

Dora Fobert, *Maria*, from the archive of Adela K, circa 1942

nyms and heteronyms art doesn't seem to be a field in which either makers or audiences are comfortable with the erasure of the author. They don't mind the idea of authorship being a little elastic, or put in temporary jeopardy, but they do mind if the elastic snaps all together. Can this be overcome?
We argued back and forth about this and finally decided to keep the identities of the real artists and writers out of the equation. Our goal was for a complete separation of the real and fictional artist – we knew the whole process would be short circuited by having the true

identity revealed immediately. At the same time we didn't want it to turn into a superficial game of who did what. If the exercise is a success (if the artists are able to abandon their usual mode of production for a short while) then you should never be able to match up the heteronym and the real artist. This remains to be seen. The festival organizers – Karol Hordziej and Tomasz Gutkowski among others – have taken a big risk in supporting our experiment. And in many ways it is an experiment that is set up to fail. We are willing it to fail. As we said before, it would be worrying if we were able to so completely abandon our own practice.
But this is turning into an interview. We want to ask you a question… as you are one of the commissioned writers/artists, how have you found the process? Were you able to overcome your own logic?

Respecting your spirit of separation, I'll answer without revealing too much about the work Polly Braden and I have been making. Like you two, we have made work jointly in the past and in many ways I think good collaborations involve the invention of a third artistic identity, not unlike a heteronym, able to produce work that is more than the sum of its parts, work that would not have been made by either individual alone (somehow we imagined this was part of your attraction to the idea). So on that level it's not been such a leap. We also decided to scramble the division between "writer" and "artist". I am somewhat shaped by a generation of people who fought very hard to be both, Polly less so, but we concocted our heteronymic artist together and we're making the art together. Without getting all post-structural we find making and thinking art fairly heterogeneous anyway. My own art doesn't really have a "signature style", and with my writing I always feel like I'm trying on new hats, new forms. Likewise, Polly is "known" for certain kinds of observational photography, but she's also collaborated with other artists to photograph their performances and installations, and also works with journalists. Maybe this is because we're both involved with photography primarily, which is such a dispersed, promiscuous medium belonging to everybody and nobody. But we're curious to see how others have responded to your invitation.

Us too! We have teamed up some remarkable and odd couples; Gabriel Orozco has been working with the oncologist and author of *The Emperor of all Maladies* (a biography of cancer) Siddhartha Mukhajee. Jeremy Deller has been working with author Jennifer Higgie, while Johan Grimonprez is taking on Pessoa himself.
This is traditionally a photography festival, but don't expect just photographs. We have been less concerned with presenting photographs as work that engages with the politics of the medium. In our central exhibition in the Bunkier Sztuki we are "using" photography rather than showing photographs. Our strategy is to print and display installation photographs of all of the works featured, rather than the originals. It's a celebration of flatness, you could say, in which the installation photograph is elevated to the status of a work in itself. Where possible they will be printed to a one to one scale! And we will not be showing original videos either, but so-called "viewing copies" which are low resolution. When installation photographs are not available, we are also using the "official views" of objects. This term "Official View" is curious. It's used by the Tate Modern archive to describe photographs of works of art approved by the artists or curators. It's a strategy that actually arose out of financial constraints, but one that we've come to love.

Maybe Walter Benjamin was right: the significance of "art photography" will always be overshadowed by the significance of the "photography of art". On the subject of copies of copies, did you invent a heteronym who then selected the artists and writers, or did you do it "yourselves"? Maybe you shouldn't answer that one.
Yes, the curators are fictional too.

It's interesting that, historically, photography has always emerged as the crucial medium in discussions not just about reproduction and originality, but also about authorship, anonymity, authenticity, agency, the status of the document, quotation, appropriation, value, democracy, dissemination and so forth. It's the medium that prompted art to rethink what's at stake in those concepts but it has also proved to be the medium best placed to articulate and express them too.

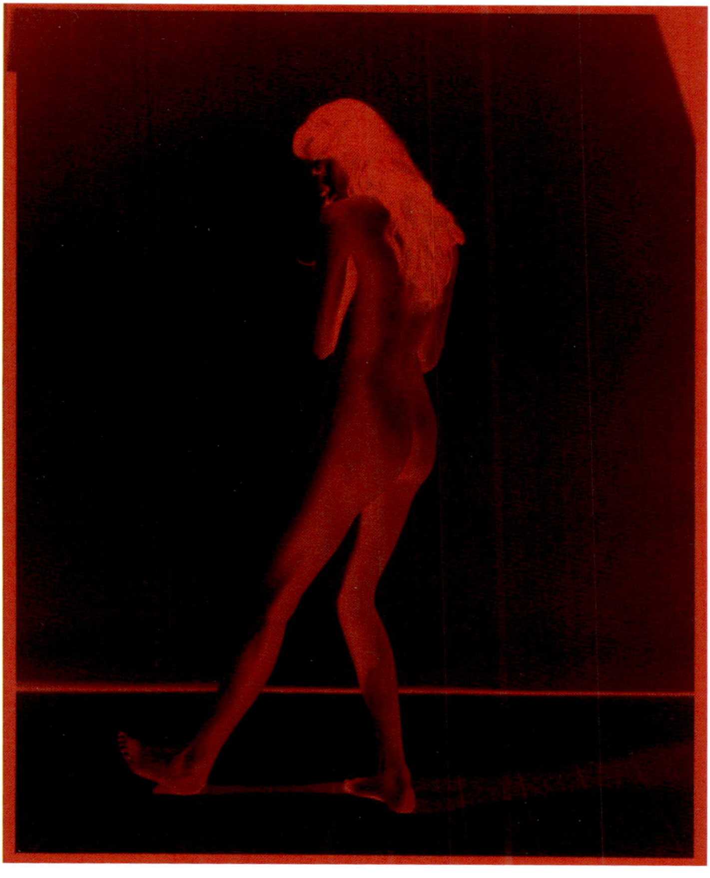

Dora Fobert, *Maria*, from the archive of Adela K, circa 1942

Daniel Blaufuks' prolific work in photography, film and writing has been a sustained exploration of the role of the image in our understanding of time, memory and place. His points of departure are often moments in either political history or photographic history. From small beginnings Blaufuks weaves complex projects that function as allegories of our often highly contradictory expectations of photographs, and our fraught reliance upon them.

Blaufuks has a deep interest of the history of photography, and the cultural and technological transformations that continue to shape it. His thinking is nimble, and his artworks are often playful, but taken together they amount to a profound reflection upon the past as it bears upon the present. This conversation began as an open-ended email exchange. It takes in everything from W.B. Sebald to the Internet, from Eadweard Muybridge to Jean-Luc Godard and Chris Marker. It was first published in Blaufuks' book *Works on Memory: selected writings and images*, 2011.

Daniel Blaufuks

Your work in photography varies a great deal from project to project, but I sense the connecting themes are "memory" and "history". Photography "as" memory and history. The photography "of" memory and history. And the memory and history "of" photography. You explore and express these themes in different ways.
More broadly the medium of photography has been understood by popular culture as having special relation to memory and history. Against this runs a more ambivalent line of thinking – from Walter Benjamin to Roland Barthes – that sees photography as something that comes to disturb the very concepts of memory and history, revealing them to be constructs, not "natural". Could you say a little about this in relation to your own photography?
Yes, I like to vary my ways of working, as I am also interested in different ways of showing images, although I think my approach to photography, or film, is always more or less the same. And yes, I am very interested in memory and history, or, rather histories, personal memories against the historical background. To try to answer your question, I think the medium, unlike most other mediums, has indeed a strong responsibility in these fields, as it creates its own constructions and meanings of reality, past or present. So, I am very aware of the importance of "reading" an image, understanding its possible layers and connections, perceiving that the family snapshot or the war image are indeed not "natural", but are as close as we get sometimes to the information lying within. That is why I am interested in documentary film, as well, having made some myself, although I consider them and my photographic work full of subjective meanings. Maybe Barthes and Benjamin would approve of that.

Looking across the range of your work, I don't so much see a common theme as a common tension. It's quite a productive, animating tension between the desire to know and the desire to speculate. The "what is" and the "what if?". You're something of a historian, a detective even, but there's also a very playful streak. Does this make sense, does it ring true with you?
Well, not long ago someone, a recent acquaintance who didn't know my work very well, called me "the curious researcher", which I took as a wonderful compliment. I am indeed someone interested in various subjects, and obviously that interest will find its way into the work, sometimes even undesired. And I do like to play, to follow a direction that some life-turn or event is leading me to. Also I don't feel, like many other artists do, that I do have to stick to one constrained subject or way of working. I prefer to imagine that I am sometimes "writing" poetry and other times fiction or essays, some more profound, some more playful. But I do know that at the heart of every project I do, the underlying theme is my interest in memory and how we deal with it.

Is it photography itself that is being memorialized in your projects, a kind of working through of the privileged place once given to the photographic image as a token of the past? I ask this because my students, and more so my young children don't seem to have this relation to photography. They see it more as a token of exchange than of memory. There's not that great endowment of the still image with the weight of history. For example your book *Terezín* begins with an image of a room you saw in a book by the writer W.G. Sebald and ends with you having followed its threads to a wartime ghetto. Reading it, I felt two things. The first was the sensation of being with a "curious researcher", as your friend put it. The second was a realization of the immense historical burden placed on the still image, which it can barely carry.
But so is text or even a single word burdened. We can regard it as a simple note or as a powerful transmission device.
Photography is an alphabet, so to speak, which contains many possibilities of depth. I agree, although our relation with the medium is quickly changing, as it becomes more and more fluid, not only in

the making through digital cameras, but in easy sharing through the internet. But not every piece of writing is necessarily literature, and not every photograph needs to carry that burden you mentioned. The question is, if we are capable of reading the language the photographer is writing, is it a song or an aria? Cinema, in a way, is going through the same period of interrogation, as we lose the habit of seeing it on screens and among strangers, and therefore are losing the reverence we once had for it. I cannot work with photography ignoring its ancient power of becoming something like an instant memory of the present. So I think I am also constantly questioning that same power, that lost aura.

In many of your projects that questioning takes the form of a movement, often restless, cursive and curious between one image and the next and the one after that. Can you say something about this?
I am not interested at all in the single image, but in the sequence or flux of images, in a kind of cinematic prose. So, while shooting one image I tend to be thinking of the previous one, which does not mean that in the end this will work out. Same with my video work: I have an idea, but not the final product in my head. That will hopefully evolve from the shooting, the editing and the thinking while doing it. In the editing, I can change everything, by not only sequencing it, but most of all by choosing and erasing whole sequences. As with video.

It's possible that editing and assembly are more integral to film and video than they are to photography. But it's fascinating how photography became a modern medium in the 1920s and 30s through a suspicion of, or a need to exceed the single image.
I think of August Sander: "A successful photo is only a preliminary step toward the intelligent use of photography... Photography is like a mosaic that becomes a synthesis only when it is presented en masse"; or Walker Evans: "After knowing what to take you have to do the editing", etc. etc. This is still the dominant attitude – very few contemporary photographers make and present images in isolation. Suites, series, ar-

chives, albums, typologies, montages, collages, juxtapositions. Painters never felt this so strongly. Are there connections for you between memory and this multiplicity in photography?
Very few photographs function entirely on their own, I would think, apart from advertising, fashion or news photography. The original image from *Terezín* in the Sebald book (by Dirk Reinartz) is very strong by itself, but I was unable to halt there, I needed to understand and later work on the context. We can present a single image of a dead soldier and elaborate a long speech on the memory of war and of private suffering just from that, but memories are so much more complex than a single vision. How many images do we see alone during one day? And how many points of view from the same subject? Memories are images from images from images. Do we need memories? Do we need photography to remind us of memory? I don't know.
Also, by creating work, we are creating new memories. An image is a memory of something the photographer saw and that is about to be imprinted on the memory (long lasting or probably not) of the viewer. That is also one of the paradoxes of photography, we are actually seeing in our present something that someone saw in the past and eventually others will see in the future. We could say the same of painting, but the fact that in photography reality does not undergo any major transfiguration or construction (like in cinema), makes this eerier.

I agree that the isolated image is always a little eerie. But this is because the stilling and muting of the world is actually a major transfiguration. But might it be that very few photographs function on their own because they've not been allowed to?
You are entirely right about the transfiguration of the world through muting and stilling. But so is the black and white photograph that we take for the absolute truth, more even than the colour image. Generally we do not perceive this transformation, same with photographs in books or magazines. We do not consider that the real object has a proper size and framing defined by the artist. We take the reproduction for the truth, which is something that does not happen with the reproduction of paintings, where we know instinc-

tively there is somewhere an original. Agnés Varda talked in her last film about the fact that her generation saw most of the paintings in reproductions in black and white, so that they had to add mentally the colours to it.

That reminds me of André Malraux's remark on the way photography invented modern art history: "Baudelaire never set eyes on the masterpieces of El Greco, Michelangelo, Masaccio, Piero della Francesca or Grunewald; [...] What had he seen? What (until 1900) had been seen by all those writers whose views on art still impress us as revealing and important". But counter to that strong critique, I think of all those moments when photography or film really has permitted us knowledge of the world, or even allowed us to contemplate it. How do we balance such things?
I don't know. Eventually by learning how to read images and trying to understand their meaning and poetry, more than their actual information.

Yes, meaning and poetry. We are circling around the central tension in photography between "artwork" and "document". It's certainly a tension that you dramatize in much of your work. Many of your most striking projects contain images of what we might call the "apparatus" of the analogue archive – the library, the postcard, the hand-written letter, celluloid film frames, files of various kinds, physical traces left behind, monuments and memorial sites. Put together they add up to an inventory of the "analogue" archive. There is a kind of politicized melancholy at work here, I sense. A kind of taking stock within reach of the spectre of the digital with its very different regime of the visual (I think of the difference between the hand-written letter and email, between the filing cabinet and the folder on a computer hard drive, etc...). The digital may produce infinitely more images but its apparatus is not so photogenic, slipping away from the visual register into the virtual. At the same time, we humans remain irreducibly physical beings with physical needs, analogue needs if you like...

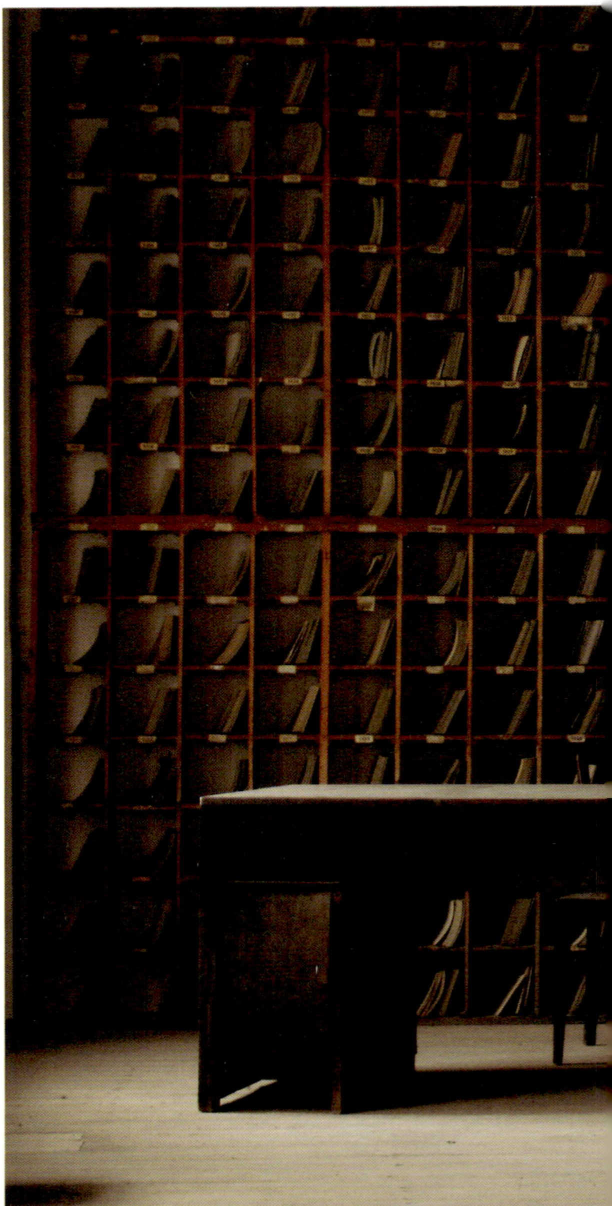

Daniel Blaufuks,
Untitled, from *Terezín*, 2007

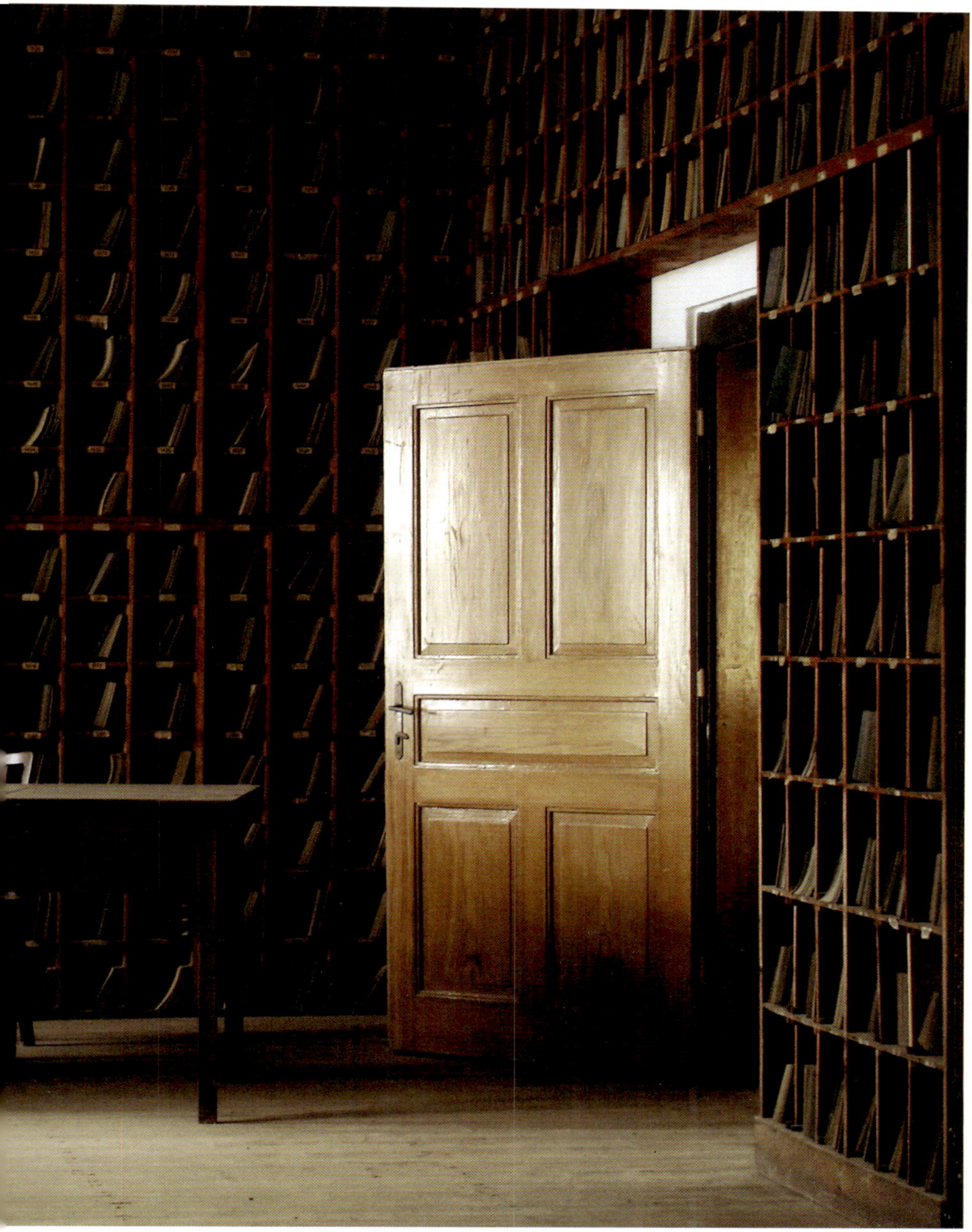

I am very interested in the ways not only photography and film are changing, but also the archives and, obviously, our memory. I am going to sound old now, but I do come from a time when we kept letters, photos, tickets, notes, etc. as mementos or souvenirs from something or someone special. Some people still do that, because they need to have things that are touchable and not virtual. But the fact is that most of our communication now is lost in computers and hard drives and it will be interesting to see how historians deal with that in the future. I was recently in an archive in Germany that contains millions of files, lists and objects from the concentration camps. I was curious to see how such an enormous event could be stored inside files, cabinets and rooms. It was an amazing experience to see the actual vastness of it. In the future memory will be different, not better or worse, but different.

Is this change in the nature or register of memory your biggest challenge as an artist? And have you noticed the change over the decades you have been making work?
I cannot answer that. But I am sure that the fact that I started out in the "analogue days" and made a transition to digital is important to my work.
I had worked a lot with instant cameras, made Polaroid diaries, so that the velocity of the digital image made sense to me from the start, but the way of achieving, distributing and perceiving a photograph has changed and therefore became a major issue in the process, parallel to the disappearance of the traditional snapshot on paper or the family photo album. You cannot ignore these occurrences.

The discourse of art implicitly demands that artworks stay pretty much the same, that they last for a long time and that they circulate under declared authorship. This seems to be in marked contrast to the promiscuous production, dissemination and ephemerality so often associated with the digital era. In other words, do you see your own artworks becoming documents of a moment of transition?
Not really, that would be too presumptuous. If they become moments of thought when they are seen, even if only for a tiny fraction

of time, I am happy. Also I think works don't stay the same, with time they gain or lose meanings and layers, even if unintended by the artist.

Some of your projects are very compact and minimal – small series of images, found photos, found objects, short films. Others are much more substantial and involved. Is the scope of a project apparent and obvious to you early on in the process? And how are projects brought to their final form? Perhaps you could describe the genesis of some of your works.
The best example might be *Terezín*, which started out as an intriguing photograph in a book by Sebald. I thought that the theatrical image of what seemed to be an office with desks and file cabinets had a lot to do with what I was doing and thinking at the time.
A few years later I followed my instinct and flew with air miles to Prague to visit Theresienstadt. Still, I was thinking I would copy that image, if I find the place it was taken and I would integrate the image in some project I was working on, the idea of the archive. But then it started to fascinate me more and more and I started to research, I found out about the fake documentary done there by the Nazis and so forth. So in a way, I followed the project that was always ahead of me. Similarly in other projects: the *Album* grew, because it only made sense as a bulk of objects, a bulk of memory of an unknown collector; others shrink, because it does not seem that they get more interesting by size. Sometimes I feel you can say everything with one image, sometimes I need a film with sound and chronology…

It seemed for a while there was something of a split in photographic art, between those who made photographs and those who preferred to work exclusively with found images. You move very fluidly between the two, often mixing them up. Do you have the same attitude to photographs you have taken and photographs you have found and decided to incorporate into your work? Or are they all just "images", first and last?
Found images or found footage have a special "aura", that is unattainable by photographs I take.
In my documentary *Under Strange Skies* I had the idea of doing just

one shot (the rest of the film is with still images and archive footage). I wanted the film to start with a view of the Jewish cemetery in Lisbon. And then I found that my great-uncle had done that already in 1968 with a Super-8 camera. So I thought it was unnecessary to do it again. Also I like the idea of transmission, and that you give a different meaning to an unrelated snapshot someone did, perhaps with no further intentions. To change the status of the image that you find in the garbage or flea market or, for that matter, in an archive.

Have you made work consisting only of found images? If you have, are the artistic parameters very different?
I have. *Memento Mori* is made from found photographs of tombstones with only a last name on it, no first names nor dates. I have made video work with found footage or from known films. And *Album* is made of found objects, so to speak.
The way of working is not very different, although the images already come with a history that "fresh" images don't have. People react to them differently, as they usually trigger something in your mind, personal or collective memory, because of how they look or where they come from. My own photographs don't have that power from the start.

Can the audience always tell the difference between found images and your images? By that I mean... is the aura you speak of a physical property of the found image or does it result from the suspension of its former use in your redeployment of it? I find "aura" is such a complicated word! Even Walter Benjamin, whose inter-war writings are still vital on the matter, seemed to change his mind as to what aura was for him. But he would certainly be interested in the function played by aura in your re-photographic work. Somehow I've always presumed you're a keen reader of Benjamin...
I would love that Benjamin would be interested in my work, if he was alive. Yes, maybe I should have used a different word, you are right. I think that the knowledge that you are looking at images that have somehow survived and reappeared in the constant flux of images, also with their technical problems, which became kind

of charming in the digital age, makes us look at them differently. Maybe aura for me has obviously something to do with time, but also with failure, scratches, dust, fading colours, etc. We won't have that in the future, will we?

We may not have it in those particular ways, because they're so much a part of "analogue" culture and technology. But the digital has its own failures and I suspect it will have its own unexpected paths towards the auratic. It's not for us to say that it won't, put it that way. After all it was only a few generations back that people were talking about the birth of photography signaling the death of aura. I don't think I can say what forms this new aura will take, but history tells me we shouldn't rule it out altogether.

You might be right, but just the fact that all prints are alike, no dust, no scratch, just pixels, makes it a bit "anti-auratic" from the point of view of today.

This reminds me now of the Persian carpet tradition, where a voluntary mistake is always included in the pattern, because only God can be perfect. The necessity of error or we could even talk about the necessity of being able to be lost in the age of Global Positioning System (GPS), the necessity of boredom in the age of Playstations and so forth.

I agree with you about GPS. Think how much great art, literature and film of the last century was premised on chance encounters and getting lost. Rodenbach's *Bruges La Morte*, Breton's *Nadja*, Hitchcock's *Vertigo*, Situationism, street photography. But I see the voluntary mistakes of the Persian carpet makers in the reverse way, with little to do with fear of offending the Almighty. Might it not be a rather arrogant declaration that perfection is within their grasp? "Even our mistakes are deliberate!"

I sense digital images are just as full of mistakes, or rather quirks of the moment of their making. The passing of time is likely to make them ever more obvious to us. Just look at how image retouching has an aesthetic that has changed dramatically over the last couple of decades.

I like your idea of the arrogance of the carpet makers. But aren't all artists in one way or another arrogant? We create objects, produce images, films and think that the world will be a better place with them and that people need them, if not by possession, at least spiritually. And, fortunately, in the case of a few artists it is true.

Art is for anyone but probably not for everyone. The art that strikes us as arrogant is usually art we don't like or care for. Good art never seems arrogant. I am grateful for good art. But what complicates this is the idea of the work of speculation, of just not knowing whether one's art will reach anyone or mean anything to them. This we can never guarantee. I sense many of your own works are made and operate this way...
I like it if I can establish some kind of dialogue through my work. Some works do that better than others, but it does not mean that they are better or worse. They are just more talkative. But, like any other work based on a mix of instinct, taste and research, this is about trial and error. It is an ongoing process, where all works intertwine and eventually become one. A few years ago I wrote that "I would like my work to cover everything that I am, everything I have seen, everything I want, everything I remember, everything I know, everything that interests me, everything I have done, everything I haven't done, everything I wanted to be".

And the viewer?
The viewer? The viewer is, in a way, responsible for the existence of a mute dialogue, of a trade between him and the work, therefore between him and me. Eventually and hopefully we create a space of silence, of thought, of suspension.

Silence and suspension are very rare commodities these days. You work both in the gallery context and have made quite a number of books over the years. Do you think the wall and the page have different relations to silence and suspension?
The experience between seeing the work on a wall or in a book is totally different. Also the disposition of the viewer varies: in a show he is usually not alone, he is less concentrated. Also books allow a more precise configuration of the work, a swifter flow of the images,

a much wider scope of the project, text if one thinks it's necessary, etc. And I am here talking about books, not catalogues, as there is a huge difference in approach. Catalogues, like exhibitions, have a short life span, but books, on the contrary, are long lasting and become eventually proud possessions. In this sense they are very democratic, as almost everyone can afford a book but not an artwork. And I think, at least in my case, books represent much more what I want with my work, than the single image. And books can be art works in their own right.

Is your interest in memory and the material/ephemeral photograph related to your commitment to the permanence of the book form? Whatever else they are, books always seem to be made "for the record".
First of all it is my love for books that compels me to make them. Then I really think most photographic projects are better served by books than by exhibitions. It's a different medium, probably the most perfect one, and you don't even have to connect it to a power source. Then I love to be able to carry and give my work away through books. And, last but not least, permanence is important, the fact that a book can be retrieved many years later, can be discovered by different people in other parts of the world. If you would choose one human invention, which would it be?

I agree, the book. But it's fascinating how there has been a renaissance of interest in the photographic book in the last decade or so, and books are being made now that are as good as at any time before.
And yet I sense this renaissance has been prompted by other things: a frustration with the limits of the gallery (despite the recent triumph of photography in art) and the displacing of the book by the computer screen... all this has alerted viewers to the specificities, the particularities, of sites and contexts – page, wall, screen.
Yes, I think photographers are more and more looking for other ways to show their work beside hanging images in galleries. There are very interesting projects on the internet as well, fully adapted to the medium and I think we will see more and more work presented

through iPads. I did a show at the Museum of Modern Art in Rio de Janeiro this year, where I showed the images in a double projection, almost as an open book. The images would flow through cuts, jumps and fades, and you would see, if you had the patience, the whole work in an hour. I felt that it was so much more interesting than the usual photographs on the wall, where you need to constrain the number of works because of the size of the space, and also I liked the fact that I was monitoring the viewing time for each image. No fast forward here, either you wanted to see it at my pace or you didn't see it at all.

Yes, I guess specificity is the key term here – the making of work specific to its context or mode of display. We can experience and return to a book or DVD endlessly but a temporary exhibition may produce a unique and memorably intense occasion for seeing and thinking. Books are intended for one person. Or one at a time.
Both cinema and to a lesser extent art are premised on economies of scale that demand multiple simultaneous viewers. As you say, the DVD operates in a hybrid space. I felt this acutely when I watched the DVD of the staged propaganda film included in the back of your book *Terezín*. A film made during the war for a very different audience ends up in a book published in 2010, and played on the laptop upon which I'm writing these words to you.
Well, against my own words, I think that this is the kind of work that will be best viewed in a room with a fair-sized projection and, most of all, an adequate sound volume, because it will bring out specific elements from the original film and from my intervention on it. The details of the decaying skin (film, pellicule) are somehow lost in the small-sized computer screen, and so is the powerful original music that I slowed down, and now sounds like a funeral march. Also it is easier to concentrate on the screen, when you are in a dark room.

I recall when Chris Marker released his CD-ROM *Immemory* in the late 1990s, he spoke of finally, after nearly fifty years, having a format that expressed his thinking, his way of

making films, making photographs, writing. A few years ago I had a conversation with Susan Meiselas. She was just about to republish her book *Carnival Strippers* (1976) and she had the opportunity to include a CD of the sound and voices she had recorded at the time. Such examples show us that while our artistic imagination operates within given practical parameters there are moments when we are making work for a format to come, a context to come.
Chris Marker is a visionary, but there is also always an excitement with new media and new forms of expression. Then again, people reconsider and go back to more traditional mediums. Maybe that is why there has been this recent hype with photobooks, parallel to the appearance of iPads and Kindles, and lots of people, including me, are shooting in Super-8. And you have the wonderful work of Tacita Dean, which can only work with film, and she is making an appeal for its continuity.
Our forms of expression became, alas, much too connected with technology and decisions of company directors. Imagine the outcry if paint or brushes were to be abolished and substituted by iPhones. Film is something you can touch and feel, something that exists, independently from projections or hard drives.

The argument that new technologies do not replace older ones certainly seems to break down the more involved and expensive they become. No, I don't suppose paintbrushes and canvas will become obsolete. 16mm ciné-film almost certainly will. But new technologies do redefine and make newly available work made with older ones. How does the fact that with the internet I can find and buy almost any book ever printed, or locate any film change those objects?
One of the paradoxes of the electronic era is that is it infinitely easier to get our hands on analogue objects such as books, films, vinyl records, old photographs, paper documents and so forth. And you and I are having this exchange via email. How much of the "research" for your projects is conducted online?
Oh, yes, I agree, nothing beats the distribution through the internet. And I do a lot of research on it. I think it's unavoidable and it is, as we all know, very useful. The fact that we can reproduce some-

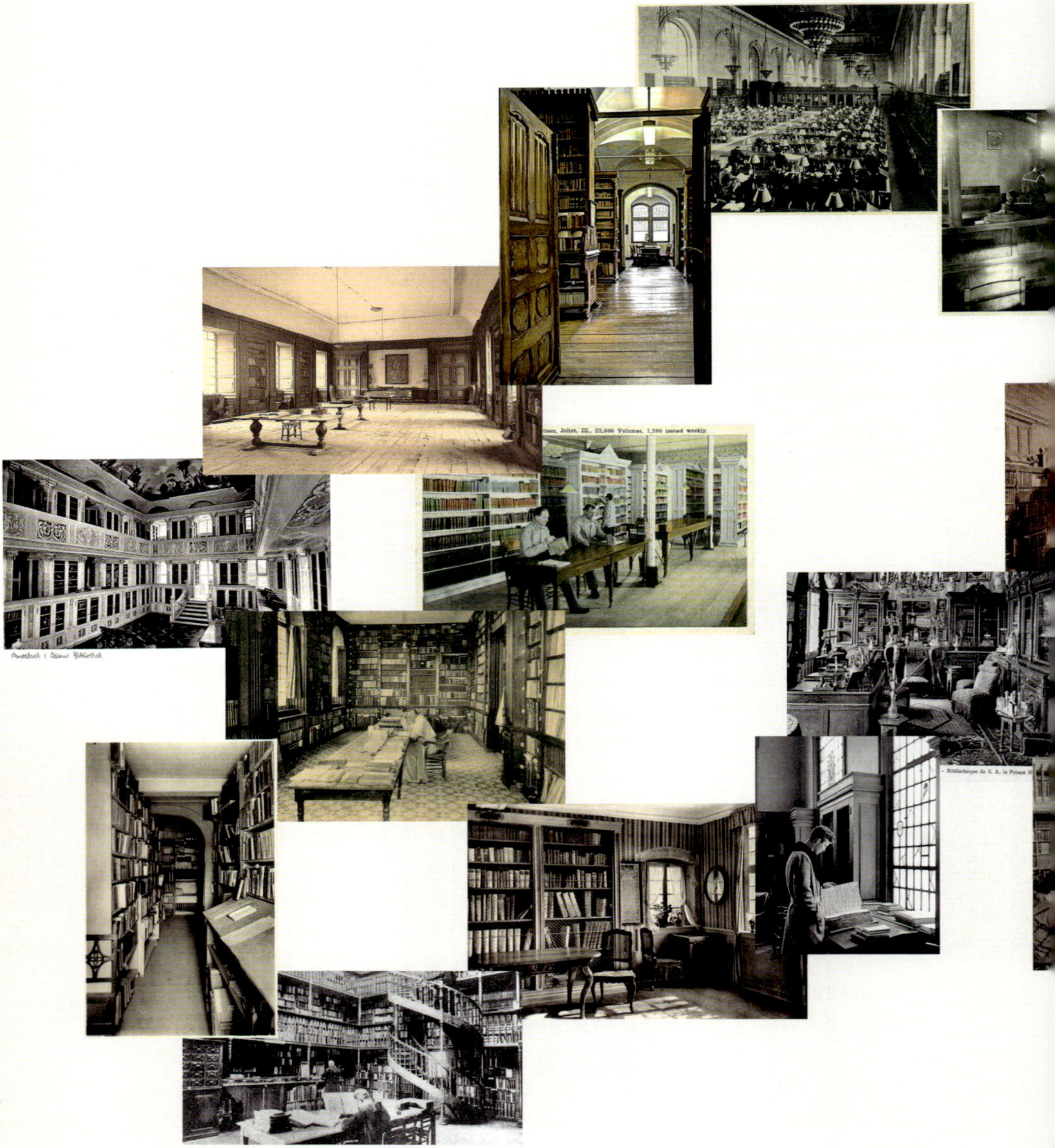

Daniel Blaufuks, Library, from *Constellations*, 2014

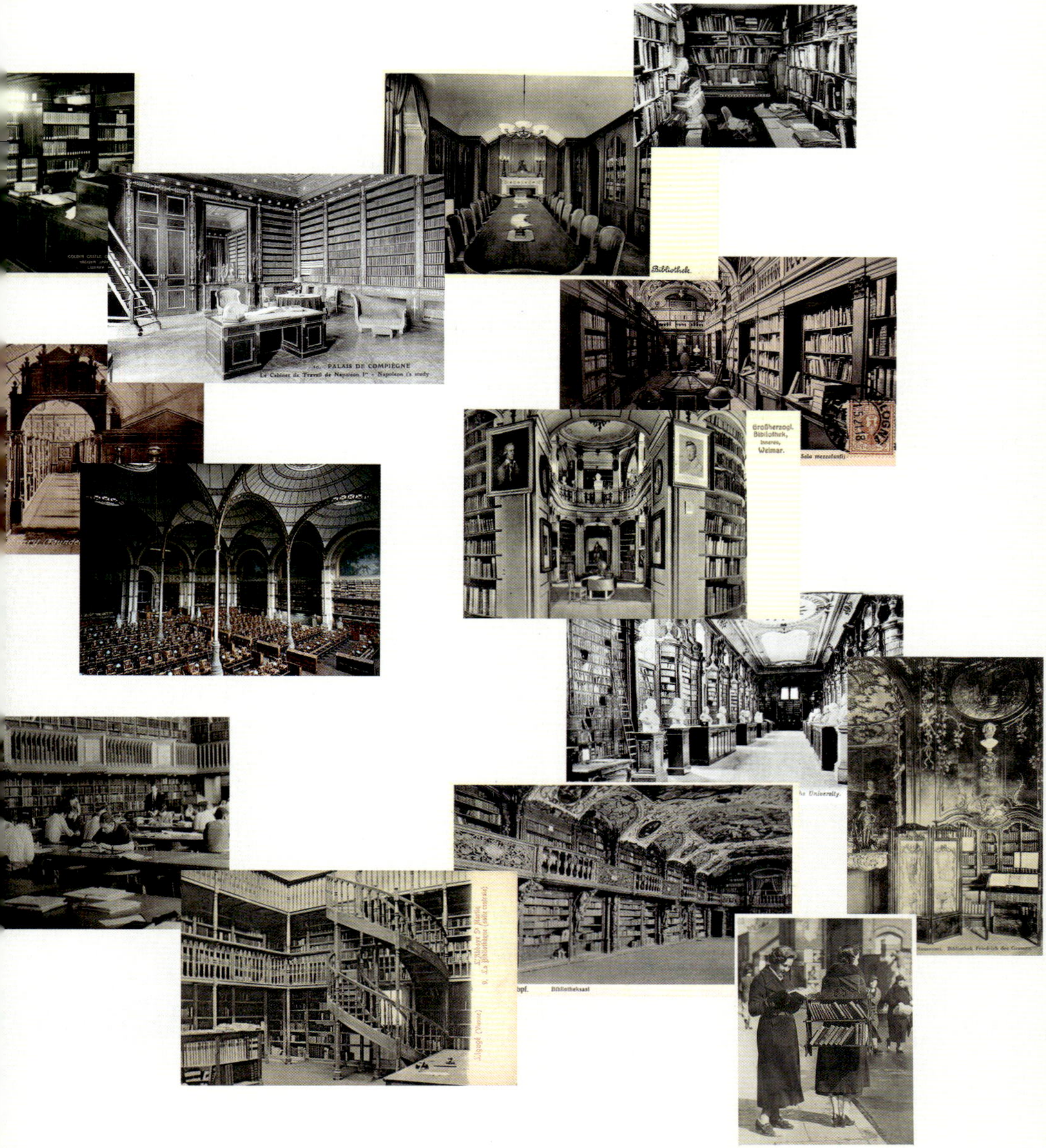
16. PALAIS DE COMPIÈGNE
Le Cabinet de Travail de Napoléon Ier - Napoleon I's study
Bibliothek.
Großherzogl.
Bibliothek,
Inneres,
Weimar.
Bibliotheksaal

thing almost as good as the original, or that in many arts we stopped having an original, is obviously shaping our way of thinking. And I know that everything changes, but what I am wary about is that technology changes the process. And yes, we get used to the lower standards, but it is still a loss. Maybe there is a point in the progress of these technologies, where it stopped getting better and instead it started to get smaller, easier and cheaper.

I came across a perceptive remark made by Walker Evans in a 1963 issue of *Mademoiselle* magazine: "Design just a little dated will interest any artist. Design current is always terrible. Anyone who has tried to find a good contemporary lamp or clock will know what I mean". It's a subtle point because he wasn't denigrating the aesthetic or technology of any era, merely noting that not-newness is what often permits artistic access. One might even say that artists are first to sense the coming obsolescence. When artists get hold of a medium, you know something has passed!

Wow, Walker Evans knew it all. It is absolutely true. But artists vary, so we have people working with the newest and others (or the same) working with obsolete media. I, for myself, love Super 8 film, but I use video most of the time and have been working with digital cameras for a long time. And recently I have been going back to Polaroids, as we have these new impossible films, who look like ghost images from the past. But it is probably nothing you couldn't do on an iPhone…

On the way to my studio this morning I bought a copy of *Intelligent Life* (a current affairs magazine). It has a photo story, shot on Polaroid, of everyday life in the Middle East. When I read the caption, it tells me these images were made on an iPhone, then converted to the colours of Polaroid and given the distinctive white plastic borders. On the magazine page the images look like physical objects. In fact they look more like objects than they would on an iPhone screen. Paper reinvents paper, via the computer. These are strange times in which social change, technological change, and change in the regime of images are all deeply interconnected.

You can now shoot Daguerreotypes on an iPhone. But it is not more than a pastiche of the real thing. The same with the Polaroid. You are lacking the whole process. They might look good, maybe even better than the real thing, but, as you say, they are mere fakes. I think we should not forget that they are not true. You can also make Super8 films with your phone, but do we really need the scratches just as a digital effect? If you can't touch it, it isn't film. If you can't interfere in the process by heating or scratching, it isn't Polaroid. It's just *ersatz*. Also, even if you are using a modern device, you are using an application that falsifies time, therefore today's pictures will look much older than they actually are, which is also an interesting factor.

I can see these concerns inform the making of much of your work in photography and film. As image-makers, we are particularly sensitive to them. Are you expecting your audience to be equally sensitive or is it a matter of introducing them to the issues?
Ah, what does one expect from the audience? When I am working, I am doing it for myself, I work because I want to pursue that path, understand something better or just because I am attracted to something. Then, once I realize I am actually showing that body of work in a public context, I try to make it clearer, either through the installation itself or through text. But different people see different things, which is also part of the game and that is always interesting to me.

That's interesting. Freund and other commentators on photography in the 1920s and 1930s – Benjamin and Kracauer especially – described very well the rupture in memory and history brought about by an accelerated world of images. This was the beginning of what we now call the spectacle of mass media. From then onwards it has been one rupture after another and, as you say, it's impossible for artists and film-makers not to be aware of, and shaped by, this condition. Hopefully viewers too. But we're at an interesting point now when the rupture seems to be as much about disappearance as abundance.

The obsolescence of certain image forms in the context of the proliferation of newer ones. Too little and too much. Again this is a dialectic I see in your own work, which often tries to resist the "generality" of images by attending with great care to very particular images, whether they are your own or rescued from history.
One has to go against the flux of images that we experience everyday. Photography is not about the "well taken" or "beautiful" image, but about the meaning of the image, be it a document, a piece of poetry or both.
The meaning changes and is often hidden or hard to convey, but there are some photographs still worth making or saving in the torrent. And one should not forget that owning a camera does not mean one is a photographer. Or that if you do videos you are a film-maker. From all diaries written in the last centuries, very few are actually literature (and even fewer are good literature) and worth saving. But in time, some unsuspicious ones, like snapshots, do become interesting enough to survive and to be seen or read again. In this sense, all artists unconsciously try to reach this kind of immortality for their works.

Why do you distinguish between the well taken or beautiful and an interest in the meaning of images? You didn't make the same distinction for literature. Is this a vestige of the resistance to photography as a pictorial art that surfaced with conceptualism? And does this relate to your suspicion about the single image and preference for the organized "body of work"?
Yes and no. I am not suspicious of the single image, but, yes, I don't think a single image means you are an interesting photographer. Anyone can take an interesting photograph, as much as anyone can write a beautiful sentence.
My grandfather took wonderful photographs, but he was never a photographer. I must say, I am also suspicious of works that collect things, which has been a trend in recent years – photographic surveys of fences, houses, trees, etc. Some are obviously interesting, but most are pale successors of the work of the Bechers. The problem with photography is that because it is well taken or beautiful,

people think it is a good work. Go to any photo art fair and see what I mean. Did I suggest the opposite for literature? Maybe, but I cannot really imagine a book made only of beautiful phrases. We also need the subtext. This reminds me that when I showed *Terezín* for the first time, someone came up to me and said how beautiful the light is in one of the images. That was really frustrating, because for me beautiful light is probably the most uninteresting aspect of the work. But, I guess, as you can catch flies with light, you catch viewers with beauty…

I, too, find many of your works very beautiful, but I do not, cannot, separate that experience from the other things I get from them: an intellectual challenge, a provocation, a philosophical meditation, a re-seeing of history and so forth. Photography is light and as such it will have an aesthetic dimension. But even the negation of the aesthetic is an aesthetic act, an aesthetic position, no?
I am not negating the aesthetic of an image, how could I? On the contrary, I am opposing that the value of an image should be aesthetic only. Also, maybe I should clarify this, I do think that some photographs function and should be presented by themselves, because some do manage to have a depth, of layers, as if they contain a whole series of works within them.
To be able to understand which ones do this is a difficult task. I don't know if it makes sense here, but I remembered the famous Iceberg Theory of Hemingway, where he is not sure what the story is really about, meaning the writing is just the surface, the tip of the iceberg. Likewise, ideally I see photographs as being just something you have to dig into, a pool of water that you can either observe from a distance or actually dive in and let yourself be part of it. Does this make sense to you at all?

Very much so. Your own work shows just how many lines of approach there can be. Photography is unusual in opening so many pathways into all of that, not least because its reference to the world – its stubborn indexicality – ensures that it can never be aesthetic only.
As photographs are mostly connected to some kind of reality, they

usually contain information, as well. Therefore they can rarely extricate themselves from the world as we know it, unlike perhaps other forms of art, which can be more abstract. Even cinema with all its information is more abstract, because it is a constructed world.

I often feel that photographs record an actuality they can never explain or account for (you can photograph a person sneezing, but the image will never tell you why they sneezed). Just like frames of a film they are forcefully factual but profoundly enigmatic. Perhaps this relates to your opening remark in our conversation about the difficult necessity of "reading" images in relation to other images, supplemental texts, history and so forth.
Your work offers the clues and something of the mise-en-scène that will make them readable.
I hope so. The image is just a fragment of a much larger world, a real one and the ones in the minds of the photographer and of the viewer. They are similar but not the exactly the same. As Benjamin said, citing the Kabala, the world to come will be just like this one, but slightly different. We just have to move things a little and eventually we will get there.

When photography became Modern, around the time Benjamin was writing, for many it was the speed of photography that seemed so characteristic. Of course, Benjamin himself went the other way – celebrating the slow, incremental work of photographers such as August Sander and Eugène Atget, warning viewers that they too would need to proceed slowly in order to read the images. Few people today would associate photography with speed. It has become a slower, philosophical medium, one that is well suited to "moving things a little", as you put it.
I agree, but at same time, it is a medium that is very connected with technology, just as cinema is. In the time of Muybridge, photography was very much related with the railroad and the telegraph, inventions that were made in order to annihilate space and time. Photography would do the same, in the sense that you can have the image of someone or something that is indeed very far away,

in fact, you can have that same image in several different locations simultaneously, unlike a painting or a sculpture. The building of the railroads meant immeasurable speed and, not by coincidence, most of the experiences of Muybridge were paid by Stanford, one of the railroad moguls and breeder of fast horses. And Muybridge was experimenting with the speed of photography that eventually became cinema. Now, we have a very accelerated technology that produces, in your words, a slow, philosophical medium. But it is also a technology that can produce fast images by the millions. Like in cinema and literature, maybe the "fight" is between what one considers art and what one would consider entertainment. And can, nowadays, entertainment be something slow or does it need to be moving quickly like Stanford's horses?

Ah, but Muybridge was interested in stopping things. This is why he's not really the "father of cinema". Cinema merely re-creates the movement it films. I see Muybridge as being on the side of slowness. Anyway I'm more inclined to rephrase your last question: Can art nowadays be something fast or does it need to be slow? There's a presumption in art and "art film" that slow must equal serious and fast must equal entertainment. I understand the cultural and historical reasons for this, but I am suspicious of it too. It's a default position that allows too many bad artists and film-makers to look credible, and it shuts off serious audiences from taking "fast" films seriously.

You are so right about that. I could argue with you about Muybridge, because even if he was interested in stopping things, in order to achieve that, he invented camera shutters that permitted him to photograph with the high speed of a fraction of a second. He worked with zoetropes and made his images move and swing. But, yes, if we look at it now, it's all about the frozen image, the fragmentation of a movement. To try to answer your question, I do think art can be something fast, if it makes us think or, at least, pause for a moment. Otherwise it will be just eye catching, and that I call, maybe presumptuously, entertainment. It can be a very thin line and I surely don't have anything against something that gives your eye plain pleasure.

Maybe this brings us back to the imperative to think about photography as a process of assembly and movement from one image to another, overcoming the single image.
Cinema and documentary film certainly had a deep impact on the development of the photographic essay as an arrangement of parts.
Yes, definitely. When you put two images together, you have a short film. All possible relations can be made from this simple exercise, which I have used in *Collected Stories*. And I added a title to these diptychs, which is kind of a third image, leading you somewhere else.

In his biography of the film-maker Jean-Luc Godard, Colin McCabe remarks "...in a world in which we are entertained from cradle to grave whether we like it or not, the ability to rework image and dialogue... may be the key to both psychic and political health". He has in mind Godard's use of movie footage in his *Histoire(s) du Cinéma*, but it's just as relevant to a photographer or film-maker "reworking" their own images – through the re-evaluation that happens with editing, sequencing and writing.
Mmmh, I am not sure how to respond to this. But surely making my photographs and work has been a good reason to be and stay alive. Lots of the beautiful and interesting things I have done and people I have met in my life have been excused by my work and not purely by curiosity. And when I work on them afterwards,
I try to make sure that only what can be also interesting for others will be used. Often I let time pass by between producing and post-production, so that I can rethink my original intents and results. More and more, I am convinced that photography is not about shooting, but about thinking.

Well, I definitely think that finding beauty and interest in a world of flattened experience and mass produced apathy is part of what McCabe means by "psychic health".
I can't remember who said it, but the avant-garde has had two tasks: to show what's wrong with the world and to find beauty in unexpected places.

I agree with that fully. And I would add another task: make people think and feel a bit differently than they did earlier that day. It's just a moment, but make it last, at least for a moment and a half.

The American sculptor, draftsman and painter **Robert Cumming** made photographs seriously for little more than a decade. But in that time, between around 1970 and 1980, he produced one of the most singular, inventive, and philosophically astute bodies of work. Mixing the techniques of highly crafted large format photography with the playfulness of conceptual art, performance and sculpture, there is really nothing else like a Cumming photograph in the history of the medium.

In my student years, I was always looking for Robert's work in old exhibition catalogues. It seemed for a while that his photographs were destined for obscurity. But there have always been a handful of people that have admired his achievement. One of them is Sarah Bay Gachot, who in 2014 put together *The Difficulties of Nonsense*, a survey book of Cumming's pictures, published by Aperture. Suddenly, many younger artists that were fascinated with photography's paradoxical qualities as both a distinctive medium and hybrid practice were able to see an important precedent and inspiration.

Robert Cumming and I met in 2013 for this conversation in Aperture's New York office. It was first published in *The Difficulties of Nonsense*, 2016.

Robert Cumming

Robert, you made your photographic work pretty intensively for a decade or so, and then moved on to other things, but the ground you covered was very rich. Are you the same person now who made that work? Do you relate to it as yours?
Yeah, it does feel like mine.

There's a lot of energy in the work.
To start off an idea, I would do a drawing, like a little pencil sketch. And I had made a promise to myself never to act on these ideas until I'd waited at least a month. I think about one drawing in five was actually made into a photograph. It was a good discipline for me because, you know, the newest idea was always fantastic, and I'd launch into this complicated prop and then realize in the middle, "This really sucks – what was I thinking?" So there was a pact to let each one simmer first as a drawing.

But do you think that something that works as a drawing might not work as a photograph, or the other way around?
Yes, that would happen. This waiting helped me understand which path to take.

There are so many translations going on: idea into drawing, drawing into objects or situations, and then into a photograph. And you need to be keeping an eye on all of those translations to get somewhere worthwhile. I wouldn't have been able to say so at the time, but I remember when I first saw your work there was something about the visual qualities of the pictures: they seemed so unlikely with the subject matter and the working process. It's overstated that conceptual artists weren't interested in craft, but your photographs had such a fascination and affection for the finest qualities of the photographic print.

It's true. But I had by that time really studied photography and its history, and I got more and more taken in by it.

You were a real bridge back then between what they used to call "photographers" and "artists using photography".
I'm sort of in the middle there. And my exhibitions were like that, too. I did some sculpture shows, some conceptual art shows, and some photographic exhibitions as well.

Did you go straight to the 8-by-10 camera?
Well, I started with a little Instamatic in undergraduate school. I was taking reference pictures mainly as, I don't know, studies for drawings I was doing.

Notations.
Notations. Notations for these big industrial landscapes – what locomotive roundhouses looked like, that sort of thing. In undergraduate school from 1961 to 1965, in our photography class, we were learning how to use 4-by-5 cameras. Then in graduate school, although it was a supposed elective, it was strongly pressed on us that it would be a good thing for us to do large format work. I really didn't like it, but later, when I was out of school, I thought, Jeez, I kind of miss this. I bought a 5-by-7 because I couldn't see lugging an enormous 8-by-10 around. But it was stolen from my car, which was great because there were no supplies. Getting film for 5-by-7 was almost impossible; I had taken maybe thirty, forty pictures on it. I then bought an 8-by-10 Burke & James, which was the main recording device through about 1980.

Did you do all your own darkroom work?
Oh, yes, and I was usaully exhibiting 8-by-10 contact prints.

I was talking to Stephen Shore recently about the necessary discipline of using an 8-by-10. He felt it was kind of cosmic because there's more information than you could ever possibly want.
Sure, that's sort of why I use it.

But the pictures have this very demonstrative, playful, pedagogical dimension. But when you use an 8-by-10, you have a great

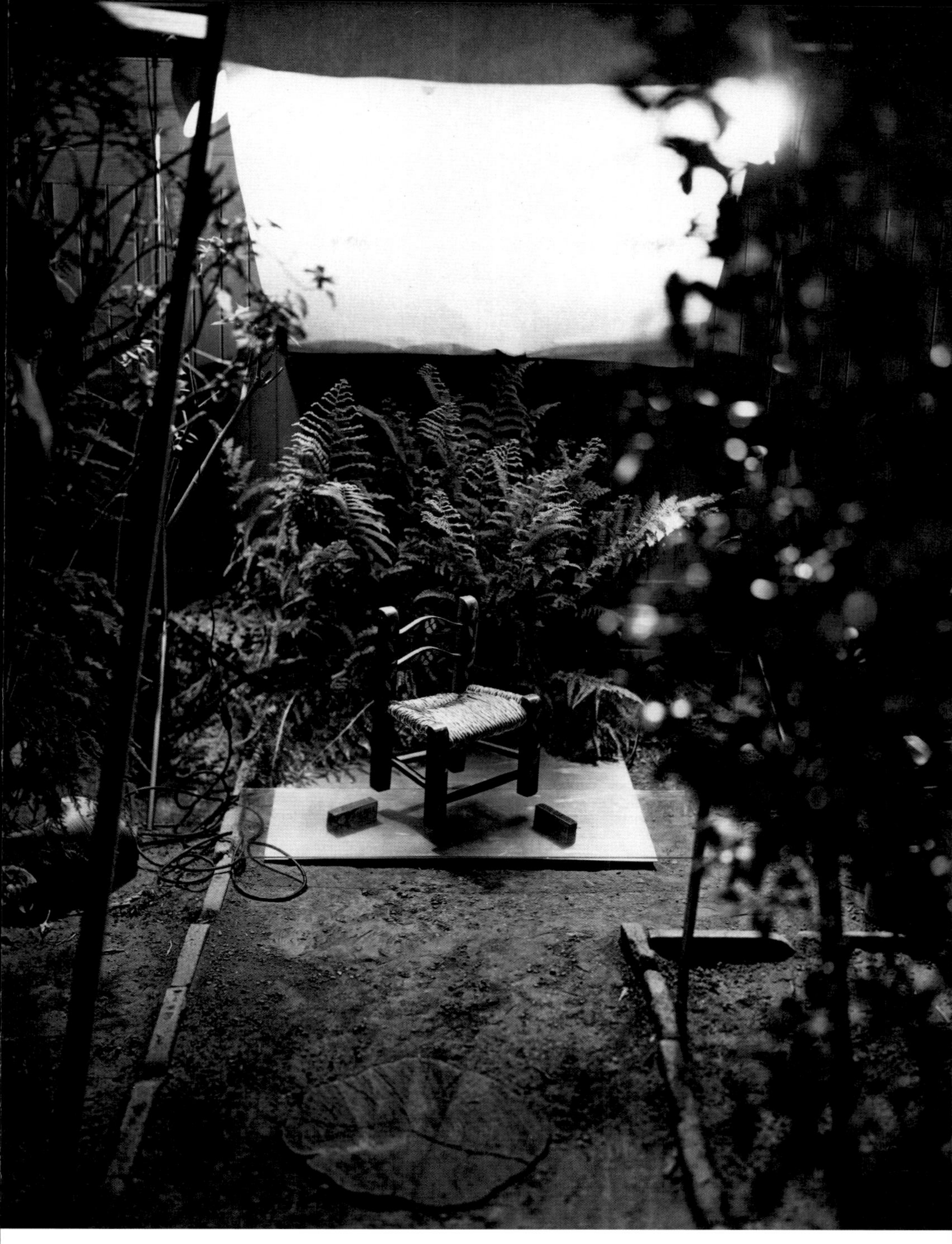

Robert Cumming, Chair Trick, 1973

surfeit of visual information that exceeds those meanings. It's just this huge richness that's... there, surplus to any obvious requirement.
There were very few exhibitions, catalogues, or books on photography when I started. Art Sinsabaugh was our instructor [in graduate school], a purist whose aesthetic I had no use for; at that point I wanted to do 35 mm collages that I'd make into silkscreens à la Rauschenberg. We had a bumpy two years together. But I'd slowly gotten sucked into this big negative thing. To backtrack just a little, it was sculpture that first prompted me to make the photographs back in Milwaukee in the late 1960s.

You were documenting your sculpture?
If you did sculpture and entered sculpture competitions or juried shows, you had to send photos. Sculpture is just too big and heavy. I always thought I had an unfair advantage because I could take a picture that could often be better than the actual piece. And in some cases other artists who did much better sculptures weren't juried into the shows – on the basis of their skills as photographers. I shot everything with the new 8-by-10.

Well, that problem has only got worse. We live in an art culture that's just full of reproductions. Sometimes I think all art culture has ended up being photographic, whether it was photographic originally or not. We see so much in magazines and on websites.
At some point, I was just happier with the photograph than the sculpture. And I could photograph them in different positions and in different locations, not just in the studio, and embellish the lighting.

You were making very photogenic sculptures somehow.
Well, the sculpture and the photography certainly fed off each other.

***Sculptures, Milwaukee* reminds me of some of the pictures that Larry Sultan and Mike Mandel ended up with in their book *Evidence*, I think. The photograph as factual enigma.**
I used to know them, though not very closely. All the artists from LA would wind up at the same shows eventually, at the same openings.

I was reading somewhere that you kept your distance from the art world. Was that just a temperamental thing?
That also describes my current situation.

There's something so individual about your work and the pursuit of the making of it. It's isolated but it's informed. You're not completely in a world of your own, but you want a freedom and space that's yours.
That's how it's been, definitely.

Although you went to art school, I sense the heart of your learning is more self-taught, more autodidactic. I don't know what I would base that on, but just looking at the work it seems that way.
Pretty much. None of our classes taught assembled, "additive" sculpture; everyone was chipping away at wood or stone, molding clay – "reductive" sculpture. I wanted to put things together with screws and nails, maybe weld. Even out of graduate school, I couldn't screw wood together properly; I had very few tools. But I wanted my objects to look like things from the real world, stuff you'd find in hardware stores: rakes, springs, brush cutters, prosthetic devices, etc. Very soon my sculptures took on that language. I liked learning how to do practical things, from the manual. Every year I'd learn a new trade: how to sew, type, weld...

It's interesting that the sculptures, kind of like the photography, begin with something utilitarian and then end up being useless. Or contemplating utility without being useful!
Yeah, exactly.

In some ways your photography is very pure and seems to be an investigation of the properties or qualities of a distinct medium. Against that notion, you arrived at photography because it's where all of your interests can come together – the writing, painting, sculpture, performance, handiwork, and the problem-solving. There's something about the way photography can be a kind of container for all of those things.
In the beginning, many of my pictures were like one-liners. Easy.

Once you saw them, you thought, OK, very amusing. But at a certain point, very early on, I realized I wanted to make more complicated pieces that would read more slowly. In other words, you'd get the main point, but then in time, on closer inspection, this other stuff would creep in from the margins, changing contexts and meanings, making the story more complex.

If you had been a die-hard conceptualist, I suppose you'd have been making all of your set-ups in a kind of blank white studio –
Right, right.

But the world comes into your pictures. The backyards, the bits of interiors, or gardens at the margins.
Yes. Often there's a staging, as if these are little theatre pieces. In *Chair Trick* (1973), the tiny "stage" is framed by my tiny backyard, only about four feet wide. It's typical California-suburban.

But you want all of that extra stuff in the frame. It's titled *Chair Trick* and there's a trick going on with the chair, but what you end up with is a picture about diffused lighting, about fauna, about backyards. There's a whole world, rather than the mere execution of an idea.
That's right. It's all in there deliberately. Actually, *Chair Trick* was one of the very first I made experimenting with the parameters of my backyard at night. Only a few feet away, a couple nights later, I made *Black & White/White & Black Rope Trick* (1973). I had found this copper wire, fine as a spider's web, that took three pieces to hold up just the one foot-long length of clothes line rope. I wanted to see if the wire would show in an 8-by-10 contact print, which it did.

That's amazing. Do you like magic? Close-up magic? Looking at these kinds of photographs is a little bit like watching somebody very consummate perform a magic trick in front of your eyes.
Yes, the pictures would give away the trick, I think.

There's often a tension between something that the title tells you to look at and something less specific to be thought about.
And sometimes my titles are intentionally misleading.

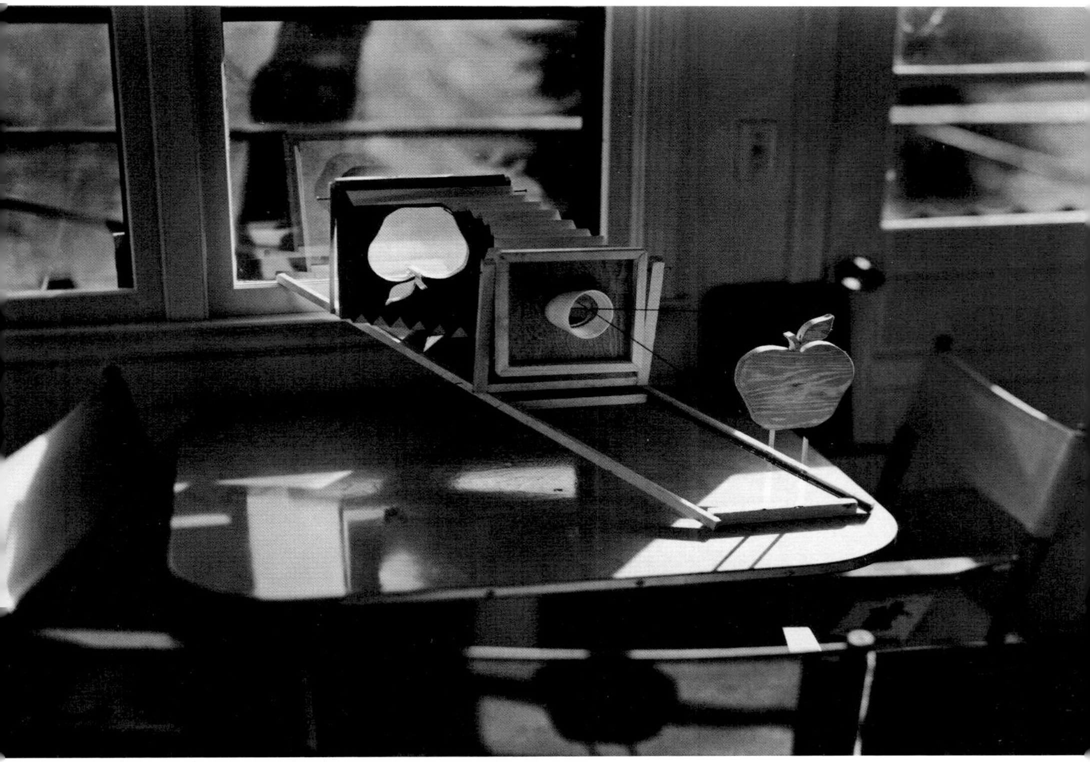

Robert Cumming, Camera and Apple, 1980

You made a piece called *120 Alternatives*, which shows a sofa on which you scattered 120 identical pieces of paper.
Yes, the text on the paper reads: "Plurally or in a Pile We Are Sculpture / Singularly, I Am a Print".

I really like it as an image. It's so much more than idea. The photographic print is very fine, with all those shades of gray. The angle is strange. You have to strain a little to read the text. Why is it that sofa? Is that the leg of a light stand?
A light stand left in on purpose. William Wegman and I were close for about ten years – as undergrads at Mass Art, roommates at Illinois, teaching in Wisconsin, and sharing a studio in Milwaukee for a couple years, before winding up in Southern California around 1970. His take on it was something like, "Cumming, you shouldn't be giving away all your tricks. You should stash all your sets and props in a big warehouse, then after you die they'll be found and it'll be revealed what a big hoax your pictures were". But for me, the whole point was the slow discovery of how the illusions worked.

The pictures are not about the riddle of how it was done. They are much more about the fact that it was done.
Exactly. The funny thing is, for all the information, all the detail and complexity, me talking about them – you can describe them to death and you're ultimately just not closer to what they're really about.

It's an incredibly rich period, Californian photography of the 1970s, there's more irony in West Coast work of that time. Or there's a kind of understanding that humour is a profound and intellectual thing. It's not the enemy of seriousness; it's another path toward it. In hindsight, what do you think about that period, making those 8-by-10s?
It's hard to encapsulate. I was working like a maniac – sort of burning the candle at both ends.

Where did that energy come from? Did you feel you were searching for something?
Well, part of it was practical. It was a difficult period. California art departments weren't putting on any new full-time faculty, which was

my main source of income. I had to work more jobs to support the artwork, and because I was doing more shows, needed more paying work, etc., etc. I was working all the time; eight art schools in eight years, janitor, sign painter, visiting artist gigs, lectures, etc. It peaked in 1980 with thirty exhibitions, fourteen lectures, a couple of portfolios, and a government jury for the National Endowment for the Arts.

Were you selling any work?
Basically, no. The work all went out to shows and all came back. Making matters worse, my first New York dealer, John Gibson, seldom paid us for work he sold. He was also the one who insisted I make editions of two or three, which I've been saddled with to this day.

Do you know which museums or collectors have your work?
Around 1982, a Chicago collector bought one version of everything – 230 prints – and donated them to four museums. So I know exactly where they are.

I've hardly seen any of your work in exhibition. I think I only know it through publications. I know the prints themselves will always be far richer than any reproduction.
Someone came up to me after a slide lecture and said, "You know that's just a trick to get people to come to your shows, telling them all the stuff you can only see in the contact print". [Laughs]

I teach students at the moment, and I show them your work and they're shocked when I tell them the dates of your pictures. It feels very contemporary to them.
Maybe it's because the work looks deconstructive.

It might be that. I think in the last five or so years there's been an opening up again between photography and other media. At the same time, there's a real interest in the craft of making pictures. So again your work is that kind of bridge we were talking about at the beginning. I think students today probably see something of that – relating to the photographs pictorially, and as explorations of ideas. There's real synergy between those two aspects. There's also a spirit that mixes the very logical and

the slightly mad. Your photographs are analytical studies that are also arcane and ritualized and obsessive.
Oh, good! [Laughs]

Let's talk a little about your making books. The books were the place where you put your different investigations together – the photographs and the writing – and in books they became more than the sum of their parts.
Maybe the self-publishing was just ego. My first book, *Picture Fictions* (1971), was a compilation of work through 1971. The second, *The Weight of Franchise Meat* (1971), I really hate. I just ran too quickly with a bad idea.

Did you approach the making of books as another discipline to learn, or did you know anything about the process before?
No – I got the idea, of course, from Ed Ruscha. He was very early on in the scene, if not the first, with *Twentysix Gasoline Stations*, and later with *Royal Road Test, Thirtyfour Parking Lots in Los Angeles*, and of course, *Every Building on the Sunset Strip*. The work is brilliant.

Did you know Ruscha at the time?
I'd meet these people at openings every once in a while, but you know, not an awful lot more than a handshake. I knew his books were published by Heavy Industry Press, so on a lark, I sent some pictures with a note [that said], "Hey, would you like to print these, make them into a book?" I got a nice letter from a woman who said, "Well, basically Heavy Industry Press is Ed Ruscha's printing company and does only his work. But good luck with your career". So I thought I'd do the same thing: publish my own stuff, starting with one thousand copies, sell lots, send them out, and it would be wonderful. Then arrived the new boxes from the printer with that fresh smell of printer's ink. Sitting there in the middle of the studio, I thought, "What now?"

Distribution is the thing.
Distribution. I hadn't even thought of distribution. Now I had to start being my own distributor. I started by charging $2.50 per copy. I'd

drive halfway across the LA basin to one bookstore. The manager wouldn't be in so I'd return home and come back on Thursday. He didn't come in – he'd called in sick – so you'd have to come back a third time. By that time, after five hundred miles on the odometer through notorious LA freeway traffic, he'd buy three copies for $7 (asking for a special discount – $5.75). It was totally, totally hopeless. In 1973 I did a book called *A Training in the Arts* with Coach House Press in Toronto, and they had a proper catalogue of titles and distribution. It actually went into reprint in 1975.

You ended up doing three books with Coach House: *A Training in the Arts*, *A Discourse on Domestic Disorder* (1975), and *Interruptions in Landscape and Logic* (1977). Those books were very "writerly", too.
Well, they're literary experiments in a way. The normal way an illustrated story operates is as a triad: illustration assists the text, assisted by the caption. All are connected. But I wondered what it would be like if one of the three connectors was clipped – if caption assisted illustration, but illustration didn't connect with the story.

I can't think of anyone else who would write in that kind of tone. It's very consistent with your visual work.
That's perhaps true. *Training in the Arts* was a parody of Harlequin romance novels – the text is so… flat. I don't know how else to describe [Harlequin books]; they're just dead. Thousands of words lying there on a page… which seem to make millions of readers happy. Additionally, it parodied a couple I knew, art-education majors for whom every damned thing was a "tasting experience" or a "learning experience". They had a way of leeching life out of everything that passed before them.

Your writing is a bit like your pictures. Flat-footed, informational prose can be very open for the reader – it gives them a lot of space. You don't feel hectored or overly guided. It's like the writing and theories of Alain Robbe-Grillet. Deadpan, uninflected writing can be a very generous writing. It doesn't force emotions on the reader.
I was very influenced by Robbe-Grillet.

You were? I sense there are many photographers who like his work. There are deep affinities. All those facts with no clear explanation!
Yes, it takes us back to the idea that you can describe things endlessly and it's still a mystery. Robbe-Grillet describes positions, topography – describe, describe, describe. But ultimately it lacks some sort of glue, doesn't adhere, just kind of disintegrates. But that's the point; it's his kind of magic.

When it's done really well, it's extremely memorable. And even though the work is kind of antinarrative, you can't help but put it into your own narrative because humans are narrative beings.
I love *In the Labyrinth*, Robbe-Grillet's book with the soldier wandering around in a vacant city. It starts to snow. And the snow comes down and down and he walks into a tavern and there's dust falling, and on the wall a print of a landscape, way in the background – a city? And the dust and the snow keep falling, glass rings in the dust…

In the short piece "The Dressmaker's Dummy", from the book *Snapshots*, he describes one room in great detail – objects, positions, angles of view – but eventually you realize that the room doesn't add up. The description is illogical. I had to draw the room to figure that out.
That's a nice way to respond to writing – draw a picture!

A question I've always thought about in relation to your work, which never seems to come up anywhere in any of the writings – maybe we can talk about it in relation to your book *Equilibrium and the Rotary Disc* – is your relation to the art of Marcel Duchamp. The technical know-how, the strange allegories, the jokes, the balance between mystery and revelation.
My work has been in a couple of shows that have tried to pair my work with Duchamp, but I really don't feel a strong affinity for him, for some reason. The last Cumming-Duchamp show I was in, a kind of Duchamp colloquium in Philadelphia, I finally figured out why… but I've forgotten [laughs]. It was complicated. If there's been an artist I've had a lasting affection for, it's probably Piranesi. There's a lot of him in my stuff from back in the 1960s. His prisons and architec-

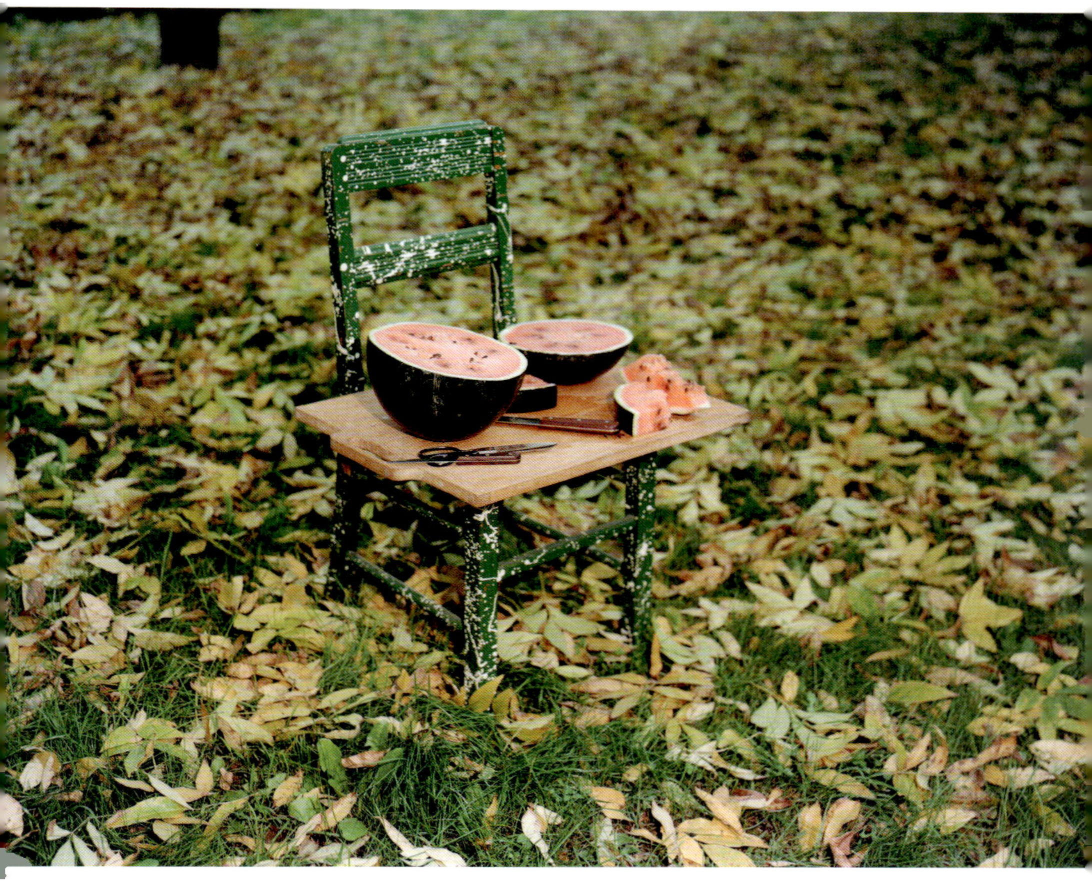

Robert Cumming, Watermelon and Chair, 1980

tural studies of Rome – all that description, like intense needlework. He also pulls a lot of funny strings, reducing his figures to make their settings mightier than they really are.

Your rotary disc on a waterfall does remind me of Duchamp's last work *Étant donnés*, but it also looks like a Max Ernst – a very lucid but unlikely vision from the nineteenth century. The viewer knows there's a central thing going on in the presentation, but again it can't be reduced to an idea.
When I was working on *Equilibrium and the Rotary Disc*, between 1977 to 1978, I was thinking of moving out of California and going back East. Part of it was the growing dissatisfaction with illusion in the work. Growing up in New England, there was a nostalgia for its history: New England mill towns, the Industrial Revolution, and the smaller scale of the mill valleys. Enthusiasm for Hollywood was starting to wane. Also, I was tired of being poor, feeling that I was never going to make a decent living.
The only chance in LA seemed to be something like starting up a studio for shooting celebrities, doing commercial work like Annie Leibovitz. But it was obvious I had to get closer to New York and connect with a New York gallery, and get closer to Europe, where there was a growing enthusiasm for American artists.

It's hard to feel one's own historical consciousness in a place like Los Angeles, where you're surrounded by the present.
Exactly. So this interest in the Industrial Revolution sparked a general renewal in history. I made drawings to show how mill towns evolved. The waterfall – the central source of energy – turned the water wheel, and the shafts and machinery inside. The workshops grew into factories, workers lived in row houses, and by the 1890s or 1900, the cities were pretty large. It was the evolution of the kind of towns I'd grown up in. I didn't understand them until I'd been away from them ten or more years and had seen them from the very different perspectives of the Midwest and the West.

Your publications are not gallery artworks. They're cheap and accessible. And there's something very nice about the drawings and the writing and the painting and the photography all com-

ing together on the printed page. I guess the issue is slightly different with the books that are more like artist's books than catalogues, because in a way they are the work itself. But I always remember a kind of famous and probably apocryphal story about English abstract painters in the 1950s and 60s: they were all making work that was never more than thirty inches wide or something, because they'd seen all of that great American abstract work in catalogues and had no grasp of the scale of the things at all.
Which is really vital. Well, with my connection with Castelli Graphics and the burgeoning 80s art market, the smaller drawings, after four shows, had grown increasingly, up to eight by ten feet. Then I started to realize the impracticality; they didn't fit through doors, elevators, stairwells.

When did you join Castelli?
Nineteen eighty-one or '82, and went through about 1990. It was a wonderful gallery. Photography galleries had asked me about representation, but I wanted a gallery where I could do sculpture and photography, where I could do everything. Leo Castelli called me, and it was a fabulous solution. A dream come true. It came to an end when Mr. Castelli died. The 80s art market was just crazy, with so much money flooding in and people buying anything. I did really well for about a five-year period in my life and got that out of my system, when I was with Castelli.

You did some very detailed paintings from your photographs.
Oh, yeah. I only did two or three of them that size. My favorite, perhaps the best of my career, *Mesh Hammer* (1977), I've never gotten tired of. Six feet high by four feet across, it's always been over my bed. Started with a pen sketch, made into several small props, photographed, bumped up, and rendered in oil on canvas. There's a chance I'd have been satisfied with a six-foot colour photo, but it was just at that point where large-scale colour printing was becoming an option for photographers.

You have a big appetite for doing that kind of thing, plunging yourself into seemingly impossible tasks.

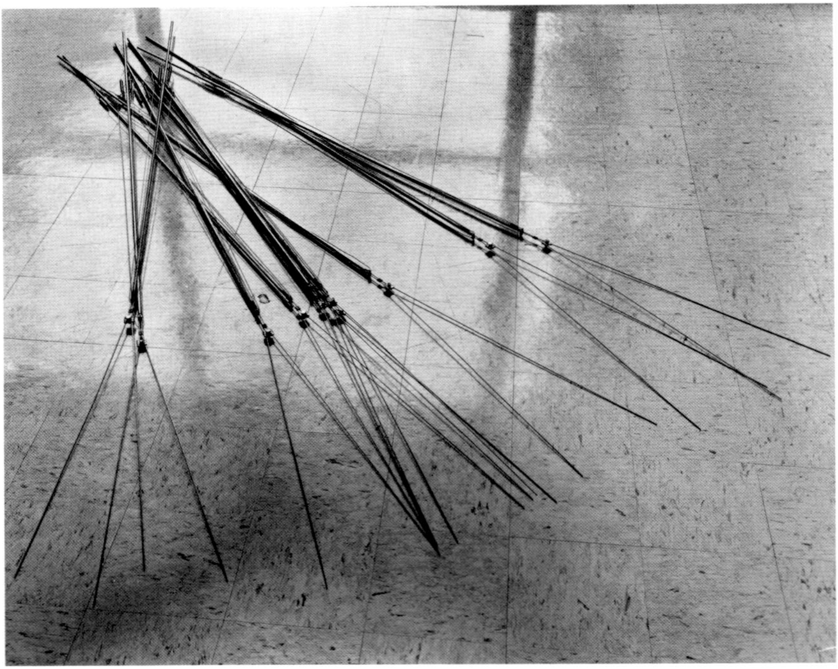

Robert Cumming, Sculptures, Milwaukee, 1969

Yes, but this really was crazy! The gridded hammer could only progress at three or four units per day [the painting was completed by imposing a grid on the canvas and completing it one square at a time]. It was wet-on-wet oil paint, so the edges of each had to be kept wet to make smooth transitions from one day to the next – for a month. Then there was the depth-of-field problem of all these crisscrossing wires going in and out of focus.

So you made three or four paintings like this and just thought, Yep, I can do that?
Yeah, despite the final result – it was unbelievably boring. So tedious being a human camera.

Having been making work for forty-five years or so, does it feel like you have circled around certain themes that whole time?
Yeah, it does. Every once in a while, I'll be just sort of sitting, looking at stuff, and suddenly – Oh, I'll be damned, this connects to that.

You've never really kept still. But you mentioned the idea of becoming obsessed and I think that's a clue to the way you've worked. You clearly have an awful lot of creative energy and curiosity, and the projects are there to get those obsessions out of your system – often in one work or a defined body of work – and then something else comes along. On top of that you have an awful lot of chops, as musicians would say, a lot of virtuosity with different materials that most artists don't have, or don't want to think about using.
The last ten or fifteen years I've been doing figure drawing. Models and such. And the drawings are people in situations which go right back to *A Training in the Arts.*

Even going right back to those photographs of sculpture from the late 60s, it seems that just about everything you've done has, at its core, the same kind of sensibility or the same kind of interest in the world around you, its objects, what those objects are, and how we perceive them.
I would hope so, but it's hard being your own art historian. In a magazine article, Chuck Hagen called the pictures "meditations".

For all your obsessions and recurrent themes, the moment you feel you are repeating... you drop it. It's almost as if those obsessions and themes are going to be there regardless of medium or technique.
They are. I very seldom worry about it. Having gotten along these last forty years, I'm still here. Must be doing something right – I'm not exactly sure what it is. But there's nothing more valuable, I think, than a person who really likes [the work]. It's a mystery to me, but...

Well, I know your art has found a very youthful and engaged audience again.
Oh, good.

LaToya Ruby Frazier's work as a photographer, film-maker and performance artist made an immediate impression on me when I saw it a few years ago. A decade in the making, her book *The Notion of Family* (2014) brought together with urgency and intelligence the best elements of America's documentary tradition with more experimental approaches. It tells the story of her African-American family struggling to come to terms with oppression in Braddock, a suburb of Pittsburgh, and the terrible physical and psychological effects of the city's steel industry. In all Frazier's work, there is a delicate balance between the autobiographical and the political, between family and society, between the human body as a site of pain and a site of hope.

The two of us have had public conversations in Paris and London, but this is an email exchange first published in *Frieze* magazine in 2015. An open-ended conversation is the best kind, but that's not always possible in a magazine, with its fixed formats. Still, I knew LaToya was articulate and to the point, and in the space of this short exchange readers are introduced to her depth, complexity, confidence and intelligence.

LaToya Ruby Frazier

Let's begin in Braddock, the suburb of Pittsburgh, USA, that is your hometown and frequent subject. Your formation as an artist and your coming to terms with the fate of Braddock are entwined. How did this happen?
Growing up in the 1980s in a shrinking steel mill town with Reagan-era policies of trickle-down economics, government deregulation, outsourcing, and environmental pollution made me keenly aware of my family's plight in an industrial landscape. My inability to articulate in words the harmful and painful effects the environment placed on my family made me turn to visual art as an outlet. I started out drawing and painting my grandmother and her step-father where we all lived together in an area known as "the bottom" by the Monongahela River, then turned to photography once I entered college at Edinboro University of Pennsylvania.

I sense in your work the rich legacy of experimental documentary: Walker Evans and James Agee's *Let us now Praise Famous Men* (1941), Roy DeCarava and Langston Hughes' *The Sweet Flypaper of Life* (1955), maybe Gordon Parks' image-text pieces for *Life* magazine in the 1950s and 60s, and the work of post-conceptualists such as Allan Sekula, Martha Rosler and Carrie Mae Weems. It's a reflexive mix of visual reporting, writing and performance.
Absolutely right. These are the artists who were mentors and influences. In fact I had the first edition of *The Sweet Flypaper of Life* in my studio while laying out the photographs and writings for my first book *The Notion of Family* (2014). My text often switches between my grandmother's and mother's, and an investigative, anecdotal, lyrical voice. At times the text functions as an image and the photograph becomes the visual language that creates a tension. They weave around throughout the book, each itself a character.

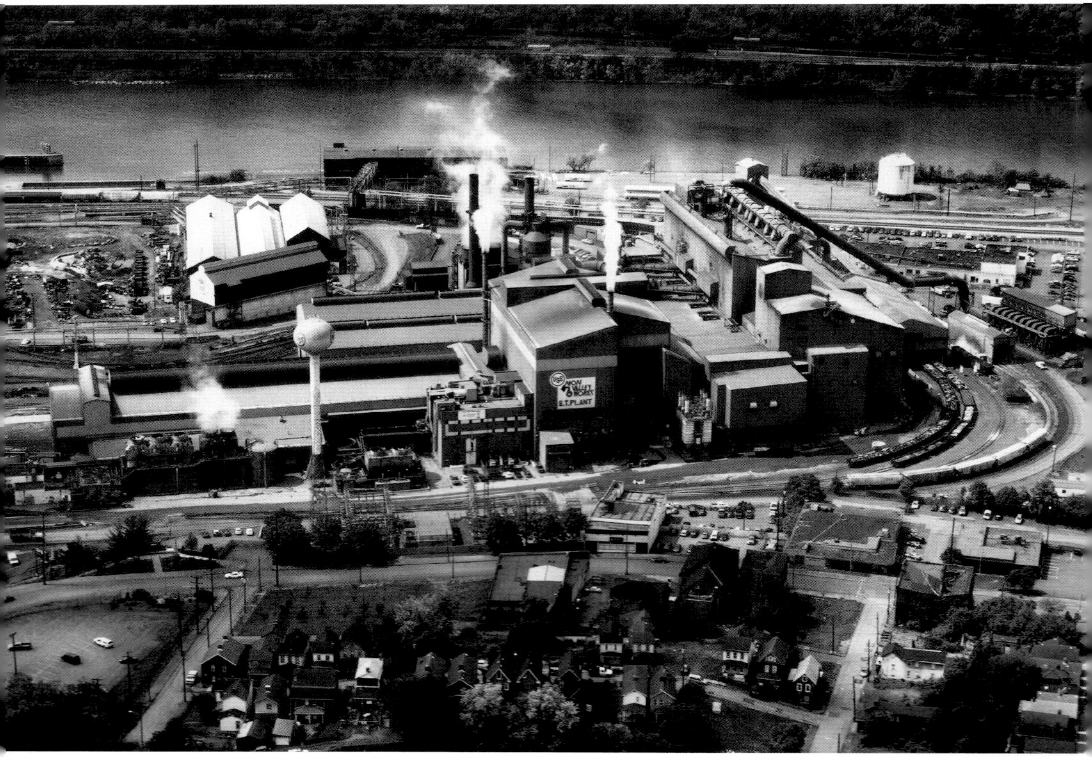

LaToya Ruby Frazier,
United States Steel Mon Valley Works Edgar Thomson Plant, 2013
(from the book *The Notion of Family*, Aperture, 2014)

Along the ancient path of the Monongahela River, Braddock, Pennsylvania, sits in the eastern region of Allegheny County, approximately nine miles outside Pittsburgh.

A historic industrial suburb, Braddock is home to Andrew Carnegie's first steel mill, the Edgar Thomson Works, which has operated since 1875 and is the last functioning steel mill in the region.

The work often depends on the nuanced interrelation of parts.
Currently I am reading Gordon Parks's *The Making of An Argument* to fully understand how Parks' photographs, which always underscored humanity and dignity, took on different meanings in the editing, cropping and story lines that *Life* magazine chose to use. If I were a journalist, I would not be able to edit and frame my photographs. I look for a narrative or context that will amplify the voices of the marginalized who have so many important stories to tell about America, capitalism, working-class life and the current issues we face under Rust Belt renewal.

The art world still seems anxious about the documentary potential of photographs. It likes artful deconstruction of the claims to truth telling but it can't really handle the more complex mix of fact and wish, revelation and enactment. Documentary gets dismissed as naive realism only to be replaced by real nihilism. Spending time with your book *The Notion of Family*, I felt you were catching the door of documentary just at it was slamming, sticking your foot out to keep it open.
I believe in the value of documentary photography especially at this moment, as we watch the mass media manipulate the issues around gentrification, poverty, police brutality and corporate violence against our ecosystem. Through government commissions and financed local business interests, the industrial past of Braddock (as an industrial suburb of Pittsburgh) was documented and contextualized by Lewis Hine, Walker Evans and W. Eugene Smith. Currently through local newspapers, social media, Hollywood and corporate advertisements by firms such as Levi's, Braddock is being rebranded. The new neoliberal narrative for the "creative class" omits the conditions of the working class and refuses the perspective and creativity of a subject like myself. Bertolt Brecht stated it best in 1931: "Photography in the hands of the bourgeoisie has become a terrible weapon against the truth". I am obliged to document and counter this reality, and ultimately re-imagine and rewrite it myself.

Brecht understood that realism must be supple and keep on its toes: "With the people struggling and changing reality before our eyes, we must not cling to "tried" rules of narrative, venerable lit-

erary models, eternal aesthetic laws. We must not derive realism as such from particular existing works, but we shall use every means, old and new, tried and untried, derived from art and derived from other sources, to render reality to men in a form they can master. [...] Our concept of realism must be wide and political, sovereign over all conventions" (*Popularity and Realism*, 1938).

I am interested in the scepticism about photography shared by twentieth-century theorists like Brecht, Siegfried Kracauer and Walter Benjamin. Kracauer felt that photographs obscured truth and fought contemplation. Benjamin was concerned that the photographic world masked the complexity of the human world. Yet, despite their harsh criticism they also felt that photography could liberate a new way of seeing and a radical consciousness. *The Notion of Family* responds to that call to suspend the passive aestheticism that turns abject poverty into an object of enjoyment.

Walker Evans has been a great influence on my practice: he established the autonomy to shoot, edit, write and design his own pages. His consciously resistant journalism at *Fortune*, countering the values and conventions of the mainstream, reminds me of the Frankfurt School belief that artists should not play a subordinate role to the culture industry.

Like Evans, you play word and image against each other. Do you write while you photograph, or do the words come later?

It took twelve years to create *The Notion of Family*. I wrote on and off for six of them. The texts come from audio recordings, interviews, research and personal writings from myself, my grandmother, mother and community residents. My book is a contribution to the long legacy of men who wrote their own narratives to address the history of Braddock. Andrew Carnegie's 1889 dedication speech of The Free Library in Braddock was a cry for his love of the town and an attempt to find peace between businessmen and working-men. Thomas Bell's novel *Out of This Furnace* tells how three generations (1880s-1920s) of his Slovak family dealt with immigration, industrialism and trade unions. Tony Buba's film *Struggles In Steel: A Story of African American Steelworkers* (1996) documents black men and women recounting years of social and economic discrimination in the steel mills. Lastly, Dennis C. Dickerson's book *Out Of The Crucible: Black Steelworkers*

in Western Pennsylvania, 1875-1980 shows how African Americans were a part of the steel industry from the beginning. Excerpts from this can be found at the end of my book, along with Dickerson's essay *Black Braddock And Its History*.
Coincidentally Bell, Buba and Dickerson were all steelworkers before they produced their writings and films. Following their large footsteps as a granddaughter of steelworkers, I needed to produce a photo-history book on three generations of women (1925–2014) that dealt with segregation, deindustrialization, environmental racism, health care inequity and gentrification.

Braddock is a very real place, but it's become a symbol for writers and image-makers. Recently the photographer Mark Neville was shooting in Braddock and in Pittsburgh's wealthy neighborhood Sewickley. Hollywood got a little interested with the recent movie *Out of the Furnace* (2013). Then there's Jean-Loïc Portron's documentary *Braddock America*. Is there a risk that Braddock begins to be generalized, even fetishized, as an emblem of a post-industrial America (we've seen how Detroit has become a magnet for so many documentarists and writers wanting a shortcut to some new America).
Dr. Martin Luther King Jr. noted that "Few people have the toughness of mind to judge critically and to discern the true from the false, the fact from the fiction. Our minds are constantly being invaded by legions of half-truths, prejudices and false facts". There are many parallel realities and narratives being told. The media / culture industry takes advantage of this, pitting one group against another. I prefer documentaries to Hollywood films. I helped Gabriella Kessler and Jean-Loïc Portron by informing them about African American families and residents that remained voiceless and invisible to mainstream media. They interviewed the Bunn family, enabling them to testify to the current discrimination in Braddock. I grew up with the Bunn family. I had been photographing the same intersection at Ninth and Talbot for years, archiving the environmental racism and aggressive dispossession the Bunn family is facing since they refuse to move out the last remaining home on a lot that has been re-zoned for light industry. The Bunns own their home through years of military service and from working in the steel mills.

Out of the Furnace (2013) is a Hollywood movie about two brothers, a steel worker (Christian Bale) and an Iraq veteran (Casey Affleck). The first scene in which they appear together is at Ninth and Talbot, in front of the Bunn's house. A shallow depth of field renders the house an impressionist painting concealing the surrounding environmental ruin. A viewer would never know that Braddock is predominantly African American with residents fighting for social and economic opportunity, to be included in the revitalization of the town. Through whitewashing, cultural appropriation and media exploitation, African Americans are being written out of the redevelopment of Braddock.

Mainstream media have a habit of recognizing social difficulty and then distorting its presentation. It's ideology at its purest: the merely symbolic resolution of real contradiction.
It's imperative we tell our own stories, controlling the framework, context and narrative. In the words of Stuart Hall, "Racism never has been put in a critical context by the media [...] When it comes to fighting racism the media are part of the problem, they perpetuate myths and stereotypes about Black people; they lie by omission, distortion and selection, they give racists inflated importance and respectability".

Opposite:
LaToya Ruby Frazier, Mom and Mr. Yerby's Hands, 2005,
(from the book *The Notion of Family*, Aperture, 2014)

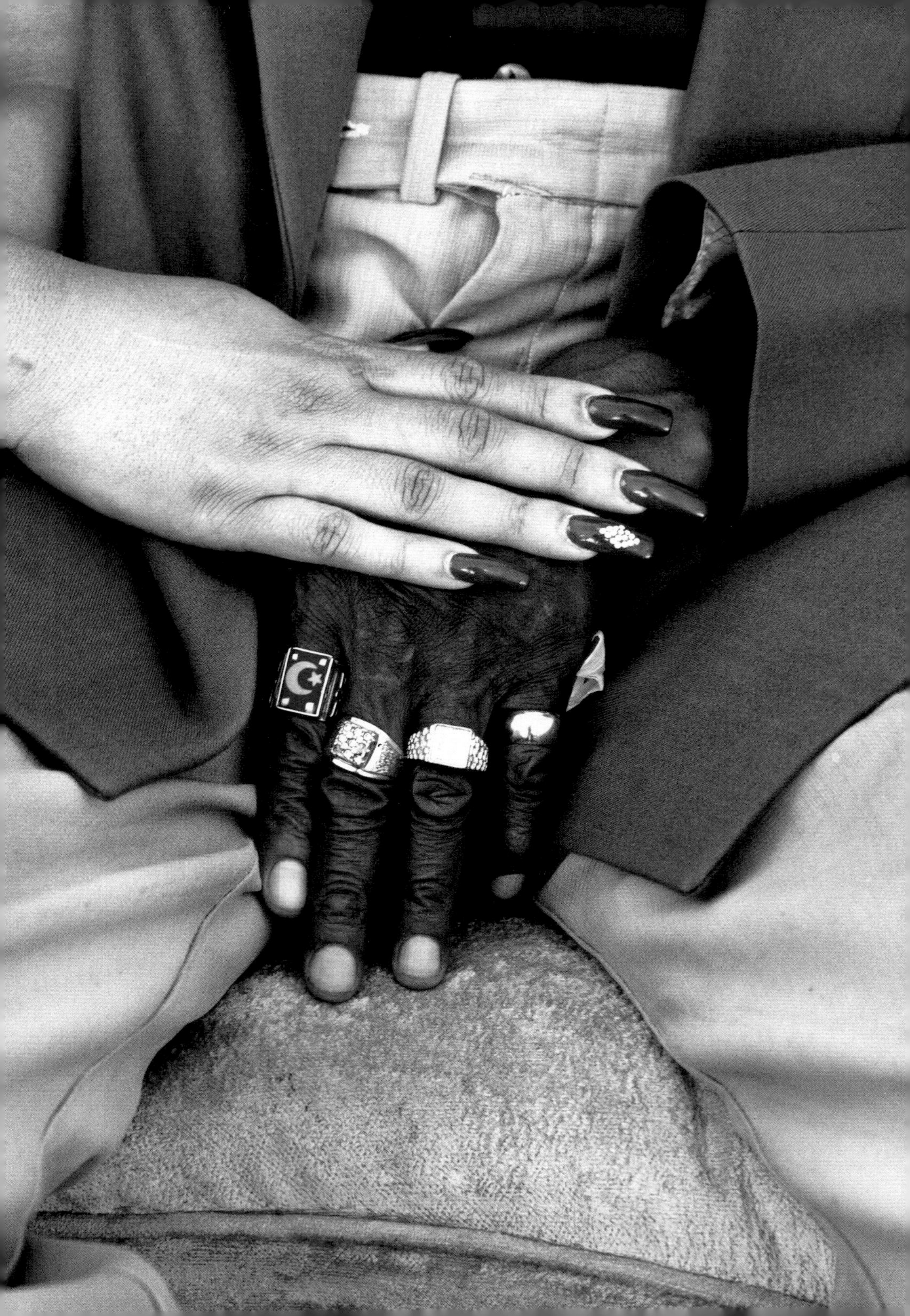

Beginning in the late 1960s, the late **Lewis Baltz** (1945–2014) occupied a singular but complex position within art, architecture and photography. While his work always showed a modernist commitment to the camera's powers of visual description, what interested Baltz was the growing tension between the seeable and the knowable. What does it mean when the surface of the world obscures meaning? How do we relate to an architecture that ceases to communicate? Baltz's serial photographic works, videos and site-specific installations dramatise this rupture in differing ways.
Like many artists emerging from conceptualism, Baltz maintained an equal commitment to the page and the wall. Each new publication was met with great anticipation and his work has been central to many important exhibitions. He also wrote about images with rare clarity. In art historical terms, Baltz's interest in the spread of modular industrial forms can be seen in the light of minimalist sculpture; his exploration of marginal or rejected spaces mirrored that of land art; his attraction to American vernacular forms was shared by Pop; his concern with the corporate forces that shape land and real estate chimed with the move in documentary photography from the recording of events to the recording of traces; and, more recently, his bringing together of different genres of imagery had much in common with postmodern montage, collage and appropriation.

In 1989 Baltz left California for France, just as his concerns shifted from images of the landscape to the landscape of images: the rootless post-industrial space of surveillance, spectacle and anomie. We met in Paris in 2014, while "Common Objects", an exhibition of Lewis's work I co-curated for Le Bal, was on display. We discussed his changes and continuities over five decades.

Lewis Baltz

In the spirit of chronology, or at least biography, let's begin with your first start in photography, which comes at a very early age.
Yeah, I was 11 when I was given my first 35mm focusing camera. Within a year I'd abandoned 35mm and was working with a Rolleiflex. I also had my own darkroom, printing all my own work. I loved it. I was absolutely fascinated by it.

What were your pictures like then?
Oh Christ, that's the bit I'd rather not speak about. They were stupid. Just pretentious landscape shots.

But what was so attractive about photography?
It seemed almost like magic to me that somehow you could make a replica. And you could represent the world, or a large piece of the world, without ever having to mess around with drawing and all that sloppy handmade stuff. This is the way it remained for a long time, I guess until the mid-1970s, when video began to come into its own. Nevertheless, photography, which really isn't all that simple, has always been for me the most direct and most automatic and most uninflected way of making a visual notation of something.

What did you want to notate?
I wasn't sure. I was just a kid. But I knew what I was looking at, even if it was very hard then, in the late 1950s, to find publications about photography. I used to be able to boast that I bought every photography book published – but that was only because there were just four or five produced every year, right through most of the 1960s. Even with all the usual kind of amateurism and popular photography nonsense around at the time, it was also clear to me then that there were in effect two trends or two positions within photography: one, of course, was Robert Frank

and *The Americans*, and the other was Edward Weston. Being afraid of crowds and also being a bit of a romantic, the Weston myth appealed to me much more than the Frank. Also, I could think of nothing better than living on one of those beautiful pieces of land in California or those southwestern states and going out each day and doing your work, your artistic work, and then coming home to find a beautiful woman waiting for you. In a sense it was a dream life. Of course, it appeared as a dream because it was mostly a romantic fiction. But Weston was also a dedicated man, a man on a mission – and if you read his notebooks, he was also something of a hard-headed narcissist, constantly writing, "Today I exchanged correspondences with Kandinsky, who told me for the first time 'I regard photography as art'". The notebooks are full of lines like this. So he was an egoist, and maybe also a bit of a bullshitter. Or both. Anyway, to answer your question, at 12 I had no idea what I wanted to notate, but I wanted to be Edward Weston. The reality is that I fell far short, but I still kept up that idea until about the age of 19 or 20.

Was it therefore because of Weston that you used to travel from your home in Newport Beach, California up the coast to Carmel?
It was partly because of Weston, but there were also all those surviving members of the Pacific Slope photographic school – Wynn Bullock, who was very generous with his time; William Current, who had been my mentor when I was just a kid; Brett Weston, who was always driving around in a Corvette with the top down and sunglasses on and a beautiful blonde by his side; and even Ansel Adams, who was a real businessman and a total charlatan. In many ways, it was a crazy thing for somebody my age to be doing – going up to the pine forests of Point Lobos every weekend to take pictures – and at some point reality crashed in and I saw the absurdity of it all; that this was all part of an older world that I couldn't have because it was gone. You couldn't do Edward Weston for the very simple reason that Edward Weston had done Edward Weston.

But outside of Point Lobos your day-to-day reality would presumably have been very different.
Oh, for sure. Most of the world that I lived in for the other five-and-a-half days of the week was much more ordinary but also somehow more mysterious, almost obscene. I mean, no one seemed to be looking at the weed lots and highway verges and gasoline stations and six-dollar motels

and what have you. And this was in spite of the fact that these things were the main presence in most people's existence. Was this in any way redeemable as an experience? I mean, if we couldn't make sense of it politically or economically could we at least make aesthetic sense of it? The answer's probably no. But that's when it all started for me, it's when I began taking the pictures that led to the hyper banal *Prototypes* series.

And did you carry this interest into your more formal studies? Did you go to art school?
Well, sort of. Just like everybody else at the time, my primary objective in continuing with my education was to avoid military service. And then again to avoid Vietnam, I went on to the San Francisco Art Institute from 1967 to 1969. At that point, in San Francisco there was the confluence of two things – at the art institute there was the continued crumbling of the school from its glory days in the 1950s with Douglas MacAgy, and of course it was also the Summer of Love. This meant we never really had any classes. You'd just go to school to hang out. I remember doing all my printing at my apartment.

And that was the beginnings of the *Prototypes*, which as you mentioned, went on for some time. But didn't they have a different title to start with?
Initially I called them *Protoinvestigations*, which was a title I stole from one of the books Joseph Kosuth displayed at his first show at the Kunsthalle in Bern, but then the title evolved somehow into *Prototypes*.

But I love the title because it raises the very interesting question of whether a photograph can be a prototype.
It was always my ambition, which I admit I didn't invent, to do a piece that would contain multiple images, and be somewhat cinematic in nature, and yet still be a single work. I was just looking for a subject that would support that kind of continued effort. This was actually no easy task. And the early stuff I was doing at the institute was, I guess, just one stop along the way.

Even though you talk about the images as a singular work, the whole series is very varied.
I think that's true. But perhaps that simply shows the effect of multiple

influences. I mean, this was a time when Antonioni first really entered my sphere of vision. I used to go over to Berkeley to watch films in the archive, and it was there that I saw *Red Desert*. I remember being completely transfixed by it. For a number of reasons, I somehow couldn't quite believe what I was seeing. One was the sheer physical beauty of the film, but it also had to do with the colour. *Red Desert* was the first film I ever saw in colour that I liked.

What else were you looking at? Or rather, what were you reading at the time? Were you a serious reader?
I thought so, yeah. But then again, if I was that damn serious – like Bruce Nauman – I would have been reading Wittgenstein. I think I was basically not intelligent enough to understand Wittgenstein, which, let's face it, is embarrassing to admit, because here is someone writing in clear and common English and yet you realise that you have no idea what he's saying. When I was young, I think the writer who inflamed me the most was Jorge Luis Borges. I borrowed a copy of *Fictions* from a friend and started to read it one evening. Didn't go to sleep till the next morning because I couldn't put it down. It was amazing. Borges' view of an idea was that its real test was not in its truth or untruth but in its beauty.

And what it might provoke.
In a number of these stories – like *Funes the Memorius* or *Pierre Menard, Author of the Quixote* – he deals with the whole question of what is cognition and language. And remember, this was all long before anyone used the word "postmodernism".

Were things like the nouveau roman also on your horizon then?
No. They should have been, but they weren't. It was only a bit later that I discovered Robbe-Grillet, but that was through film.

By your early Twenties, you had gone from someone who wants to be Edward Weston to someone who somehow wants to directly confront the reality of the 1960s.
I'm not sure I wanted to confront it, but there just seemed to be no other choice. I mean, I'm sure it was different for you in England, but I was restricted by the experiences of growing up in Southern California. Where I lived – the place I was raised – was just a small suburban town built

around a rich man's boat harbour. It was incredibly under-populated. It's called Orange County because most of it was just orange groves. But by the time I graduated from college in 1969 it had a population of four million and had just elected a president – local boy Richard Nixon. So there was incredibly rapid growth. And you couldn't just take it or leave it: it was really being shoved down your throat. So I started to think of what I was doing as a way of shoving back. It was a reaction. Not by making things or by shouting out obvious moralisations, but by doing what I thought was the very worst thing that anyone could possibly do, which was to hold up a mirror to this place. You know? "This is the world that the richest and most powerful country has given to its citizens. This is as good as it gets".

Talk me through that, because the really interesting thing about a camera is obviously that it is constructed around a mirror. And as an apparatus this mirror is undiscriminating – one day you can be shooting the trees on Point Lobos and the next day can be photographing a seedy gas station, and technically speaking you're doing exactly the same thing in both. But of course, as a photographer, you're making big decisions about subject matter and about how it might be pictured. So what exactly might constitute a "mirror back"?
Well, some of its physical characteristics would be that it should be very high resolution. Photography *per se* should be transparent. It shouldn't be grainy. It shouldn't in any way use the effects of photography.

For the grainlessness, your pictures really look like photographs.
Oh yeah, that's interesting. But what does that mean, though? What else could they look like?

Well, Jeff Wall once told me that his work was always "trying to make photographs look like eyesight". When I pressed him on this he said, "I know it's a complicated thing, but when you look at an Atget" – and it was clearly important to him that Atget was the reference – "you know you're looking at someone who's very conscious about the translation into the photograph"; that is, he was not thinking about a mimesis of eyesight. And so given what you said earlier about your interest in the facsimile or replica, your

pictures therefore often feel highly photographic, and in feeling highly photographic they don't simulate. They draw attention to themselves as photographs and their difference from vision. Or at least, that was my reaction to your pictures of industrial parks when I first saw them. They really felt like photographs.
You've got me here. I don't know how to answer. But it's really interesting. I mean, most people who were pulling the strings and deciding what was and was not photography, and what was and was not worthy, would have either said my pictures didn't look like photographs or they looked like very bad photographs. I suppose if there's a model for that, it would be the kind of photographs that used to be in real estate office windows, as opposed to the mainstream model, which was the American snapshot and family album.

Sure, but both the snapshot and the real estate picture, or even a study of industrial architecture for that matter, are two versions of a kind of anonymous, nameless practice. And maybe that's why people don't think they look like photography.
But this again raises the question of invisibility. And it was this question that was really on my mind in the late 1960s and early 70s, certainly with the industrial parks series. I'll give you my five-minute screed on this: the question "is it photography?" was in effect just a child of the industrial revolution. In fact, there's a very persuasive argument that says photography was never really invented; it was simply a number of separate techniques that were brought into being, brought together because there was a commercial and a social need for them. But whether legitimate or illegitimate, photography was still a product of the industrial revolution, and what is especially interesting is that photography soon found itself photographing industrialism – that is, it turned its glass eye back on its horrible parent. And what it found there was something discernible to the human eye. It found a world of pulleys and levers and Aristotelian principles that a reasonably logical person could look at and figure out. This, I think, is comforting in a certain way. And then at some later point, probably around the time I was in school, we passed from the mechanical age to the electronic age, where nothing is revealed to the eye. I mean, that's what intrigued me about Irvine, California, where I first photographed all those industrial parks. Among other things, Irvine was the most highly praised and decorated planned

industrial environment in the world. It therefore became the model for many others, not just in the US, but all over the place. For me, this also went beyond Walter Benjamin saying "you wouldn't know what goes on in a Krupp factory". No, you wouldn't know what goes on, and it's no coincidence that you don't. This is really an architecture and a planning of concealment.

But my feeling is that this doesn't come about with the shift into the electronic, but it arrives with modernism, particularly in architecture. Because in modernism while there's a commitment to the idea that form might follow function, there's also a kind of rationalising, modularising of architecture where once there was only a kind of symbolic language – wherein a house had to look like a house and a bank had to look like a bank. With the modern, a hospital and an apartment and a school and a factory all begin to look like each other.

Yeah, sure, you can trace and project these ideas from Le Corbusier's writings forward, but in physical reality you don't really see the consequences until after the Second World War. Because it is only then, to be as crude, as literal, as possible, that some company in Nebraska has to figure out what to do with a hell of a lot of aluminium technology it had previously used for manufacturing cargo planes, or whatever. And in applying this prefabrication to more everyday uses, they know that they can produce on a certain scale. But still, the public had to accept the spaces that they were inhabiting. So we end up with these industrial parks. And they're all so cheap. This, I guess, is one of the major points – that unless you're dealing with an architect with real ability and a real sense of luxury, most modern buildings reveal themselves only as more cheaply made than their predecessors. Take the Portland building – you know, the one Graves did in Oregon. It replaced a building which was a tiny and perfect little Beaux-Arts structure. But this was a style the world couldn't wait to get rid of. And so in its place we got something that looks like what it is. Cheap and tacky.

Let's talk about technology, which similarly never used to be cheap or tacky. I read that the industrial parks, or maybe all your photographs up to that point, were shot using a 35mm SLR on extremely slow film.

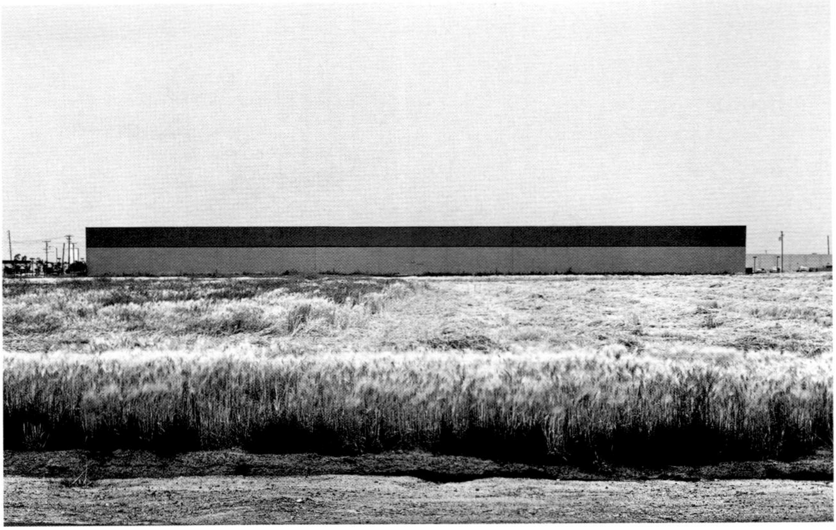

Lewis Baltz, East Wall, Western Carpet Mills, 1231 Warner, Tustin,
from *The New Industrial Parks near Irvine, California*, 1974

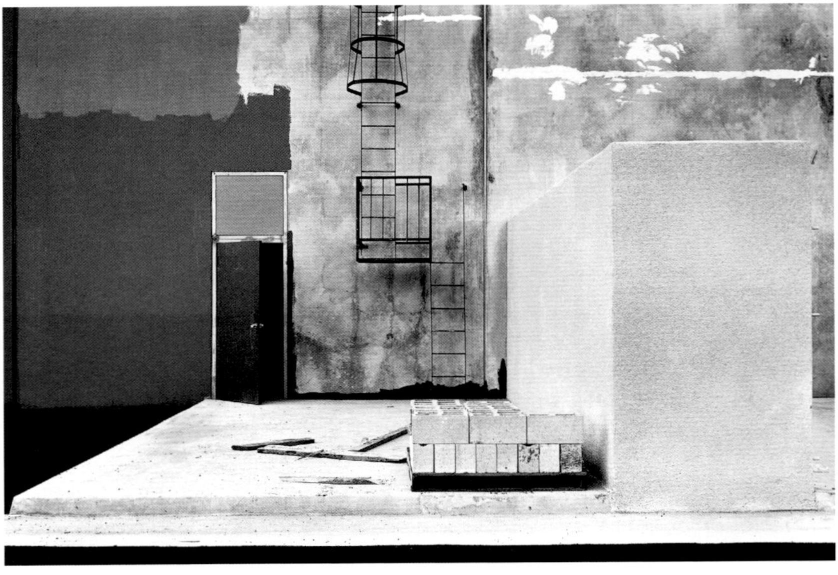

Lewis Baltz, East Wall, Western Carpet Mills, 1231 Warner, Tustin,
from *The New Industrial Parks near Irvine, California*, 1974

That's the secret to them. They were all shot on a Leica using microfilm developed for continuous tone.

What, really low ASA, like five or seven?
Yep.

Wow. How did you arrive at that?
Because I didn't like looking into the ground glass of large-format cameras; because I didn't want to learn how to develop cut film; and because I didn't want to carry around all that heavy equipment. I wanted to be more mobile. With a Leica and this really slow film it seemed technically possible to achieve the results I wanted, and so I thought, why not? Of course, this meant I was freer in the field, but much less free when it came to actually realizing prints.

And over how long a period were the industrial parks shot, considering it's a world that's changing very, very fast?
Probably through most of 1973, and going back three or four years before that.

For all your mobility, it's also a very fixed body of work. There are precisely 51 images in total. How did you come upon that number?
Because 51 equates to three rows of 17.

But they are not always exhibited like that. I often see the series as five rows of ten and a one. Regardless of their display, though, how did you determine that you had adequately covered the subject? I mean, when does a photographer say "that's enough"?
I've been asking myself that same question for years.

If you're Jeff Wall, you make just one throw of the dice and you try to capture an idea in a single picture. But he's probably the only photographer who works this way. Just about everyone else works in series. And so this 51: it's really quite a big number. That's a lot to hold in your mind when looking at a sequence of images in a book or exhibition. And it feels as if it's complete. I feel like I'm with a mind that's thinking about covering something in its entirety.

I'm sure my pictures never exhaust a subject. Fifty-one probably just exhausted my engagement with the subject, or what I felt I could do. And the thing about the industrial parks was that they were not put together chronologically. They were assembled in an attempt to make the series as non-narrative as possible, even if you always get a narrative feeling anyway – I mean, you take 25 pictures and shuffle them like cards and every time you deal them out it looks like there's a narration. But it was supposed to come full circle. Or at least, its ambition was to come full circle, even if in some of the pictures you start to see me drawing away from the buildings and focusing more on the empty flood plain that they are sitting on.

Were you thinking of it as something to be published or exhibited, or both?
Both. Always both. The book – *The New Industrial Parks Near Irvine, California* came out in 1974. It was designed by the photographer Tom Barrow, who I haven't seen for so long.

The book is pretty extraordinary as a design, but didn't you want to design it yourself? I've always thought of you as really quite a keen graphic designer. There is a number of artists of your generation who have a very distinct graphic sense.
Well, Tom was very nice about this. Basically I told him what I wanted and he produced it. We had to work this way because I don't know any of the technicalities of graphic design – this was before any of the desktop publishing programs. So I just explained to Tom what I wanted and we went through each page, one after the other. It was all done in one mask. It's about as austere as anything I could think of from that time.

How come it was published in English and German?
It was in part because I'd seen the Bechers' work and realised that there might be some interesting things going on in Germany and some interesting people in Germany or an audience who would appreciate my work. And guess what, 35 years later and this audience did appear.

Well, it was not even 35, it was pretty soon after you released the book. And today, of course, almost all your titles are produced through the German publisher Steidl.

Oh yes, Gerhard Steidl is not just a printer or publisher but a patron. He's interested in projects. And the scale of his ambition is almost like Tintoretto – he wants to cover every wall in the house. He's therefore patron to every possible kind of photography book, including quite a few he thought he really didn't want. And his ambition is not only to print these but to print them beautifully. Beyond that, he just hopes to make enough money to keep going.

Back in 1974, who were the other photographers you were looking at? Did you know people like Robert Adams, for example?
I did. The first time I went to New York – to show my work to people who in turn showed it to Leo Castelli who, to my astonishment and unbelievable pleasure, would eventually decide to take it on board – I saw two things that were really heartening to me. The first was a bizarre show at MoMA – bizarre in the sense ... well, it was Peter Bunnell's idea to always oppose things and he did this by exhibiting Emmet Gowin next to Robert Adams. So with Rob you had this unbelievable purity, while with Emmet you had these dark foresty scenes and his wife peeing in front of a tree. Robert's work, especially, was amazing, totally fantastic. His book, *The New West*, came out shortly afterwards and I reviewed it for *Art in America*. The second was a show at the Sonnabend gallery of the Bechers, which of course just delighted me. It was sort of like Robinson Crusoe finding the footprint. Before that I had gone through a period in my life when I felt like a minority of one – a mad man, who nobody gives a shit about, producing work nobody wanted to engage with. So when I came across something or someone who in some way touched upon my interests, I found it an enormous validation. And when the work was so good, like with Robert or the Bechers, it gave me even more validation.

And within a year you and Adams, the Bechers and six other American photographers are all curated together by William Jenkins in the "New Topographics" show.
That was just a moment of perfect confluence. If you think about all those people now – photographers like Nick Nixon, Frank Gohlke, Joe Deal, Stephen Shore or Henry Wessel – you could never have shown their work from five years earlier or five years later. But at that particular point in time it all came together.

So it felt significant at the time?
I'm often asked that question, so I've gotta know, right? It opened at the Eastman House in Rochester, upstate New York. I remember they did this very clean, beautiful little catalogue. But nobody came to see it or review it. They finally invited a critic up from *Art in America*. He stayed for a week, looked at the show, and then wrote a good, intelligent review. That seemed to be the end of it. The exhibition did go on to the Otis Art Institute Art Gallery in Los Angeles, and then to the art museum at Princeton. When that ended nothing more was heard about it. A few people even started talking about a "backlash" against the show. I never got that. I mean, how can you have a backlash when you never even had a frontlash? But anyway, things went quiet again until the mid-1980s when Jonathan Green wrote a book on American photography and called it the single most influential photography exhibition of all time. I have to say I was incredibly happy about that, but also totally astonished.

I think it gets caught up with a certain kind of art history that's always looking for landmarks rather than precedents.
It's also a reflection of an art world that has thrived on movements, most of which have been named by their enemies. So if it was just Stephen Shore and Robert Adams, then that's interesting, but if we put them and the Bechers and Baltz and Wessel and Joe Deal together, then it becomes a movement and people will pay more attention. And they did.

But arguably, I'd have thought you were closer to what Jenkins was after in curating the show than anyone else in the exhibition.
That's a good question. Although, in actuality I think I was somewhere in the centre of that spectrum. If you look at someone like Henry Wessel, you'll find a photographer with a strange and beautiful eye, and someone whose world is full of objects which are not mute. But if you push a further in his direction you get more traditional street photography.

Henry is also a shutter photographer, whereas the rest of you are lens photographers.
Henry was one of the few who didn't use a tripod.

The cut of the shutter is what makes the picture. Things are moving and then stop, which has never really interested you.

I could never move that fast! We used to play racquetball, he and I – he's a lot quicker than I am.

There's also an interesting ambiguity to this moment. Having got into the medium at 11 through Edward Weston, and with your very obvious affection for photography, there comes a point in the mid-1970s when like a lot of others you're saying, "I'm not a photographer".
Are we talking about photography, or are we talking about the world of photography and its history and its historians, its networks, its personalities, its gods... because I don't credit any of that. I think as a medium it's brilliant. And it's brilliant because of the simplest things that it does, and does well.

But not everybody's interested in that.
Ha ha, I know, I know, I'm aware of that. But you know, if you speak to photo historians they can tell you everything about when Stieglitz reprinted his pictures of Venice and made the water black so as to bring forward the plane of the buildings in accordance with cubism, but then they can't tell you anything about cubism. Photography has always been presented to us as a separate creation which has nothing to do with anything else. Yet it very clearly has a great deal to do with other contemporary forms of expression, in art, cinema, what have you. It also has a great deal to do with the objective social realities and conditions in the time of its making. At MoMA John Szarkowski really fostered the whole idea that photography was something special (along with a really distasteful nationalist sensibility); that it was a different creation. I don't believe that for a second. I simply think there are people who don't want to confront this. I also don't think of it as the major medium of the twentieth century.

Secondary mediums are still significant.
Sure, it's a significant medium, and it's still a medium in the sense that you can't replace it with something else. It's like trying to whistle the Seagram building. Impossible.

Beyond the case of "New Topographics", what's your feeling as to how your photography was understood and received in that

period? I ask this because I was talking to Robert Cumming recently, who like you was with Castelli, and he said, "Well, you know I got lots of invitations to go with photography galleries, but I didn't want to because I was also making sculpture and I was making paintings and I was making video".
There also wasn't a photography gallery around at the time that was any good. So maybe he was just being diplomatic.

But were you in shows that made those connections explicit? For example, shows alongside minimalist sculpture?
No, that only really came later. At that stage there was a distinct apartheid between photography and the rest of the arts. But this also meant that a lot of people who were being made out to be second-class citizens actually enjoyed this undervaluing, because they could be very important players in a very small field. As a case in point, I was in the Paris Biennale once upon a time. I don't know how they pulled that off because the Paris Biennale didn't have photography, and the reason they didn't have photography was simply the logic of the marketplace. In other words, if they saw a photograph by Robert Frank it was valued at $700, but if they saw another photograph by Sol LeWitt it was $4,000. The result was that your viewer or potential buyer would be mystified. They'd scratch their head and leave without buying either. Of course, there's always been an audience for photography, but it is only fairly recently that there's been a market. The thin end of the wedge into that market now is work like Jeff Wall's or Andreas Gursky's. In other words, tableaux images, photographs that most resemble paintings.

What about the argument that's made about photographers not having quite embraced scale the way they could have done, because they'd somehow internalised the page?
But in the 1980s those opportunities were not so available.

But it could be done. It was possible to get hold of big paper and some photographers and artists did it.
Who? And who on a consistent basis? It was only really the Becher students who were the first to seriously commit to making large-scale work.

But when Szarkowski does the Walker Evans retrospective at

MoMA in 1970 or 71 he gets very worried about audiences having to look at two hundred 8x10s, so he has 12 of them blown up mural-size and mounted on Masonite – although he says these are just graphic punctuation, as if a spectator would complain that they were not the real thing.
Deep down everybody's Edward Steichen, huh?

But in one sense he's right. I mean, in many ways I find detailed, rich 8x10s incredibly difficult to look at in a gallery. I'm 12 inches from the wall. That's not a comfortable position to stand in.
But ask yourself this, why are they 8x10? Why aren't they, for example, 6x13? Because that's simply the size the paper comes in.

I understand that, but surely artworks should come in the size in which they are produced, whatever that might be. And yet it is also very interesting that when certain photographs are blown up they look grotesque. For example, I've occasionally seen a Cartier-Bresson big or a Winogrand big, and they fail. You realize that the pictures only work at the smaller size. Somehow those photographers had internalized the page as their scale.
Yes, but everything does that. I can't think of any images that work beautifully at all different scales. For example, my gallerist in Cologne has a little print by Gursky, of the port at Salerno. It's a wonderful picture, about what commerce represents in Europe today. The print he had was really small. It was very lovely, but it had almost no power. But when you see the same image measured in metres rather than centimetres you'll find that it's still lovely, but it now has tremendous power.

I agree, but I also think there's something about the relation between the architecture of the space in which the work is exhibited and the work itself. You've always managed to balance this by thinking of the artwork as an ensemble – as a sequence or as a grid. Of course, this also comes back to the question of the gallery versus the book, and the two different ways of representing your work.
It was never my ambition to make a career out of making tableaux. I mean, I've always had too much fascination for cinema to create singular images, and so I wanted my photographs to be like paper movies.

Not necessarily narrative in structure or composition, although what the hell does narrative actually mean, because we can compose a narrative out of any two things placed together. But in a grid it's interesting because you can't control the order in which people see things and the emphasis they give to them. The grid becomes a screen and you'll be drawn to one thing or another, but there's no guarantee. In a book there is. *Candlestick Point* as a book is different from *Candlestick Point* as a wall piece. That was the first time I ever did anything like that.

The obvious thing about your grids is that they are punctured with gaps or voids; sections of blank space that become almost panoramic.
It's about reading something in a certain way. Where I felt like *Candlestick* finally succeeded, and where I felt there was a form of culmination, has to do with the fact that there's not a standout picture. There's not a single image that someone could make a strong case for being a really great picture, meaning by definition the others are not so good. Rather, they all seem to be on a level. I like this and I like that. Whereas in *Industrial Parks* the picture on the back of the book is a picture that everybody loves.

Wouldn't that be an argument for kicking it out?
Yeah, perhaps, although I didn't see it that way. Maybe I wasn't tough enough. There's actually another image in there, which I think is much more interesting – the shot of the long building on the horizon. It's a personal favourite. This also reminds me of a time I was in Castelli and the curator from the Boston Museum of Fine Arts came by, saying he had received authorization to purchase just one of the pieces. I had realized a little earlier that people were buying complete sets of images and were then breaking them up into individual images. I thought "Fuck that. Why should they do it, and not me?" I used to figure that as long as I could keep the images together as a book, or as long as I could have a few complete sets in museums, then it would be okay. But then this Boston curator kept asking me for my personal preference. "What's your favourite among those that are still available?" And so I showed him this image of the building on the horizon and he said, "Well, I don't really think so". He finally bought something, but I can't remember now which one. He also gave me these filthy looks for the rest of the day. It dawned on me

later that I think he imagined I was trying to sell him the dog, the one that nobody else wanted – let's see if this guy from Boston will fall for it.

But in a way that's kind of true, or part of the reason you like it. It is one of the most delicate but it's also one of the most belligerent images.
It's a little hard to get into, yeah.

That's an interesting aspect, the hard-to-get-into – the idea that a photograph might be impenetrable while at the same time showing you something. I'm sensing this tension is one which has animated you for more than a decade.
I've always been interested in trying to understand how much of a context we can really create for something, and generating a kind of legibility without actually using text. Of course there later came a stage when I did use text because it was the best and clearest thing to do. But at that point in the late 1980s I avoided it. This was also partly in reaction to the artist and photographer Allan Sekula, who was using a lot of text and making really feeble images and claiming that one couldn't be supported without the other. My thought at the time was perhaps if he'd made better images, they wouldn't need the text. But then later Sekula did a project called *Fish Story*, which again combined the two, but the images were so much better and the thing was really good. In *Fish Story* you no longer feel that when an image falls short he's there to do with language what he had failed to do with the camera. It's leaner somehow, and much more critical. I think MoMA just bought the whole thing.

What's interesting is that in Sekula's writing the practices he holds up as beacons are always experimental filmmaking and documentaries. It's never photography. There was no good photography, if you asked Allan.
Well, he certainly didn't like my work. He wrote about my work twice and both times he was highly critical. But I was sorry when he died. A good adversary is hard to find these days.

Victor Burgin. His is an interesting parallel path to yours, in that you both move away from photography into other practices: montage, collage, mixed-media, video, text. You also share a great

interest in architecture, or at least architecture understood socially, economically, politically. How close do you feel to Victor's work?
I'm a big fan. I have been since I saw his poster work "What Does Possession Mean to You?" in the mid-1970s. He's also very good company. He's back in England now after all those years in California. I could never imagine him in Santa Cruz. He is so un-Santa Cruz. That's the only spot in northern California where you get beaches and surfers. It's a beautiful little town, but it's really only for bliss-ninnies and airheads.

Did your own move away from photography similarly correspond with your physical move; this time, away from America and to France?
Yes. At a certain point, in effect immediately after doing *Candlestick Point*, I felt that I had done everything I had wanted to do or was capable of doing in that direction, and I wanted another method of making that work public, plus another family situation, another country, another continent.

Did you speak French?
I still don't. Or at least not a version of French that any French person would understand. At the time, I just remember wanting everything to change. By the end of the 1980s I was pretty disgusted with the way the Reagan world had taken over the art world. We had all this crappy tenth-rate stuff like the *Neue Wilde*, who were not all bad guys, although most of them were. All the rigour had gone out of the art world. The rift between the bourgeoisie and the artist, which began around the time of Manet, had been healed. Now the artists were completely bourgeois themselves. But I hated capitalism. I still hate capitalism. And out of that I came to the idea that France, Europe, anywhere in Europe, would be a more socially democratic place in which to live and work.

But with this move to France, the world that you're attempting to picture or articulate also changes. There's a good line in the Le Bal catalogue about how you moved from images of landscape to the landscape of images. So it's no longer about a place just outside of Reno, it's more abstract.
It's also a question of history. Everything that I photographed in the US,

and the American West in particular, is in so many ways ahistorical. Its history – at least its white settler history – is very short and pretty ugly. And in a certain sense it's not getting any prettier. There was this creepiness there – partly because every place had grown up so fast, like mushrooms in spring, and they could also disappear just as quickly. Everything was transitory. I therefore never felt that there was any security in being in a city. There was no monument of continued human endeavour. Whereas here in Europe, of course, it's all monument.

But arguably your European work becomes more dystopian in character.
Yes, maybe. Most of my more recent pieces were also made as public works, which meant I had a responsibility to make something that someone could encounter on the street, which I think is different from the responsibility of making something for a museum. I mean, we're not dealing only with consenting adults, we're dealing with a person who happens to be stuck in a traffic jam who happens to look at a billboard. It all became a little less subtle in the sense that it was easier to read and figure out.

It's interesting that you talk about your new audience like that. On the street. The vision I have of you is of an artist who, when he's in America, is slowly stalking these alienated, entropic landscapes, and then when you get to Europe, it's a different kind of social interaction, of local meetings and community groups.
Well, I was fed up with the Marlboro Man model of the artist. It's lonely. Do you think it's a picnic walking around Park City, Utah for four months?

But historically, so many photographers have been socially dysfunctional outsiders. They like it there. They go to graveyards. They go to the banlieue. They like the edge. And nobody is making them do that.
I didn't say I didn't like it! I just got lonely. In total I spent three years doing stuff on Park City, and for at least one of those years I was all by myself. Doing what – being heroic? Printing the largest edition ever printed of anything? (Until some Japanese guy saw it and immediately made an even larger one).

If you were making work now what would it be?
If I knew that I'd be making it.

Would you? I somehow felt you decided to put an end to making.
No, of course not. I would probably be looking into making work that is situational, transient, ephemeral. This seems to be the possibility now for art. The other end of the spectrum would be to make really polished items for undereducated billionaires. Although it can't be much fun doing that, and even less fun trying to do it and failing. You know, turning out some neo-pop thing that's even dumber than the guy who's gonna buy it – it flatters his intellect by being dumber than he is. So, no, I'd probably be making something non-marketable.

Did you live off sales? Did you teach?
I did everything for a while. I came from a family that had middle-middle-class money, but I was a spoiled only child, and so I got some money from my family and bought my own house. Didn't have to pay rent. At the same time I was always teaching whenever I could get a job, and I was always selling work, although this never really gave me enough to live on. Not even enough to pay my expenses in doing it. This went on until about 2004. And then suddenly my work started to skyrocket at auctions. This was work I had made 40 years earlier. Maybe it was a question of it finally being presented to a public that has a different understanding of it than before. My German dealer Thomas Zander tells me that he has never once sold anything of mine to a photography collector. And I've also only ever made things in very limited numbers – many of which I give away to friends – perhaps three or four prints at most. Of course, every artist you interview will always say the same thing: "Among my collectors I have some very intelligent people. And the people who collect other people's works are idiots". Or words to that effect. All artists think only their own collectors are geniuses.

It must have been heartening to suddenly have this great interest in your work.
It was, it really was. For the first time in my life, aged about 55, I was finally able to make a kind of living from my work. By 60 it was a good living. I'm 67 now. I've never hit the stage when I can drive around in a Ferrari, but in my old age I have a certain degree of financial security.

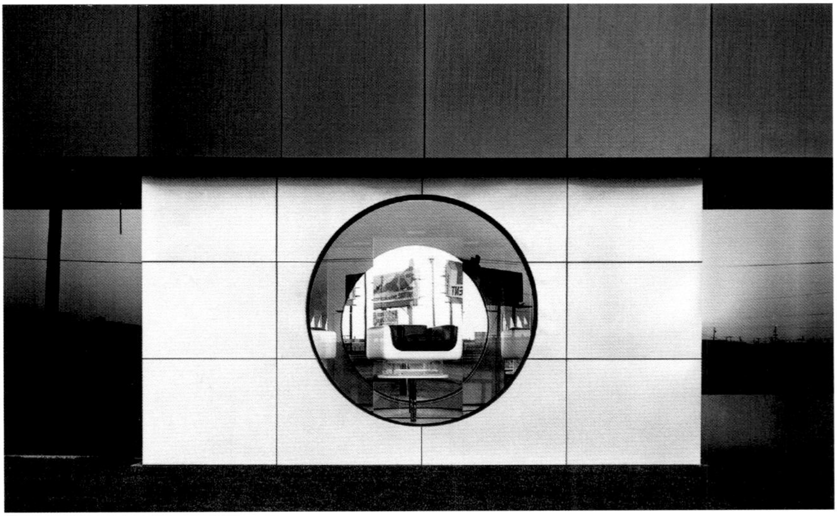

Lewis Baltz, North Wall Steelcase, 1123 Warner Avenue, Tustin, 1974, (from *The New Industrial Parks near Irvine, California*, 1974)

And the good notices we have received for the Le Bal show are also, of course, incredibly pleasing. It seems that the people who perhaps didn't quite get my work have retired and a new generation of younger curators has arrived for whom that boring old distinction between art and photography never even existed.

There is also a degree of nostalgia now, which in itself creates problems. I once spoke to Stephen Shore about this, who admitted to a certain apprehension about how a diner from the 1970s or industrial park or whatever is suddenly romantic. It worried him that there is now an exoticism that absolutely wasn't there at the time. The "old problems", as Brecht would say.
I think for better or worse Bill [William] Eggleston's work plays to that all the time – an older, gentler way of life that supported itself by using other human beings as slaves. For me, it's a little hard to feel nostalgic for that now. But still, he's working, and if Brecht was right, we know that the one thing about those problems is that we have survived them.

John Stezaker has been making collages for over forty years, often combining just two found photographs, or even simply removing an element from one photograph. Precise and psychologically charged, his art has strong ties to the history of Surrealism, Situationism and Pop, but it is uniquely his own.

Stezaker's starting point is the wildness, the deep ambiguity at the heart of *all* images. This quality is usually tamed by text and context, but under the right circumstances it can be released, and at that moment the viewer is also set free. The kinds of imagery Stezaker uses as source material are among the most clichéd and familiar: picture postcards and generic film publicity photographs. But from these humble and banal artefacts, Stezaker is able to draw out a world of repressed fantasy and possibility.

Although John and I are almost neighbours in North London, we choose to conduct our various conversations as email exchanges. It allows us time to contemplate our responses and draw our thoughts together. This one was first published in *Frieze Masters* magazine, in 2013.

John Stezaker

You have been making collages with photographic material for over forty years. Where did the interest begin? You attended London's Slade School of Fine Art in the early 1970s. Did you go there with an interest in the photographic image, or was it a matter of discovering a new direction once you were there?
I already had a collection of photographs before I went to college; postcards mostly, a sepia dog calendar that I remember with affection, and my mother's old shopping catalogues. The first paintings I did, when I started at the Slade in 1967, were enlargements of tiny collages made from shoe adverts. I found the enlargement process slavish. The paintings were not as interesting as the collages, and the collages were not as interesting as the original images. This led to a crisis in my first year, which resulted in my giving up painting. I decided that nothing I could do with these images, which I found fascinating, improved on them, and that, in order to be fascinated by an image, it already had to be there, it had to be found. The processes of enlargement and media transcription only seemed to diminish the power of the found image. This was when I began to see my process of collecting, fragmenting, and reassembling images not as my preparatory activity but as my primary one. And I quickly expanded it, scouring secondhand bookshops and the dustbins of the film studios in Soho. I discovered Situationism around this time, which offered some justification for what I was doing.

Did you feel you needed justification? Was that to do with the politics of vanguard art at the time, and its suspicion of fascination? Or, was the need for justification more to do with the complicated relation between "finding" existing images and the creative act?
It is more complicated. My tutors and everyone else thought my

paintings were "pop", and, though I had an interest in Richard Hamilton, I wanted to avoid that association. By stopping painting, the association disappeared. In the political atmosphere of the art-school occupations that occurred that year (1967-8), situationism and the process of *détournement* seemed to justify my collecting activities, which my tutors saw as "giving up". Re-captioning images suggested a critical relationship with the found image that was absent in pop's unquestioning celebration of consumer culture. But, in the end, the captions and their political justifications became obstacles to my image fascinations, and they took a lot longer to dispense with.

Fascination is, almost by definition, beyond will, beyond conscious intention. I get the impression your collages come from the fine balance you seem to strike between accepting your fascination with images and wanting to reflect on it, like a dreamer, contemplating their own dream.
Yielding to fascination means overcoming the habit of *using* found images, of consciously manipulating and controlling them. I resist subordinating the image to any concept or legible use. My aim is to free it, to let it reveal itself from behind the cloak of familiarity. I have found following my own image fascination difficult. It is always in conflict with my conscious intentions and leads me into unexpected, sometimes unwelcome territory. But fascination has become the only rule in my work – to follow it wherever it might take me. That is why digression is so important as a way of escaping conscious control. Collage is a way to create the circumstances for digression and for attention to the unintentional or inadvertent, as you say, for allowing a conscious contemplation of the image in its dream state.
I only started using the word fascination after reading Maurice Blanchot and Georges Bataille in the late 1970s, early 1980s. Fascination is a relation with images divested of conceptual content and intentionality, images which have lost their connection with everyday legibility – after images. Bataille associates fascination with such images; images that have, in a sense, died. He defines fascination as a form of "morose delectation". Blanchot, similarly, describes fascination as being for what is left behind in the image, in the mortal remains.

You've worked extensively with old film-publicity stills and old postcards. Symbolically, the film still dies once its publicity function ceases. The postcard dies after it has been bought, sent, and received. But when images die, they do not automatically disappear. Many persist, zombie-like, to continue the metaphor. But when you talk about this being the state in which it is possible to "free the image" – "in order to let it reveal itself" – this, too, is a metaphor. The meanings, ambiguities, and energies of images are not literally in them. They must be in us, no?
In us and outside us – that is the ambiguity of the image. In Blanchot's words, the image is "between here and nowhere". In other words, when we read an image, we do not necessarily see it, or, if you prefer, we see only what the image is designed to show. Blanchot went on to describe the way utensils "disappear into their use", only to appear in their obsolescence or dysfunction. The same applies to images. As they fall out of use, we see what was previously invisible or neutral. It is a matter of seeing what is betrayed by the image rather than what it transparently signifies.

This accounts for your interest in the kinds of imagery you use, the "raw material", but what of the cuts and collage? Are these additional means of bringing out what is betrayed by the image? Or, do they bring extra significations?
Both. With the image fragments – where I remove part of the photographic image and the resulting image remains rectangular – they become new photographic images, each with a new central focus. We are left with the setting, a body without a head, or a familiar gesture or pose that seems to betray something of the relation between self and photographic representation. Where it works, it estranges the familiar, and this is a transformation as well as a betrayal.
This metamorphosis is more obvious when the subtraction is internalised as a hole, as in the *Tabula Rasa* series (where an empty canvas or a shining screen replaces a central character in a film still), or, in the *Circle* series (where a spot-light blinds out the centre of interest in the image). Then, you could say that there is a transformation of one narrative into another. But, however transformative these devices may be, they are just other ways of displacing atten-

tion from the centre to the surroundings – the setting of the image. This is another way of allowing the image to betray itself, its "set-up". In rendering "the star" invisible, these works bring to the fore the minor actors and extras, whose role is usually to disappear into the background.

This relation between the purported subject and the "set-up" or surroundings is always a little unstable when the image is photographic, because the camera takes in everything, without hierarchy. Open the shutter and the world-as-light floods in. The camera has no conception, no way of knowing what is important in the image and what is marginal. Things like composition, lighting, or focus are rhetorical devices that indicate conventional ways to read the image. But, conventions are only conventions. They cannot exhaust the possibilities of the photographic image. So, in a way, your shifting the emphasis of the image, from subject to setting, reorients us back, to the mechanical indifference of the camera. Would you agree?

The collages exploit this "mechanical indifference" of the photographic image, as you put it. It allows the collage devices I employ to redirect attention, from one part to another. But, even though, as you point out, the camera has no way of knowing what is central or marginal, the photographer does. The film still and the publicity portrait are some of the most convention-bound and staged genres of photography, where hierarchies of image legibility are clear. With the stills, the star tends to be at the centre of any complex arrangement of characters, and, with the portraits, the focus tends to be on the face in the upper middle. (Women's faces tend to be less central, because of the need to include a secondary object of attention – the bust. I find it easier to "behead" men, because their ties, their folded-arm gestures, and whatever else is revealed in the lower part of their portraits do not constitute a secondary object of interest in the same way).

In films, extras disappear into the background. The still photographer, engaged in the second photographic "take", often finds it necessary to recompose the scene so that the star doesn't get lost in the crowd of incidental details that the photograph indifferently registers. I have a collection of images that were rejected because the star got lost in the crowd. They are wonderful. You find yourself searching for a recognisable face in a sea of extras. It is a bit like spotting Jesus in Bruegel's painting, *Christ Carrying the Cross* (1564). Although Jesus is dead centre and literally marked with a cross, he is always difficult to find. This makes me think about another device used in my collages – hiding. It raises other issues connected with this idea of "mechanical indifference".

In your collages, there's often a fine balance between the seductive and the monstrous. Perfectly benign images, originally made to be attractive, become demonic when cut and combined. That effect was always an aspect of collage, going right back to the 1920s. But, in your work, which is often as simple as collage can be – one cut, the combination of two parts – the balance is refined, exquisite even. There is a purity to your minimal means. Is this to do with your affection for your source material, with wanting to show it and celebrate it as much as alter it?
Yes, but I am not sure if it is an affection for my source material. I am certainly attracted to it or fascinated by it, but what draws me to it is usually some hint of the uncanny. The starting point is not knowing why I find certain visual material unsettling. Perhaps there is an inherent strangeness in images of worlds that have vanished, which I never inhabited; for example, 1940s film stills or Edwardian postcards. However, creating the monstrous out of the benign is not just tapping into something that is already there, but usually the result of combining other images. I use other images as another way of interrogating my found images and the source of their unsettling nature, but combination always leads to a more extreme disjunction. With two images, it becomes a mutual estrangement, and this leads to the combination straying radically from their original contexts and meanings. For me, holding these divergent images together requires an overtly simple format. Often these combinations come about through the failure of originally subtractive cuts. Once they have failed as subtractive collages, it is easier to use them as material in collage combination. That's why I don't worry too much about failures, as they always provide the grounds for new combinatory possibilities. (In mathematical logic, there is a maxim of "minimum mutation" in the process of

simplifying formulae. There is a similar principle at work in what I do. It should be called "minimum mutilation").

Aside from the literal cut into the image, there is the metaphorical cut that comes with moving an image from one context to another, or the cut that comes from plucking an image from obscurity and placing it under a new spotlight of artistic attention. This brings us close to Marcel Duchamp's idea of the "readymade" – the nomination of a commonplace artifact as a new work of art. The object remains materially unchanged, but the new context, the new frame of reference, allows it to be reimagined, re-experienced, rethought. You have explored this yourself with certain photographs that you don't alter at all, and in your decision to exhibit a series of hands from old mannequins. Looking back over your work, I get the impression that the paths opened up by Duchamp have been important to you.

Enormously. In the early 1970s, at the height of conceptual art, it was issues of nomination and the contextual conferral of art status that interested me. But, by the mid-1970s, I had begun to discover Duchamp the surrealist and the "re-imagining" of the found image or object. As you say so eloquently, this is a cut in several ways. It is, initially, a gesture of violence, then a reparative reintegration. I think of my *Marriage* pieces, where the half-face has to find its "other-half". In my work, the broken mannequin hands seem closest to the Duchampian readymade. I found a box of them in the street, having just read a passage in Giorgio de Chirico's memoir about his revelatory encounter with a broken disembodied pointing-hand sign.

Duchamp writes of wanting the viewer's reaction to his readymades to have the force of a snapshot – recognising something instantly, but out of context. So, there are interesting oscillations here between objects that behave like images and images that behave like objects. On this point, I've noticed that, though your collages reproduce exceptionally well as graphic impressions, on the page it's difficult to capture their status as objects. Framed on the wall, you allow the images to curl a little, and the decades of accrued wear and tear are all part

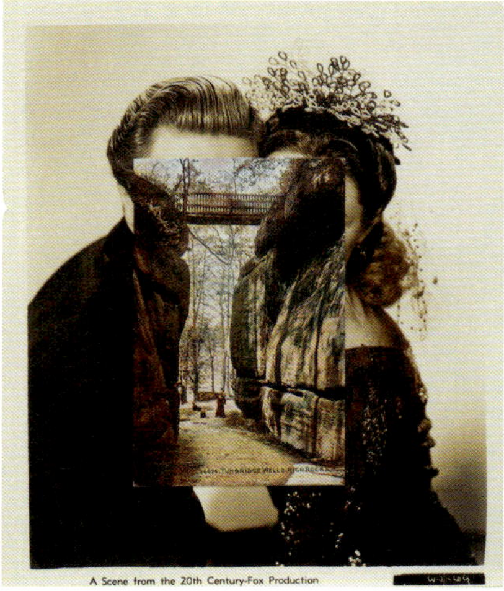

John Stezaker, High Rocks IV, 2014. Collage 24.7 x 20.4 cm

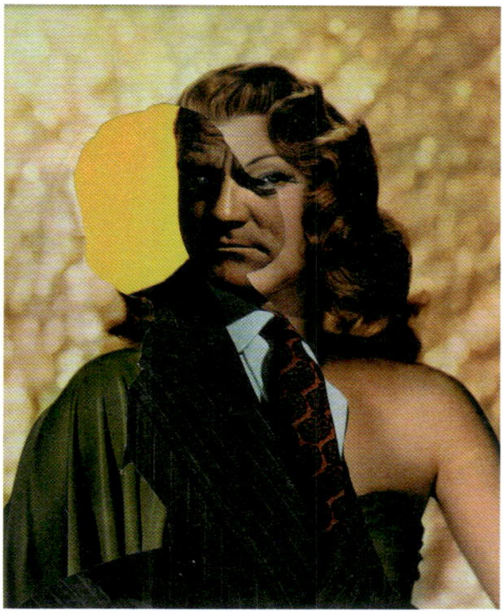

John Stezaker, Film Portrait (She) VIII, 2005. Collage 24.4 x 19.3 cm

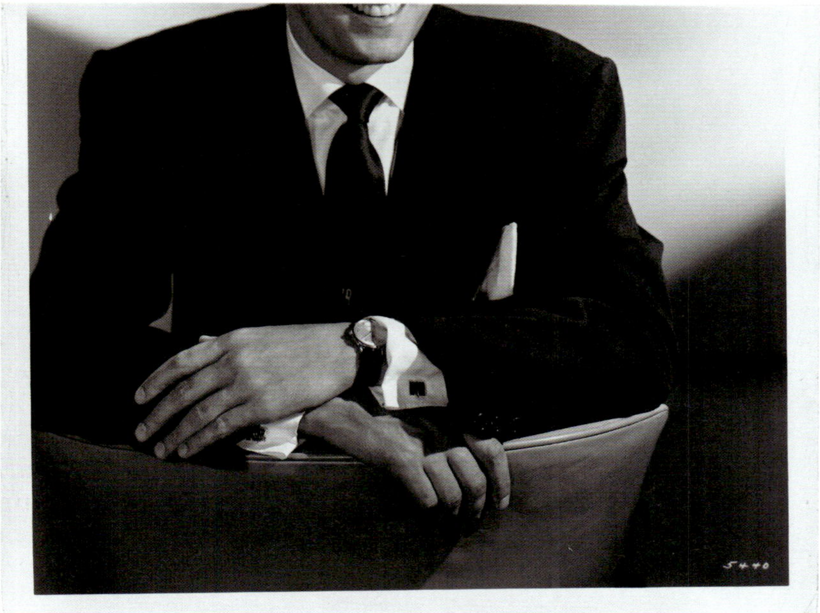

John Stezaker, Untitled, 2010. Collage 15.5 x 20.6 cm

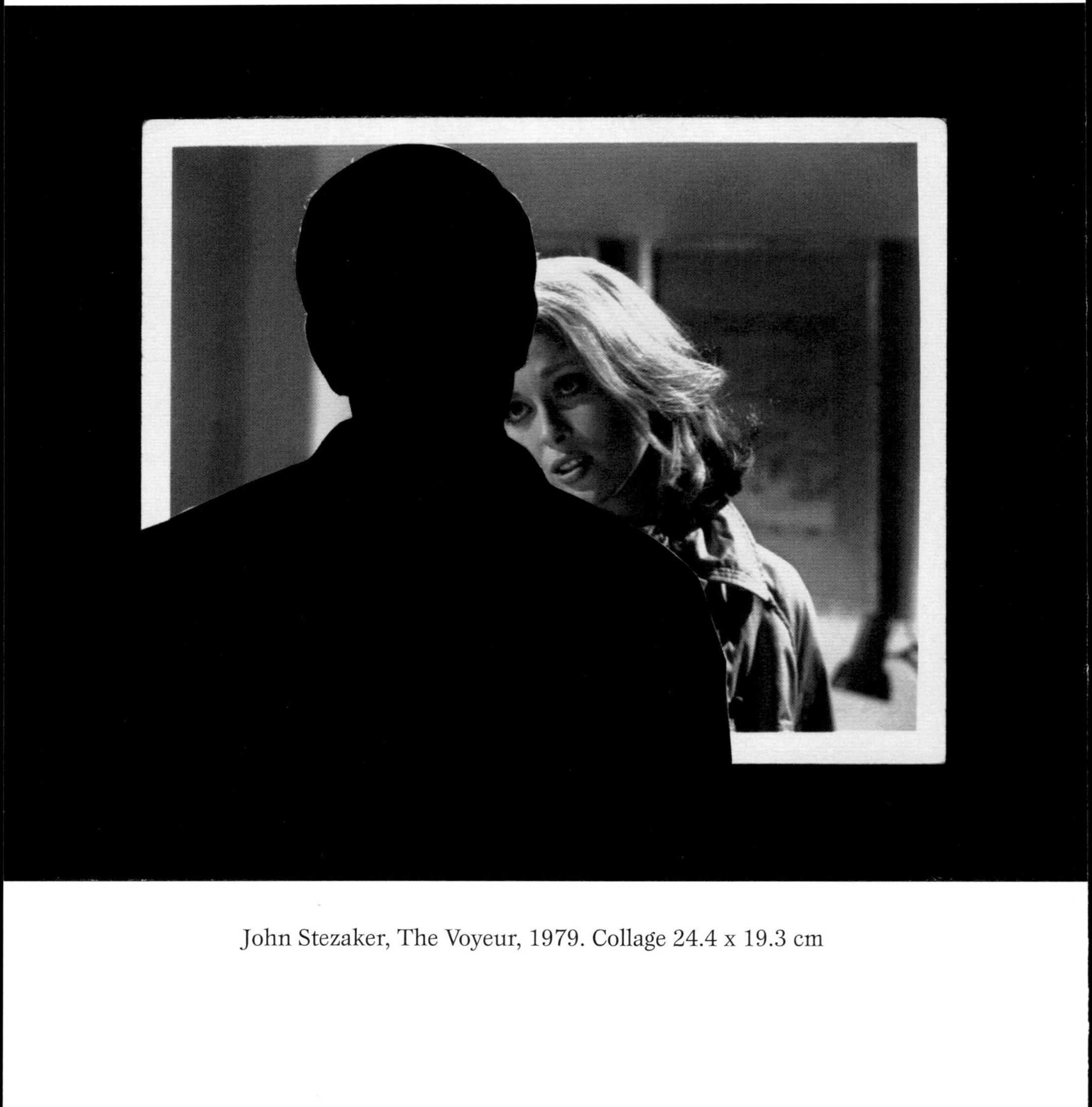

John Stezaker, The Voyeur, 1979. Collage 24.4 x 19.3 cm

of the experience. Plus, of course, a cut is a cut into an object as much as an image.
Yes, they become graphic in reproduction. The physicality of the work is difficult to reproduce and is important in the experience of these ruins of images. The snapshot idea has always interested me – the way an object in its dysfunction or contextual orientation becomes an image; it seems to become an image of *itself*. Duchamp also called these encounters arrests, stoppages, and delays. He saw them as decelerations of our contact with things that allow us the distance to see them as images. I suppose, in your terms, they achieve objecthood at the expense of their temporality. I have always made the connection between cutting and arresting the image. In fact, one of my earliest groups of collages, titled *Cut*, was a play between my own act of cutting and the film director's command. Cutting, after all, arrests the still image's indifferent legibility and transparency. I like to think of my *Damage* pieces – found damaged photos – as readymade eruptions of physicality in the midst of the momentum of our everyday encounter with images. As film stills stand in as arrested cinematic moments, this makes these found and cut objects images of images, or arrests of arrests.

A cut is a peculiar kind of intervention. There and not there. It's not really a "mark", like a brushstroke. It can be very apparent or hide itself seamlessly. The kind of montage we see in narrative cinema and in advertising hides the cuts. The avant-gardes have always tended to keep the cut active, palpable, thinkable. It is interesting that, at the same time, that the surrealists turned to collage, they also turned to filmmaking. In films such as René Clair's *Entr'Acte* – made in 1924, the year the journal *La Révolution Surréaliste* was launched – the audience is given a thrilling lesson in the associative potential of editing; what one shot can mean in light of another and another. Although you have been interested in film for a long time, it's only recently that you have made films yourself. What prompted this?
Actually, I made films as a student in the late 1960s and early 1970s, and, in 1973, on my first adult trip to Italy. Having discovered Giorgio De Chirico, I started to collect postcards of equestrian statues in

silhouette. I hoped to animate these as a flip-book, but nothing came of it. More than a decade later, I came across a book, the *Stallion Annual*, containing hundreds of identically formatted images of horses. And that's when the idea for the film *Horse* (2012) occurred to me: hundreds of images of horses projected, each for twenty-fourth of a second. It was several years before I found a second *Annual*, and it was only with the advent of the Internet that it became possible to collect enough of these publications to make the film. I thought of it as a reverse Muybridge. Rather than breaking down and re-integrating a multiplicity of images into movement, I was starting with a multiplicity of horses and attempting to create stillness. At the same time, I had been collecting images of steam trains with a similar aim in mind. But rather than stilling, I wanted to create a slow-motion version of the approach of a train composed of thousands of different trains. I was thinking of the Lumières's *L'Arrivée d'un Train en Gare de La Ciotat* (1895), the first film to be screened publicly.
Along the way, as an experiment, I wondered what would happen if I didn't have a singular central object of attention. The results were the films *Blind* and *Crowd* (both 2013), which opened up a new dimension in cinema: the experience of inapprehensible multiplicity. It seemed that I had stumbled upon a cinema of discontinuity, one that does not make us see the same thing but exposes us to difference. Every time I saw these films, I was aware of having a different experience. No two people see the same film. At the time, I had thought of my films as explorations of the purgatorial dimension of the cinema of blindness, of an inability to see because of the speed of succession of images. I was surprised, however, that the experience was the opposite – of the indelibility of the image received at this speed. I remember, years ago, the art critic Stuart Morgan saying that the connection between collage and cinema in my work was obvious, that there was a self-evident connection between physical cutting and cinematic montage. But I never found out what was so obvious to him and so mysterious to me.

That's fascinating. The experimental film-maker Hollis Frampton once imagined an "infinite film". It was not quite a loop, but it did go on forever. He wrote: "The infinite film contains an infinity of endless passages wherein no frame resembles

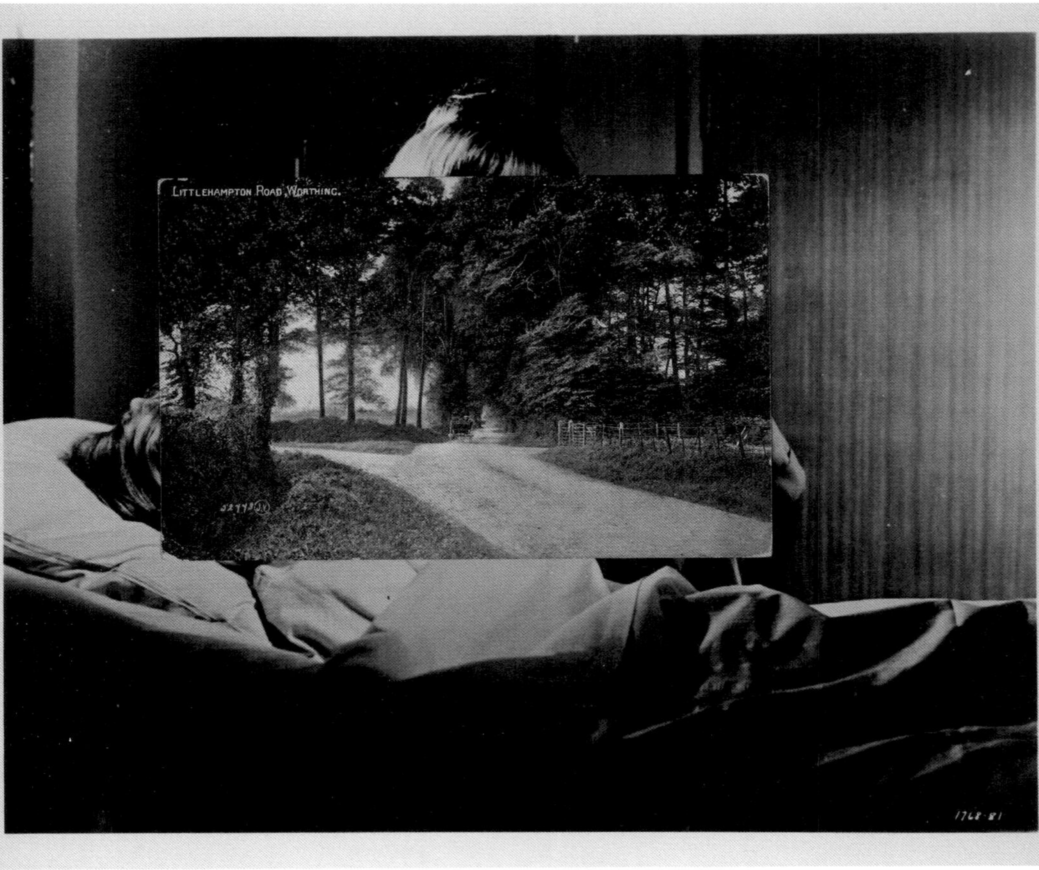

John Stezaker, Untitled (Film Still Collage) XXIII, 2009. Collage 20.6 x 25.4 cm

any other in the slightest degree and a further infinity of passages wherein successive frames are as nearly identical as intelligence can make them". Popular narrative film stays away from endless difference and endless sameness. It occupies a small mid-ground of "sentence-length" shots, neither too short to be incomprehensible nor too long to be intolerable. By contrast, avant-garde cinema gravitates to those two extremes. At one end, there is the film built up from rapid cuts, and, at the other, the long single take. In general, the shorter a film's shot, the more like a photograph it gets, until one ends up with shots comprised of single frames. The longer the shot, the more like a photograph it gets too; the continuous "stare" of the lens giving us a "picture in motion". ***Horse*** **bypasses or combines both, with endlessly different frames, producing the feeling of static sameness. But, coming back to Morgan's point, while I see a relation between your collage cuts and a film-maker's cutting, which is underscored by your use of still photographs derived from movie productions, in the end the two are profoundly different. Combining printed photographs is really nothing like consecutive shots of a film on a screen.**
I made a number of "still films" at college. They were mostly sequences of words, but the final one, *The End*, was made using a still postcard image of Big Ben at sunset, composed similarly to Andy Warhol's film, *Empire*. With the avantgarde logic of the time, I thought of *The End* as superseding *Empire* by extending the twenty-four-hour film to one which was potentially infinite, as well as picking out everyone's favourite part of *Empire* (the sunset), and freezing the alternative British emblematic tower. The film was never made because the rostrum camera at the Slade had been reserved indefinitely for Marcel Broodthaers's film works. Finally, I left it as a series of vertically arranged, identical still images, in the manner adopted at the time by structuralist cinema. The collage, which is owned by the Tate, is called *The End, The Film*.
I love the point you made about how, at either extreme – with slowness and speed – the film resembles photography. And that is what I felt I was doing with these films, carving out territory between two kinds of stillness, between instantaneity and incessancy. It is also between conscious control (holding on to something at the centre of

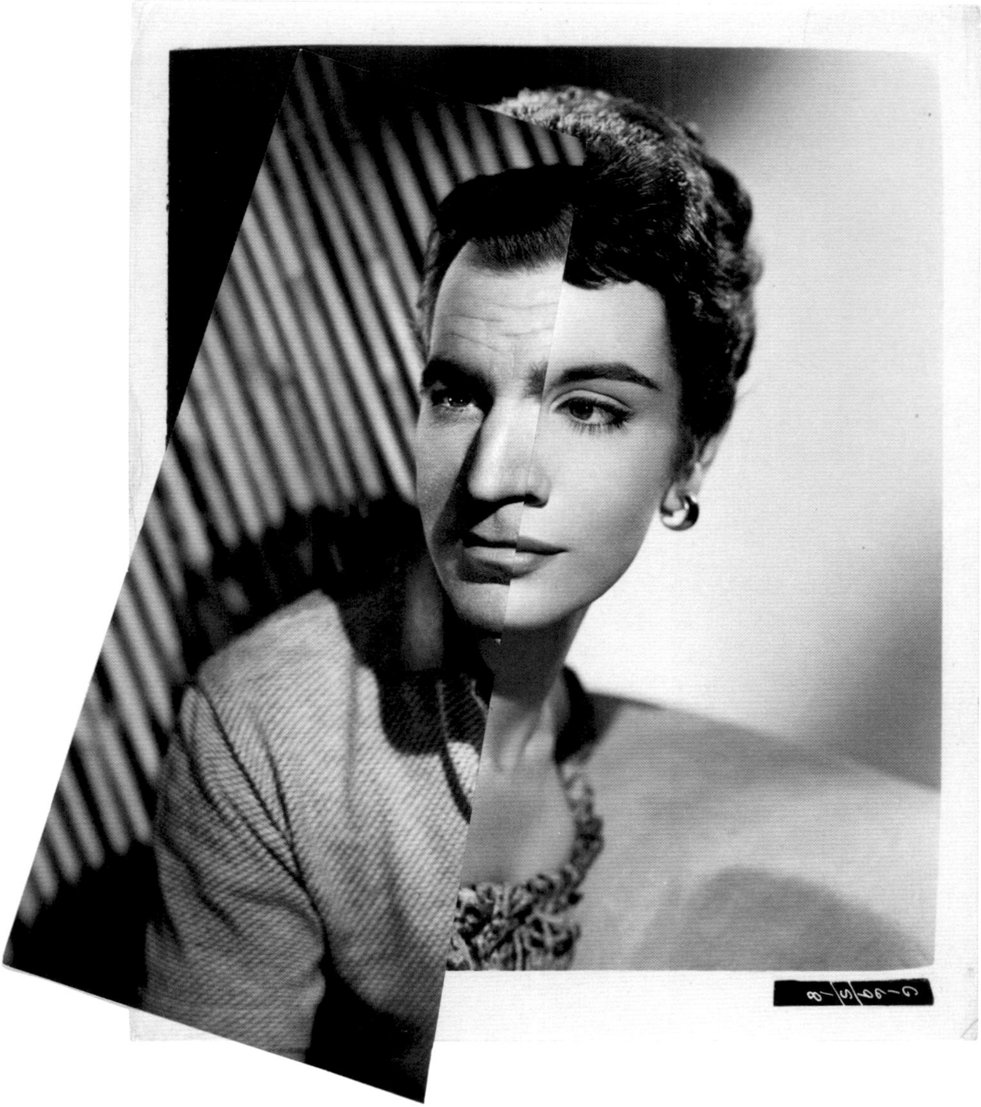

John Stezaker, Marriage LXXVI, 2012.
Collage 26.9 x 23.8 cm

perpetual difference) and letting go (allowing for the accidental to engage the unconsciousness). Each film project is trying to achieve a different kind of balance between consciousness and unconscious reception, and, as you have said, between different aspects of the photographic. I like the idea that the film collages can open up something like that within the photographic. (With my suggestion, that editing is like carving, I was thinking about my films like *Cathedral* (2013) and *Crowd*, where I start with a lot of quite unordered material and create a central image or continuity by cutting out extraneous deviations).

The collagist's cut and the film-maker's cut are alike: excised parts are brought into a relation with each other. Of course, a film-maker is usually stuck with a consistent frame shape. With your collages you are interested in cutting into or across the frame.
Physically, cutting occurs across the image, but it is interesting that you use the phrase "cutting into". From the beginning, I thought of my collages as cutting into, opening up. That is why so many of my early titles related to surgery: *Incisions* and *Excisions*. I wanted to open up a space that I thought of as closed; in other words, to introduce a seam into what was seamless about the media image. Perhaps it was a way of making bodily contact with what seemed remote from touch. Somehow, the cut, in creating a sense of here, also helps create a feeling of depth – of there. Certainly, the use of two images is about creating a "before" and a "behind". I think this applies both to my intercut film stills, where you see an image behind, through an aperture in an image on top, as well as with the postcard *Inserts* and *Masks*. In the context of filmic material in front and behind inevitably become metaphors for temporal succession or perhaps they satisfy a demand denied by cinema of simultaneity. Over the years, I have been drawn to cinematic images, mostly from the 1940s and 1950s, and to postcards from the interwar period, so there is also an historical regression in the spatial unfolding of depth.

Let's go back to the question of fascination, with which we began. Is there something about fascination that is beyond the temporal? Although your work has changed across the

decades, your central fascinations have remained remarkably consistent, unwavering.
It probably looks more unwavering from the outside. I sometimes feel defeated by the sheer scale of my collection and the multiplicity of my image fascinations. I feel pulled in too many directions at once. But, once I overcome this, usually by picking up on one of the many loose ends left in the processes of sorting and cutting, I find the sifting process a way of overcoming these pressures. Usually, through a couple of digressions and diversions from the first point of entry into the work, I am lost in it. Everyone who has been lost in their work knows that its pleasure is an escape from the usual order of time. It is different from the arrest that occurs in finding and this is where, for me, the time of fascination takes over, perhaps when just momentarily we are robbed of the power to make sense of what we are looking at. Blanchot believes that the promise of the image is in making contact with the eternal: in the image "we find, as pure pleasure, and superb satisfaction, the transparent eternity of the unreal". I am open to all these suggestions.

A key figure in the emergence of colour photography as a serious artistic medium in 1980s Britain, **Paul Graham** soon went on to international recognition. From his early projects such as *A1: the Great North Road* and *Troubled Land*, to *New Europe* and *A Shimmer of Possibility*, he has been remarkably restless. While all his photographs are based on direct observation of the world around him, no two bodies of work have been alike. Each has its own way of noticing, and its own way of photographing. In this way Graham has remained committed to the idea of an experimental documentary practice, one that allows for the innovations and finding of new forms that are necessary for the renewal of oneself as artist, and for the renewal of the medium of photography.

Graham moved from England to New York in 2002. Many of his influences had been American – Walker Evans, William Eggleston, Garry Winogrand – and in some respects, it was those influences that had helped to make Graham's European work so distinctive. His first project in the US was *American Night*. This was followed by *A Shimmer of Possibility*, conceived as a set of edited sequences of photographs of everyday street life. *Shimmer* was recently voted the most influential photographic publication of the last fifteen years.

This public conversation took place at the Whitechapel Gallery, London, on the occasion of major survey exhibition of Paul Graham's work in 2011. With the various projects freshly installed, Graham was in a reflective mood, taking stock of three decades of continuous practice.

Paul Graham

Paul, your work has been very influential internationally. And here it is a kind of retrospective, at the Whitechapel Gallery in London. There are projects that I don't think have been shown in the UK since they were first made. Since the early 1980s, each new project has started afresh, almost like a tabula rasa; you don't rely on what you've done before. Do you think about the arc of your career to date? In such a retrospective, does your work make sense to you?
I don't know if you're asking the right person really! Well, it's funny, I look back over my work and see all the early British projects grouped together – the Irish pictures – *Troubled Land*; the unemployment offices – *Beyond Caring*; the A1 road – and they do kind of fit together. There's a coherence. Then I see this bigger symmetry in connection with later work, *A shimmer of possibility*, where I'm peripatetically wandering around the USA, and I see how that connects with A1, which was me wandering around the UK. But to come back to what you're saying, yes, it is important for me not to repeat exactly the same idea again and again. For me, when you prove something to yourself as an artist it means you now have to do something fresh that will scare the bejeezus out of you because you're starting from zero once again.

Are you constantly assessing your past work, do you think about it much?
No, I prefer to look forward. It's very lovely to see it all together here in the Whitechapel, but I'm looking forward to putting it all back in crates and not seeing it again for years.

I guess when you were starting, most serious photographers were thinking about their work in book form. Now for a lot of

photographers it seems to be the other way around. They make work to exhibit.
It's changed. *A1* is my oldest work here. I started it in 1981, and all you had then were dedicated photography spaces such as The Photographers' Gallery in London. The art world was not embracing or accepting photography so we created this separate community, with its own creative space where you published books. That gave you a dialogue, and gave your work a longevity. It was democratic as well, because people could buy this book for £6 or £10 and own your entire project, and it gave your work a life, an international life. That's how I learnt about photography, that's where I saw it. I would go to the library and find books on Walker Evans or Garry Winogrand or Robert Frank or whatever, so it was great to contribute back into that dialogue.

And what about making colour photography back then?
What's strange about seeing the early work now is how invisible the colour aspect is. It was something controversial in its time – I don't want to call it radical, but some people found it so. To them is was very troublesome that my pictures were simply in colour. Now that debate is so old and so over that it's invisible. People felt that *Beyond Caring*, the pictures I made in English unemployment offices, was a topic that should be done in black-and-white. Period. And to the work I made in Northern Ireland, the reaction was: "That's a serious situation and one should treat it seriously with black-and-white film in the camera, not colour".

Most of the names you've mentioned so far have been American, and it seems that from very early on you were filtering an American sensibility into an English, British and European landscape.
Yes. I mean the pioneers of contemporary colour photography were virtually all American – William Eggleston, Stephen Shore, and so on. I was taking that sensibility, and putting it together with the unique, innate sensibility we have here in the UK, the engaged photographic history going back to Bill Brandt through Tony Ray-Jones to Chris Killip, Graham Smith, etc. The development was in uniting new colour photography with the British classic social documentary consid-

erations. Dammit! I've brought the D-word in – "documentary" – and I didn't mean to.

Perhaps the term "documentary" is a problem only because it sums up a very narrow set of connotations for people. But there is an experimental documentary tradition. There have always been experiments in documentary, often crowded out by the mainstream models of the photo-essay or a visual report.
True, and also a problem concerning documentary work is that it's become used as a tar brush by the contemporary art world for dismissing pictures of life as it is, unstaged pictures of the world. That's unfair. You don't call cooking with ingredients that came from the garden "documentary cooking". It's just cooking! As far as I'm concerned, it's just photography and that's that. We don't stage them, we don't make things in our studio. We go out and take pictures in the world. I think that is the purest of photography. Let's give it the main place, *photography*, and have special modifiers for everything else!

Let's stay with "photography". In your restlessness, there's a change over time in the way you notice things, and a change in understanding how the viewer notices things. In *Troubled Land*, the details that matter are very small within the landscapes, and the viewer has some work to do, but in doing so becomes alert to every inch of the picture. A small British flag in a tree. An army checkpoint so tiny in an epic Irish landscape. I remember at the time that seemed like a risky venture – where photography was supposed to be about immediate messages, for you it was about something one might almost overlook, the way one may not have noticed those details there in the Irish landscape itself.
Yes, but then of course you can use tricks to seduce people into engaging with the images. You can use the beauty of the landscapes, the Northern Irish skies, the Constable-like fields and hedgerows to seduce people into engaging with a picture they normally wouldn't look at. Suck them into the seductiveness, the sentiment towards landscape that we all have in us, then they engage and then you can flip things around to something else.

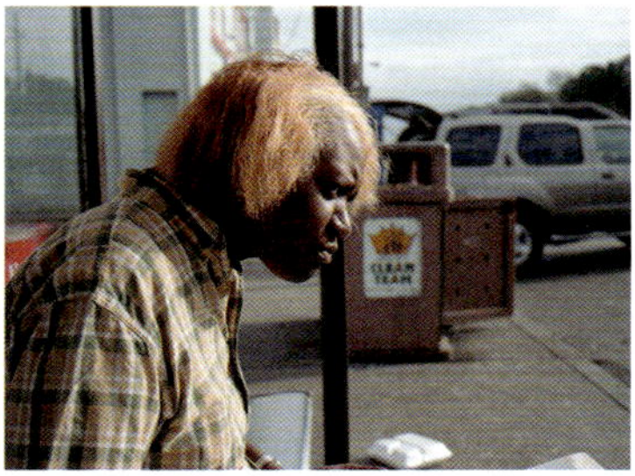

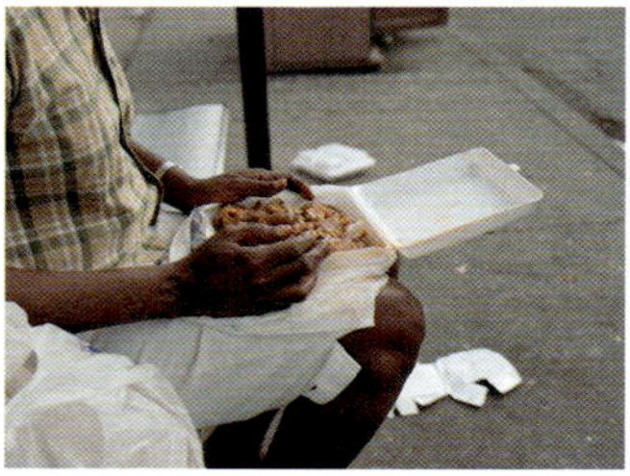

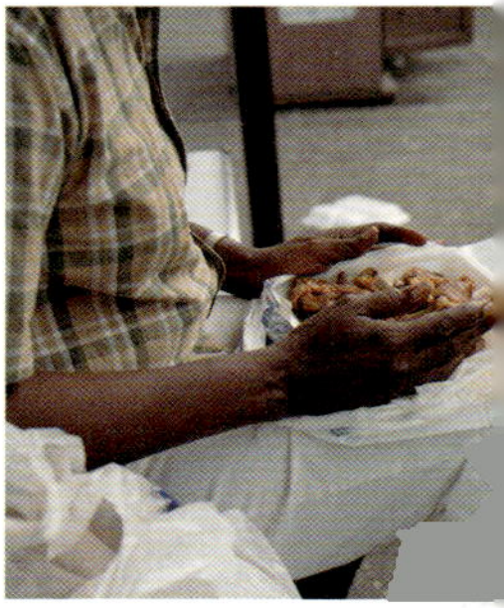

In a lot of your later pictures such slight things matter – the way someone's hair curls around their ear, the way a piece of graffiti suddenly slips out of focus.
Indeed… or the way that in the white overexposed images in the *American Night* series there are almost invisible people who are quite tiny in a giant, 8-foot wide picture.

Was there a point where you started to think about a photograph as something that belongs on the wall and not on the printed page?
I think it works in both – people read books in their lap or on a table, and they look at pictures on a wall in a different way. For example, *A Shimmer of Possibility* is a work that has one life in book form and another on the wall, and yet they mirror and connect with each other. The work on the wall is not the book on the wall, and the book is not the gallery layout in book form. For me it's a matter of finding a harmonious way to do something.

Ireland figures three times in the show, could you say more about that?
The first time I was in Northern Ireland was 1984. Quite difficult times then. From 1984-85 I was working on *Troubled Land*, then I

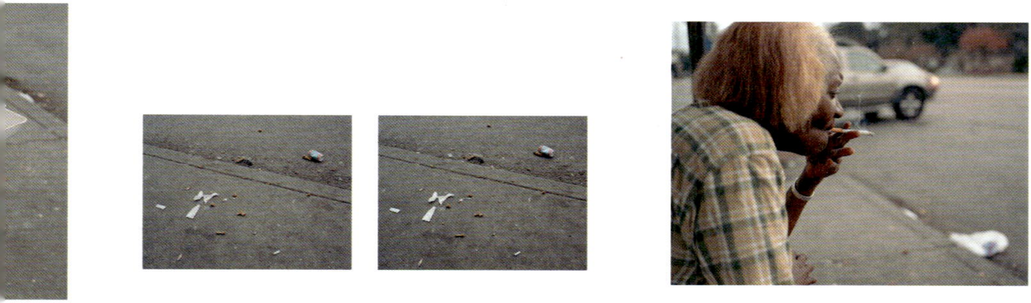

Paul Graham, New Orleans (Woman Eating), 2004,
from *A Shimmer of Possibility*, 2007

went back in the late 1980s working on *New Europe*. You see those pictures are a lot closer, and it's very interesting how subconsciously I go from distant details and then suddenly there's the woman smoking a cigarette, for example, very close, very intense, much more direct. The last series is the *Ceasefire* skies, which actually wasn't a ceasefire, but a "temporary cessation of hostilities", to use the beautiful British governmental euphemism for it, where they had a first and brief moment of peace. They held it over the Easter weekend, I believe, in 1994, and they agreed there would be no killings or bombings. Being the contrarian I am, I jumped on a plane knowing that because nothing would happen, I had to take some pictures precisely about that.

Those Irish sky pictures somehow politicize the cloudscape genre inherited from British painters such as Turner and Constable. It's a self-consciously symbolic gesture. That's so different from your more recent projects, such as *Shimmer*, where you are trying to make photographs akin to the experience of noticing.
Thank you, I agree. It's trying to simulate the experience of looking and noticing and time passing. That's a lot to do with what photography is about, trying to simulate the experience of noticing, that breaking moment of awareness. If you go back before photography to representational painting and the Dutch Old Masters, their paintings

were like "Behold: Look at this person in front of you". Photography has picked up that mantle and is running with it now. It's the same artistic idiom – "Look at the wonder of this person, this object, this landscape". It's about the beautiful irreducible fact of the thing right there. With *Shimmer*, it's trying to tap into that and appreciate the way that life moves around you and past you, and how moments of awareness drift in and out. Your consciousness drifts from one to the other. So, you're right, it's very much about trying to represent this flowing element of life, but then hoping people will take that out of the gallery, and walk out onto the street and see something similar.

If one has affection for photography, whenever one sees a show one really likes, it starts to have its effect immediately. You step out the gallery and find the way you are seeing has been affected. It's something that art criticism cannot comprehend, and something photography has a privileged kind of access to. It can have a very immediate effect upon experience.
Sure, sure – but then as a photographer you have to shake off that point of view and find your own awareness of what's going on around you.

How has it been photographing in America, and what's it like living there? You talked earlier of so many of your influences being American…
I was dead scared of taking a camera to America the first few trips. In fact, for the first ten years I was visiting America on and off, I didn't bother packing a camera at all. It sounds ridiculous, but I was so in awe of what had been done there I thought: "What can I do? It's pointless". And after about ten years, I thought, "This is silly, I really need to take the camera with me". So, I did and started to do small pieces. And everything ebbs and flows.

Your more recent work seems to be about the almost nothing of the everyday. Do you think some of the big, emphatic themes and subjects that had informed your earlier projects aren't there so much?
Things move along, you know. I'm less interested in the pictures being so obviously *about* something, as they were in unemployment of-

fices or Northern Ireland. I've done that, it's a good few years ago now. The stuff that interests me is the everyday ether of life running past us. They can be really important things, but not so obvious they can be summed up in a catchy phrase. It's that dance between the photographer and life – you might have some idea about what you're going to do then life slaps you across the face and says "No, that's not interesting, but: how about this?" You can have this dialogue, this dialogue with life, and you can come back with something far more interesting than you ever could dream up in your own little ideas.

That's an interesting way of putting it because one of the inevitable fictions of a mid-career survey show like this is that everything starts to look like an immaculate gesture. All strategic and perfect.
Right! It looks like you knew what you were doing all along, you had it all planned beforehand. Whereas actually I went to Northern Ireland and thought maybe the curb stones were painted red, white and blue because they'd just finished with the Queen's Jubilee. I had no idea. It took me a long time to figure it all out!

That's what makes photography so particular. I know you've written something of a polemic about this, an essay titled *The Unreasonable Apple*, which is about that mercurial lightness of observational photography, which still gets it into trouble in contemporary art, according to your argument. Contemporary art prefers the kinds of photography where the artist's labour, the intent is clear.
If you as an artist stage the entire scene with thirty actors and thirty lights, set something up and you take a picture of it, they understand that that is a creative activity, because you control everything and organise every inch of the picture. But the same picture taken by someone as wonderful as Robert Frank or Garry Winogrand, someone who "just" walked down the street and saw it and photographed it… what did they do? That's the conundrum you find with some people, that it's "just" street photography, or "just" documentary. At the same time, as you just said, so many of the greats of photographic history have been exactly this. Where would we be without Robert Frank's *The Americans*, without Garry Winogrand's *Public Relations*,

without Robert Adams' pictures? There are photographers who go out and ask the same questions that photographers have been asking for a hundred years – "How is the world?"

It's interesting you say one hundred years. I remember there was a big show of American photography at the Barbican [*American Images: Photography 1945-1980*, 1985], and the photographer Lewis Baltz wrote a beautiful essay for the catalogue suggesting the art world gets interested in photography like a child picking up a toy then putting it down again. And this happens every decade or so. There might be a more solid understanding of photography now and one of the real bonuses of this might be a reopening of the photographic tradition, a re-understanding of the continuity of the medium's history, that image-makers in the 19th century were working in very similar ways to what we do now. Photographers have always understood that there's a great lineage that goes right the way to the beginning, and that photographic art didn't begin in the 1960s with conceptualism. And we're in this interesting moment where I guess you find yourself being both a contemporary artist and a historical figure at the same time. While you're busy making new work, I see that *Beyond Caring*, a book from the 1980s has just been reprinted and there's an audience for it.
It is strange to see the parallax effect of history apply to yourself. Pictures of unemployment offices that were once contemporary suddenly disappear down the corridor of time and end up as historical artefacts, representing an era – mid-term Thatcherism in 1980s England. That's a very strange experience, to have something shift in that way.

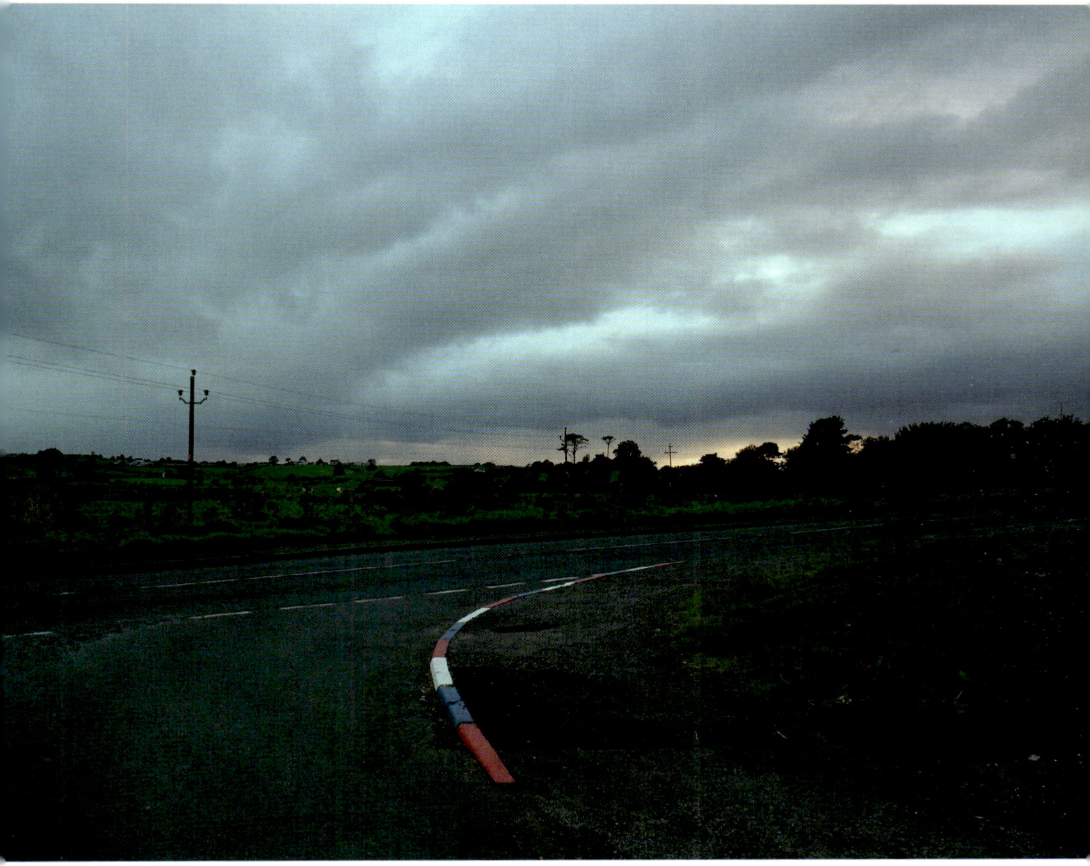

Paul Graham, Unionist Coloured Kerbstones, at Dusk, near Omagh, 1985

I first met **Rut Blees Luxemburg** in 1994, when we were fellow students on the Masters programme in photography at the University of Westminster. Rut was already deep into a long project, photographing London on a 4x5 camera, in colour, at night. Occasionally I would accompany her, carrying the camera or tripod. Sometimes we would go with no equipment at all, just wandering, exploring how familiar places become strange when the sun has gone, and the sleeping city is bathed in very different hues.

For this conversation, made for the fun of it in 1999, we walked through the night, visiting the various locations where Rut had shot her photographs. She had made 35mm transparencies of each of her large-scale pictures, which we looked at on a little battery powered viewer that she carried in her pocket. This way we could compare her images with the locations in front of us.

We were both at an early stage in our careers. Rut knew where she was going. I had no idea where I was going. But looking back it is clear that many of the concerns that still interest us both were already present, nearly two decades ago: the tension between the photograph as document and expression; the image as a space of imaginary projection; the desire – both individual and political – to reinvent the modern city; and the mix of enchantment and estrangement that often seems inherent in the camera image.

Rut Blees Luxemburg

It's Saturday night and we're at the foot of Hungerford Bridge in Central London. Rut, you are preparing an image of the underside of the bridge. You've made a small 35mm study which we have here, so we can see your image and the bridge itself. Was there an obvious way for you to make an image here? By that, I mean, do places strike you as images?
Well, this study already has a title which is *Die Ziehende Tiefe*. It took me a while to figure out the title, which means *The Wandering Depth*. And *ziehende* also means pulling, so there is this play between "wandering" and "pulling", and that's exactly what I felt about the water here. It sort of pulls you, as well as moving along. And with this long light exposure you suddenly see something below the surface, and that is what I was interested in here. So, yes, there was an obvious way for me to shoot this scene.

Seeing the place for myself and your image of it – which is quite a transformation – leads me to think that you are able to see places in terms of how long exposure will render them. I guess this comes with experience. There is often a tension in your work between what is there and what is not there.
Yes – that is certainly an experience that guides my image making.

This seems partly a technical matter to do with long exposure – some things are rendered crisp, others disappear – but it is also to do with how people see at night, or don't see.
That is the pleasure within my practice: the camera allows what you called a transformation. Something other than what you can see during your mundane, everyday experience of the city can emerge. Something which is there, but can be sensed better than it can be seen. A camera allows this to be unveiled or shown. In this photograph I had to work

out the schedules of the river, the tides. When the tide is low, another hidden layer emerges.

You mostly make 35mm studies first before moving to a large format camera. This is quite interesting in the sense of your relation to the site or location. It means that when you come to actually make the final image, it's already a return to the site. You are going back.
I don't think of it as a return. The moment of making the study is more of a pre-moment and the real moment comes when I make the large-scale exposure. Why don't we walk along the river? I have made an image called *Liebeslied* or *Love Poem* about a quarter of a mile further down.

We are at the foot of Waterloo Bridge looking at a flight of steps you photographed in…?
1997.

It's changed since then. The text that appears on the wall in your image, that looks like a poem that has been crossed out or covered over, has almost disappeared. What first drew you to this site?
Liebeslied has become the overall title for a body of work and for my second book. For me the *Liebeslied* was this elusive writing on the wall which seemed always more than just graffiti or some quick communication. Even when I first saw it, it was indecipherable. I think that the writer tried to eradicate it, just after writing it. And now it has become a stain or trace, adding to all the other stains on the surface of the city. I like the curves, they are so baroque that they suggest something much more palatial, or sacred, instead of a cold, outdoor space.

It looks like a very private form of communication, the opposite of most graffiti or street writing which might tend to be a disenfranchised citizen announcing something to the world in general. The poem seems like one soul speaking to another soul but within a public place.
Yes, that's why for me it became a *Liebeslied*. It is very considered. The scale is intimate. It is writing at the scale of the body. So I came and photographed it. It seems private. I'm attracted to the *Heimlichkeit* of a space in public. A space that allows for a moment of repose.

Rut Blees Luxemburg, The Wandering Depth / Die Ziehende Tiefe, 1999

Do you think that repose comes from the places or from your images?
From the places, most definitely. It is hard for me to photograph places where I don't have that feeling or relation. The images then try to trace that sensibility.

I think of your work as almost the opposite of street photography, which we associate with bright daylight, people, grabbed chance instants and speed, instantaneity. Here we have long duration, emptiness, a shell that becomes a content, rather than the other way around where in street photography people become generalized ciphers of the masses. In your work the population is either moving through – coming or going – or absent.
The 4 x 5 camera is the opposite of what the street photographer would use. It requires slowness and concentration and the exposures are long. Ten, fifteen, twenty minutes. It's another kind of street photography. Or maybe "street" isn't even important. "Public" photography is better.

Your photographs are often of streets or contain streets.
Well, in the newer work the street is becoming less significant for me. In my earlier work, collected in the book *London: A Modern Project*, the street was much more important. Now it's other places.

There is generally much more intimacy in your recent work. You have moved away from the great heights and the monumentality of the built city.
That's a deliberate move. The idea of the *Liebeslied* suggests that intimacy of communication. An attention to another experience of the public. Not the great, grand declamation but the small theatrical spaces and gestures. Shall we go further along the river?

OK, we're at the site of a picture called...?
Nach Innen or *In Deeper*.

The title seems to refer back to a quote by Roland Barthes that Michael Bracewell used in the introduction to your first book.
Yes, yes: "To get out, go in deeper". It became the motto for this newer work, in a way. Deeper, closer to the ground.

You can't get much closer to the ground than the water, or sea level.
Well the interesting thing about the sea level is that it moves, as we saw, it changes within a couple of hours.

This suggests interesting questions of duration and long exposure and the subtleties of changes. I'm reminded of a great little essay by Jeff Wall called *Photography and Liquid Intelligence*. He's talking mainly of how the instantaneous picture can show forms that are unavailable to human vision, but I think the long exposure of moving water does something equally specific to photography. This soupy, syrupy quality.
And here a very golden quality to water as it is lit. This image is also very much about absence. You see the footsteps on the mud? They are expressive of something that runs right through the *Liebeslied* series, which became about a possible poet who is wandering the city in a way that is in contrast to the *flâneur* made famous by Baudelaire. The *flâneur's* relation to the city is very much about a pleasure or diversion. The poet's wandering is more about an encounter.

There has been a lot of recent discussion about the *flâneur* and the contemporary city, partly as a response to new forms of spectacle, and partly, for political reasons to open up the city and break the alienated, uncreative habits into which city dwellers fall or are coerced. But the wandering of the poet is far more contemplative, it seems. Perhaps more difficult or painful.
I wouldn't call it difficult. It's a different daring. To dare to have this encounter, which might be an encounter with the self, or with what goes beyond the experience or appearances. It looks deeper to levels of experience beneath. In that way it can be much more political than the *flâneur* whose distraction fits in so well with the city's diversions.

The more recent work is spatially more intimate. It is also slightly more mute. Of course all photography is mute, but your previous work conjured up sounds of passing cars or anxious voices.
The newer work is not mute. You just have to listen more carefully.

The American photographer Robert Adams once said:

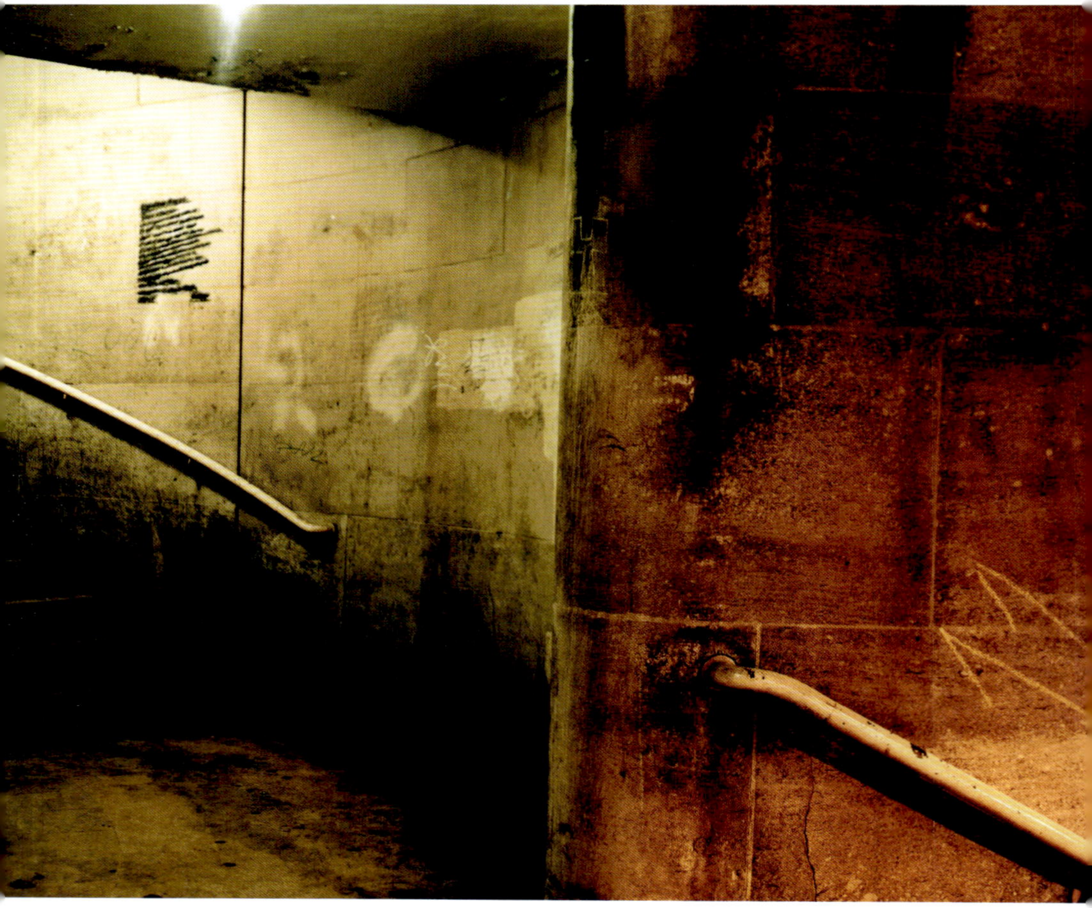

Rut Blees Luxemburg, Liebeslied / Love Poem, 1997

"Still photographs often differ from life more by their silence than by the immobility of their subjects. Landscape pictures tend to converge with life however on summer nights when the sounds outside, after we call the children in and close the garage doors, are the small whirr of moths and the snap of a stick". The idea of a picture taken of a silent world is perhaps more realistic than a photograph that shuts off noise. The silence of photography is consonant with a silent world.
I'm not sure. That's debatable. But within my work of course it's all taken at night, which has a very different level of silence or noise.

It's a John Cage-like idea that the quieter things are the more significant the sound. This would run counter to Adams. Do you want to say something about the significance of the river coming up again and again in this new work?
Hölderlin had some interesting ideas about the river. The river is this wonderful moving entity, which combines places and joins them up together and brings them to the sea. Hölderlin understood the river in a relationship to the sky, through the reflection of the sky in the water joining the two different elements together. For him the river was almost a receptacle of the gods. Do the gods come down through reflection and the rain?

Water at night is a very powerful image.
It suggests an immersion. In my past work I was very interested in vertiginous sensations. In this one I am much more interested in the sensation of immersion. Of course the river reflects, so it has this curious relation to photography. Water appears in another image called *Feuchte Blätter* or *Moist Sheets*. In German the word has a double meaning again. *Blätter* means leaves on the trees but also sheets, perhaps waiting for the text.

This is a big break from the permanences of the world of concrete and steel that characterized *London: a Modern Project*. The newer work is more intimate. It welcomes nature and looks to the ephemeral.
The ephemeral did surface in *A Modern Project*, usually in the lights on buildings that would go on and off according to people moving around.

Now then, you've brought me to a rather swish but smelly public toilet. We've paid twenty pence and now we've entered one of the city's more intimate spaces! You've made an image of a very similar space.
Yes. The image is called *Orpheus' Nachtspaziergang* or *Orpheus' Nocturnal Walk*. This isn't an ordinary toilet. It's one of these modern generic city toilets, a capsule. I think as an image it is very lush, which I like. These toilets have never been successful. No-one dares to use them. I don't use them! But I like the privacy they offer within the city. In a very public situation you suddenly have this incredible privacy.

And the marbles and metals of this interior are so similar to the cafés springing up all over the city.
Absolutely. But it feels strange. I like the beautiful round mirror. I shot it from the outside glimpsing the inside, from the position of a walker. Nietzsche said "Only the thoughts formed during motion are worthwhile".

Let's return to this idea of the walking poet in contrast to the *flâneur*. For Hölderlin, or the poet, walking involves responding to the world around them while being wrapped up in, or preoccupied with, other thoughts.
In a way, the motion of walking induces a certain state of mind. It's not dreamlike, but it is almost meditative. So shall we walk a bit further?

We are looking down at a tennis court you turned into a photograph titled *Corporate Leisure*.
The tennis court is on top of a building owned by de Beers, the diamond merchants.

It's in one of those courtyard spaces that exist around the back of the impenetrable looking facades of so many big London buildings. How did you come to be here?
I think the impenetrability of the city is more of an illusion than a reality. You can actually find access to these places and enter them. This has been very important for my work – penetrating sites that at first suggest inaccessibility. What is so frightening about these places is the future they suggest – the fortress and the control that emanates from it. But I think they can be entered.

We've arrived at what looks like a shallow excavation site. I guess a building once stood here but now it is being used temporarily as a car park. You made an image here called *Das Offene Schauen* or *Viewing the Open*. It is a cinematic image, something like an establishing shot. Frame shape varies a good deal across your work. Does the cropping come afterwards or at the act of taking?
It varies, as the image requires. This place felt something like a Western in a way, with a swooping panoramic expanse. A vista.

Questions about the medium of photography and related technical matters have surfaced already in our conversation. Now, I have this sense that the serious amateur, in coming to grips with the medium, encounters the long exposure as probably the first "trick", the first magical bit of photography, where the camera itself is helping to produce an estranging effect. It is giving a kind of duration that is longer than normal, producing its own forms in the image. And on that level there is something about all long exposure night photography that contains something of the fascination that the serious amateur has with the camera itself.
Well, for me, it's not so much a fascination with photography, but a fascination with the possibilities of the large format camera and the long exposure which allows me to let chance enter the work. The long exposure leaves space for unexpected things to happen while the shutter is open. So contingency is a big part of my way of taking images, of letting in that which is outside of my control.

This is an interesting way to use a large format camera, which we usually associate with the height of control and pre-meditation.
The serious amateur would be horrified by certain results I get in terms of colour balances and uncorrected perspectives.

Control and chance. This is somehow quite similar to your overall strategy of walking through the city at night and seeing what happens. It is a framework in which new possibilities can arise.
I set my own constraints, but they are open for whatever can happen.

The street photographer, whom we mentioned earlier, has historically shot an awful lot of images, and probably a lot of awful images, to get what they want. You don't work this way.
No. I edit before I shoot, which means I take a very deliberate number of photographs. The consideration and the chance come before taking the image and during the image but not afterwards. For me it is much more interesting to concentrate on less, and perhaps in one image enough happens to keep you engaged for a longer period instead of moving onto other images.

That means you have an output that parallels a painter more than a photographer. And you also make preliminary studies, which is quite a painterly activity, as a way of preparing or pre-editing before committing to the time and expense of a big image. Are there many images that don't make it to the final stage?
Yes. Not many but there are a few. But sometimes I go back to them and think about them again.

Could you talk a little about titles of your photographs?
The titles open up the work for another reading. These other readings are often literary, or mythical or allegorical.

Again this is more like a painter than a photographer. Let's take an image like *Mount Pleasant*, a beautiful image of some rather savage metal fence work running along a high wall.
It was taken in Mount Pleasant, but the name is also evocative of another sensation. In the *Liebeslied* images I've gone back to German. Not intentionally, but somehow it came over me to use them, because often the German words have the quality of being equivocal, and in translation a gap opens and another layer of meaning becomes possible.

This plays against how mass culture puts image and text together to clarify, to contain what Allan Sekula once called the "fragmentary, incomplete utterance" of the photograph.
Yes, but my titling is not an obscure act. It is something which opens up something else.

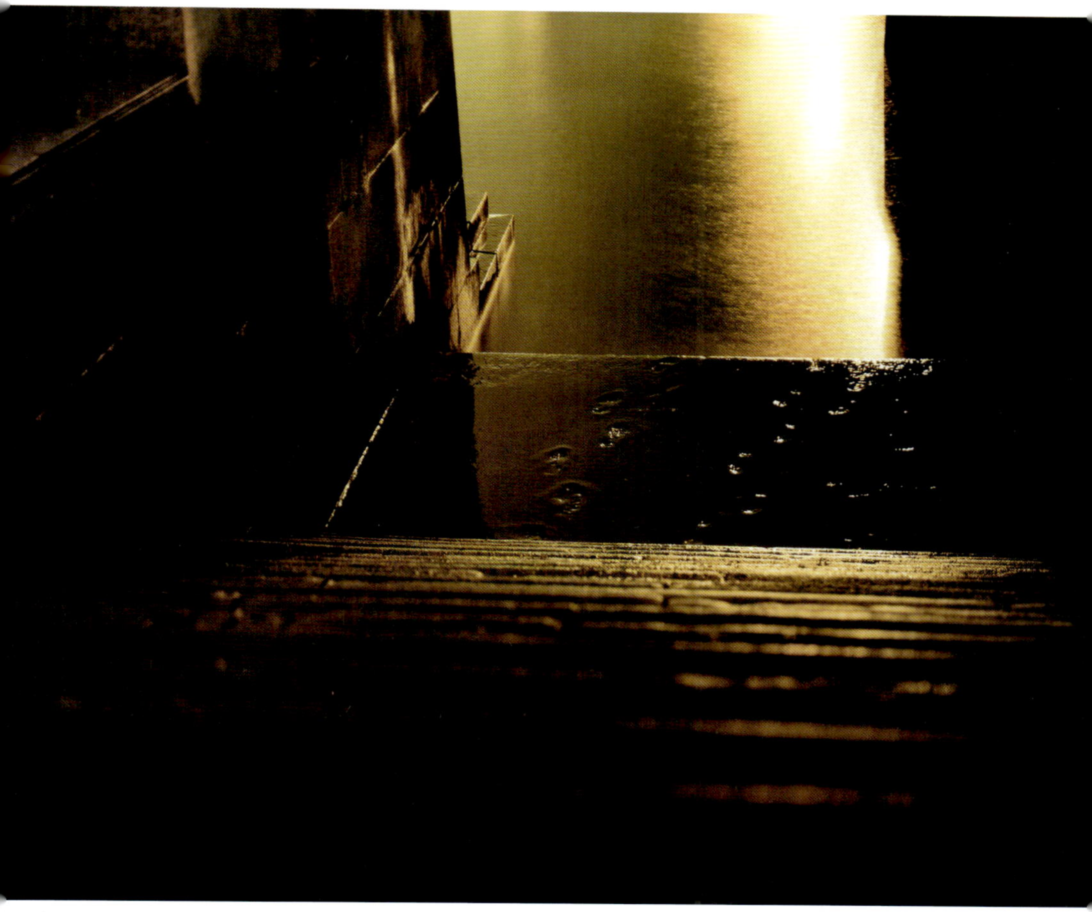

Rut Blees Luxemburg, In Deeper / Nach Innen, 1999

In the late 1970s, when **Jeff Wall** began making tableaux images presented as transparencies in big lightboxes, nothing could have been further from general expectation. Few photographers were working at large scale, few were working in colour, and almost none were thinking about images that worked alone, outside of any series or set. Today he is one of the most significant photographic artists.

I first encountered Wall's images and his highly original writings when I was studying photography and film in the late 1980s. I found his mix of pictorial ambition and critical thinking truly galvanizing. I didn't always agree with it, but it was undeniably exciting to see an artist ask so much of himself and his medium.

We first met around 2001. Eventually I ended up writing a book about just one of his photographs, *Picture for Women*, from 1979. But along the way we have published several conversations. "The Domain of Occurrence" is one of the most recent. It was commissioned by the Spanish *Concreta* magazine in 2014. We explore a number themes that have interested us both for a long time; the photograph as "picture" and "document"; the shifting attitudes to photography in and as art; and the relationship between subject matter and pictorial challenge.

Jeff Wall

Jeff, in the past you have spoken of picture making as a set of challenges that often float free, or *almost* free, from subject matter. You explore a certain pictorial form or method and the ostensible subject matter may be secondary. It's close to the way some figurative painters work.
But you *have* circled around certain subjects, making different kinds of pictures of them at different times. For instance *Ivan Sayers* (2009) has affinities with *Picture for Women* (1979), made thirty years earlier. *Mimic* (1982) has elements in common with *Figures on a Sidewalk* (2008). There are many recurrences or returns of motifs. Do the changes in your pictorial approach correspond to changes in attitude to the subjects you are depicting? *Mimic* and *Picture for Women* are forthright and confrontational. *Ivan Sayers* and *Figures* are more openly affectionate.
I think the pictorial problems emerge from the accidental encounter that reveals the subject. They aren't free of it, they are born from it. But, it might be that I am wanting to deal with some kind of pictorial question, like, say, the closeness of a face and figure to the picture plane. But I'm not really aware of it or if I am it is a vague impulse. And then that might help me to notice something that I might not otherwise have noticed. Or, it is really just a random encounter that sets the whole thing off in a direction I wasn't involved with at all. I never know. Certain things probably attract me more than others, as well, and I don't want to get very much control over that, either. So the subject is never secondary but at the same time I am not indebted to it the way some other photographers can be. Photographers often want to treat a subject extensively, devote themselves to it, and make groups or sequences of pictures about it. I do it in one image, and clear the debt in one throw of the dice.

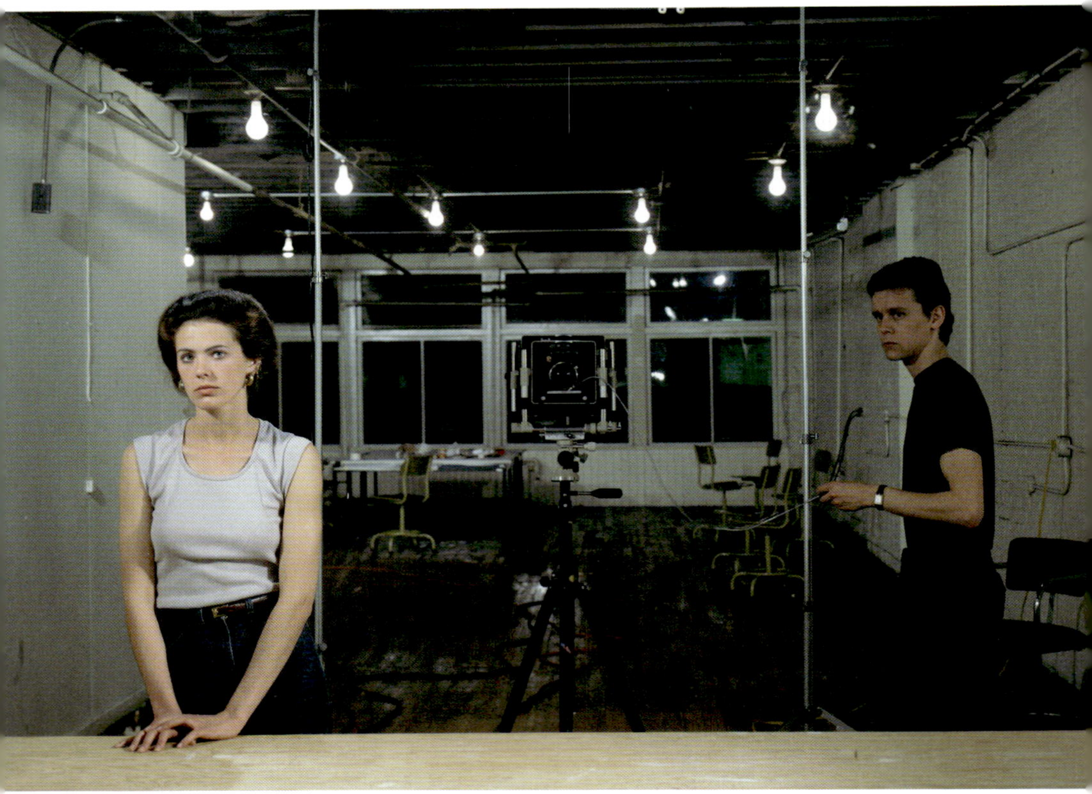

Jeff Wall, Picture for Women, 1979. Transparency in lightbox, 204.5 x 142.5 cm

My attitude seems to be changing all the time, and not in one direction, but in some tangled way. I feel great affection for the people in *Mimic*, not much different from how I feel about those in *Ivan Sayers*. The affection is for how they appear. You need the same affection for everything you depict, or you can't see it well and depict it well. Depiction as a process or a mode of art seems to me to be based in sheer affection for appearance as such.

Do you ever feel a tension between this affection for appearance and what they used to call "the politics of representation"? Back in the 1970s and early 1980s you seemed to be interested in depictions of situations where there was some overt social tension or unease. Those tensions have their own kind of pictorial energy. I sense that today, or at least currently, you make fewer images of that kind. You seem more at ease with that "sheer affection for appearance as such" and this has opened up other pictorial possibilities.
If you are just talking about subjects, I think there are quite a few I've done recently that are in the same range as pictures from the 80s. But I am probably doing them somewhat differently now. Those kinds of subjects might have their own specific pictorial energy, but I don't think they require any predictable way of being shown. So I'm looking for ways of showing, ways of creating an appearance of something, whether it is a scene of tension or of something else. Also, I don't feel that there is any preferable kind of subject, especially since subjects usually come up by accident.
If you think about the generic subjects of pictorial art – like still lifes, portraits, nudes in interiors, landscapes – it sometimes seems to me that they are sort of stand-ins for their having to be a subject for a picture. Any slightly unusual subject would likely have to come to the artist through some sort of unexpected encounter. In the absence of such an encounter, you can still keep working by using one of the generic subjects as your starting point. Once you've started, then you're at work again and facing the problem of how to make that particular subject into a good painting or photo or drawing. This is probably more the case with painting or drawing, but it is still a strong factor with photography. I think it's perfectly possible to, say, work on some arrangements in a studio when you might be

lacking something else to do, or more unique to do, just the way a painter might, and that those pictures are just as likely to be successful and good as anything else you might do. So, just to keep busy, just to keep working, moving, looking, you would try this and that for as long as it seemed to be the most immediate possibility. And, as we know, that kind of studio photography has become very popular now, and maybe it is because that space presents a constant set of possibilities that don't rely on some occurrence in an unpredictable world of occurrences. The interior of the studio is by nature a sort of space-frame of occurrence – the occurrence of something there to be photographed in some way.

I think you're right about this tendency, which is currently widespread in art photography, to accept and work with that older notion of the stand-in subject, the generic subject. But what's striking is how recent this seems to be, or at least it's recent in the form of the "expanded studio" practice as you describe it. It used to be that photographers with an urge to make pictures but no particular idea about a subject simply went out with their cameras and found it in the world. Maybe not the nudes in interiors but certainly the still life, the portrait, the landscape, the streetscape. The picture-maker in the documentary mode, I guess you might call it. And in that mode, the photographer really does stumble upon their subjects and genre possibilities. You have made pictures that way but generally, as you often say, you "begin by not photographing", by noticing something that might lend itself to the making of a successful picture. Then comes the "preparation and collaboration".
Are you noticing generic subjects? If so, what does it mean to notice the generic, rather than the particular?
It might be that we are all working in the wake of Garry Winogrand's last years. If the accounts are true, he was simply more interested in making photographs out in the world than he was in printing them, assessing them, even in developing his film. Winogrand, as he put it, "said yes" to the elemental encounter with unforeseen occurrences, said "yes" to being there, somewhere, pulling the trigger on a moment, capturing it on film.

After that, photography was for him seemingly finished and maybe he didn't want to spend the slow, excruciating time poring over all his contact prints looking for the best ones. Maybe at that point he figured that if there were "best ones" they'd eventually come to light through the study and judgment of other people, people he guessed he would never know. And he seemed to be perfectly OK with that. Now, because of his show at the Metropolitan Museum of Art in New York, people are worrying over the fact that other people have selected some of the pictures from the material Winogrand never looked at, wondering where the authorship is. I think this is just great for photography – it reiterates that there are simply NO RULES. There is no reason why Winogrand couldn't have felt somehow, foreseen somehow, that this process would itself become a great moment in the understanding of the art form. You could say that Winogrand wanted to keep as far away from the generic subject as he could; that he wanted each picture to be the result of a very specific encounter with something, some occurrence. So he could be seen as the important counter-model to any notion of photography needing to engage with the generic subject, or genre. Maybe, but its more complicated; maybe for him the endless encounters with what can seem like infinitely reduced occurrences, the tireless recording of them, often without looking through his viewfinder, maybe that process got to the point it did because he was in a state of recognition that "occurrences" themselves are a single sort of thing – brief concatenations of human or animal energy forming erratically though often in structured spaces, and in the presence of a recording device.

Or – also – instances of the absence of those concatenations – or of the failure of the recording device to capture one and so it captured only its wake after it had vanished – and so on. "Occurrence" itself becomes generic – the pictures just show an endless stream of the thing we come to recognize as "an occurrence" – including its absence, or its having passed without being caught on film. Maybe that's why he could shoot without looking – because he already knew that he was in the domain of the occurrence as such and that the image could not fail to capture that or fail to fail, either.

Winogrand shows us that nothing that we consider necessary to photography as art is indispensable – this is his very radical lesson and we can accept it seriously from him because he got to the position of being able to experience that by working as rigorously as anyone did to "capture a unique occurrence and make a great picture" in the street-photography way. And he seems to have worn through the backcloth of that space into a very abstract space and a very abstract relation to photography. I feel that my "beginning by not photographing" has always been very close to what Winogrand was doing in his last few years, up to 1984.

I see it as even more radically open than that perhaps, because I think we must include the photographic act itself among those potentially infinite "occurrences".
When we look at a Winogrand, yes, we sense the world was/ is ongoing in its patterned but unpredictable ways but really the world itself has no sense of its own occurrence. It is only the act of observing it, putting a perceptual, or symbolic, or photographic frame around it that can turn it into occurrence. Winogrand's camera conjures "something" out of the "nothing" of everyday life. But unlike, say, Henri Cartier-Bresson who wished to impose a strong pictorial order (a strong observation, a strong perceptual/symbolic/photographic frame), it seems that Winogrand was flirting with the idea that the photographic act will always and inevitably transform things into a picture and that "composition" is entirely secondary to this phenomenon.
So I accept what you say about your own work, that however much preparation there is, however much "composition", if you are photographing living things, or even just photographing in changing light conditions, you can never be outside of the unpredictable gift of appearance. The shape a body takes. The way light hits something. The way fabric folds. An expression on a face. A chance alignment. This itself is radically, disturbingly and freely beyond authorship.
The world itself is richer, stranger, more complex, more exciting, more frightening than any art, but photography has some kind of conditional access to this non-art. Does this ring true to you?
Sure… but let me add that, maybe the issue, in relation to what

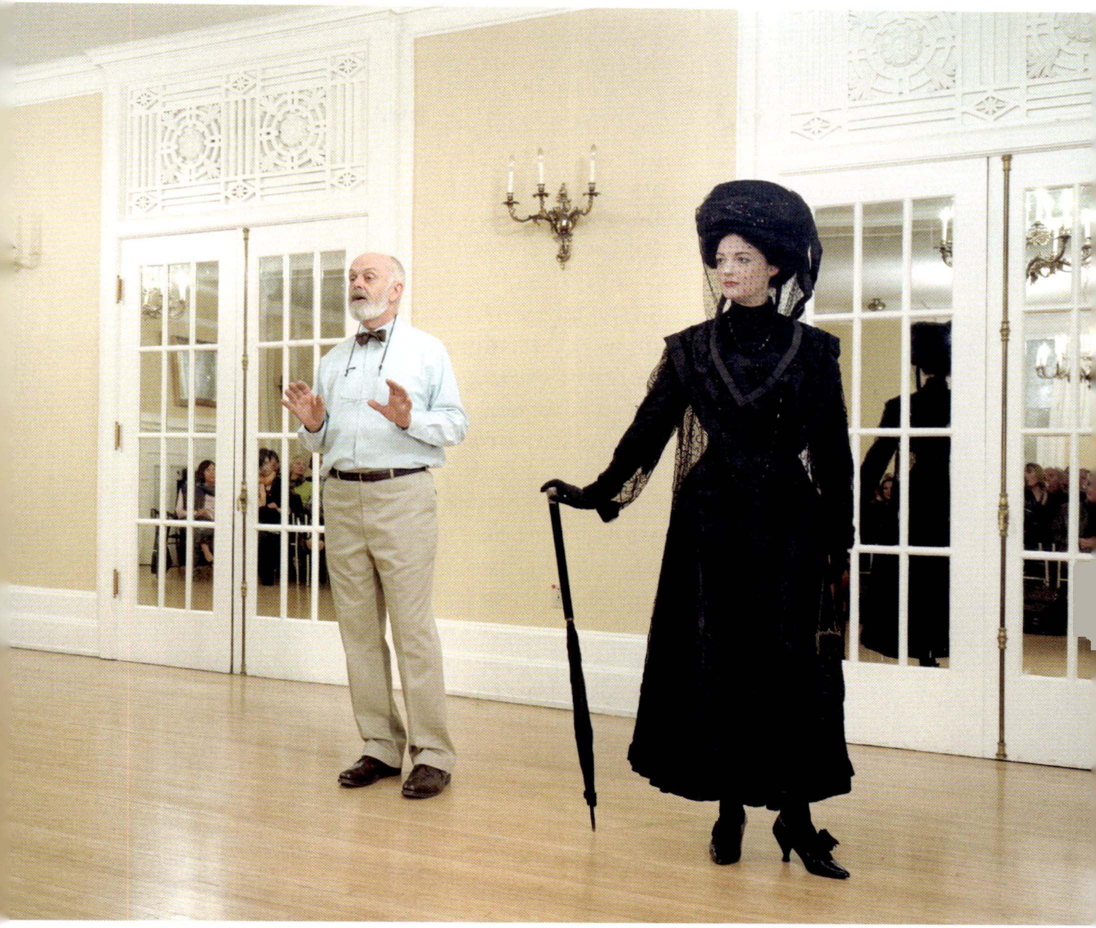

Jeff Wall, Ivan Sayers, costume historian, lectures at the University Women's Club, Vancouver, 7 December 2009. Lightjet print, 182.5 x 224.3 cm

we're saying about Winogrand, is to do with the tableau, that form. Not every image is (or wants to be, or needs to be) a tableau. The tableau can be thought of as a particularly acute act of composition, and when an image isn't as acutely composed, it has less presence as a tableau. Winogrand's experiment, if that's what it was, had to do with seeing how little deliberate composing one had to do to end up with a tableau, seeing how much automatism could be involved. And he showed that there is an infinite amount. Because there are no rules, only examples, any random capture can result in a convincing tableau. The tableau form, like any identifiable artistic form, can't be made – or made interestingly – according to rules; it just gets made somehow and if it's good, that's it. That's one of the reasons it's so interesting and long-lasting, it can appear anywhere at any time, can be composed with extreme deliberation or none at all, and so on. And chance, or accident, is always hovering in the process, to play some part or other. So, in that light, there is only a difference of degree between Winogrand shooting without looking and without processing, and my version of deliberation. His version of chance can appear during my work process at any stage, and often does, and his level of deliberation in working so hard not to compose anything but still to spend many hours a day moving around and operating his camera is just a different form of what I do.

Let's say, just for the sake of this discussion and not to make any particular claims, that his approach is one limit and mine is the opposite and everything else lies between them. Across the spectrum of gradation between these limits we have the domain in which occurrence becomes tableau. And so, if we imagine say 1000 photographers, each occupying a point on the spectrum, taking an image we'd get the 1000 shades of the tableau. And if we did this experiment, we'd ask the 1000 all to photograph the same thing in order to be able to compare the results. And so, in the experiment, the occurrence, or subject, being photographed would just stand for "the occurrence" as such.

That's a way of seeing that the relation between occurrence and tableau is completely structural and aesthetic, and therefore there is, at least as a structural model, such a thing as the occurrence in the abstract, or the occurrence as such. Then, moving from that abstraction back to the actual practices of various photographers, we'd once again get the variety of pictures being made, but we'd have a sense of the common ground on which they get made.

I am struck by the way the case is made (and unmade) for the tableau form in photography. The making of the case calls upon two related but different forces. One is artistic will – the desire on the part of the photographer to fashion something artistically convincing. The other centres on the viewer's "will to form" – the desire, conscious or unconscious, to relate to a photograph as a tableau regardless of intention. But then there might be something else – the conscious or unconscious desire to see past form to an engagement with the subject, or something "in the picture".
Last month I showed to my brother-in-law Stephen Shore's book *Uncommon Places*. His main interest was the recurrence of MGB convertibles in Stephen's pictures. He didn't mention Stephen's gift for composition, although clearly composition will always condition our engagement somehow. Stephen was coming for lunch that day and my brother-in-law asked him if there were lots of MGBs in the Midwest in the 1970s or whether he had been drawn to them somehow. Stephen replied that he *was* drawn to them. His wife had an MGB, he liked that type of car and he always seemed to notice them when he was out making pictures.
Just as there is nothing to stop any photographic document being viewed as an artistic photograph or tableau, there is nothing to prevent any tableau photograph being read as a document. Every photograph is and is not a tableau. Every photograph is and is not a document. I am simplifying of course, because what is so fascinating in photography is the tension or dialectic between artwork and document. And so many of the great photographers of the past worked in ways that drew from or dramatized that tension. Weegee, Evans, Cartier-Bresson, Helen Levitt, Arbus, Frank, Klein, Shore, so many others. They all occupied their own space between reportage and art. It's almost as if there was an understanding that a weak claim to art could be really productive but a strong claim might crush it. Evans was once asked if pho-

tography was Art. He replied that it was *an* art. I suspect you might disagree with this.
Well, I agree that photography is an art, like all the other arts, not "Art" as such. But I don't agree about the weak or strong claim dichotomy. I don't think there's a better or best way to make any art that can be known in advance and turned into a guideline or criterion. The weak claim is valid but it can't stand as anything more than one possibility among others. It also reflects the circumstances – and the sensibilities – of that generation of photographers. Because they did so much, their approach can appear to be the much preferred or even the only valid one. But that can never really be the case, even if just because times and circumstances change.
The "weak" claim reflects or expresses a certain ambivalence about art that was characteristic of the avant-garde, or the avant-garde period. But things have moved on from there and now there's less reason to want to undermine art, especially "Art", and more reason now to want to preserve it as a possibility, since it is to an unprecedented extent threatened with a kind of dissolution into a mass culture or a global digital culture. Art with a big A seemed like an accomplice of imperialism etc. a hundred years ago and to some extent it was...but by now it is the nuanced distinction between the works of art themselves and the culture in which they were made that seems more important, and that sense of nuance is maybe what "Art" has handed on to us and what we now probably need to get closer to than we have been. The "weak" claim was an important means to reduce the pretensions of – if not the art itself – at least the aura around it and the way societies received and manipulated the art, and that, as part of the self-critique of art, has given us a completely new way of appreciating the art that was once considered so pretentious. It doesn't seem so pretentious anymore – at least not the good art. (The less good always takes on that sense of pretension because it's pretending to be better art than it really is). For example – notice the revival of interest in nineteenth- and early twentieth-century Pictorialist photography over the past several years, something that wouldn't have been likely without a real change of mood and attitude. Anyway, the "weak" claim is now a permanently valid approach but it doesn't have the exclusivity it had say in 1930 or even in 1970.

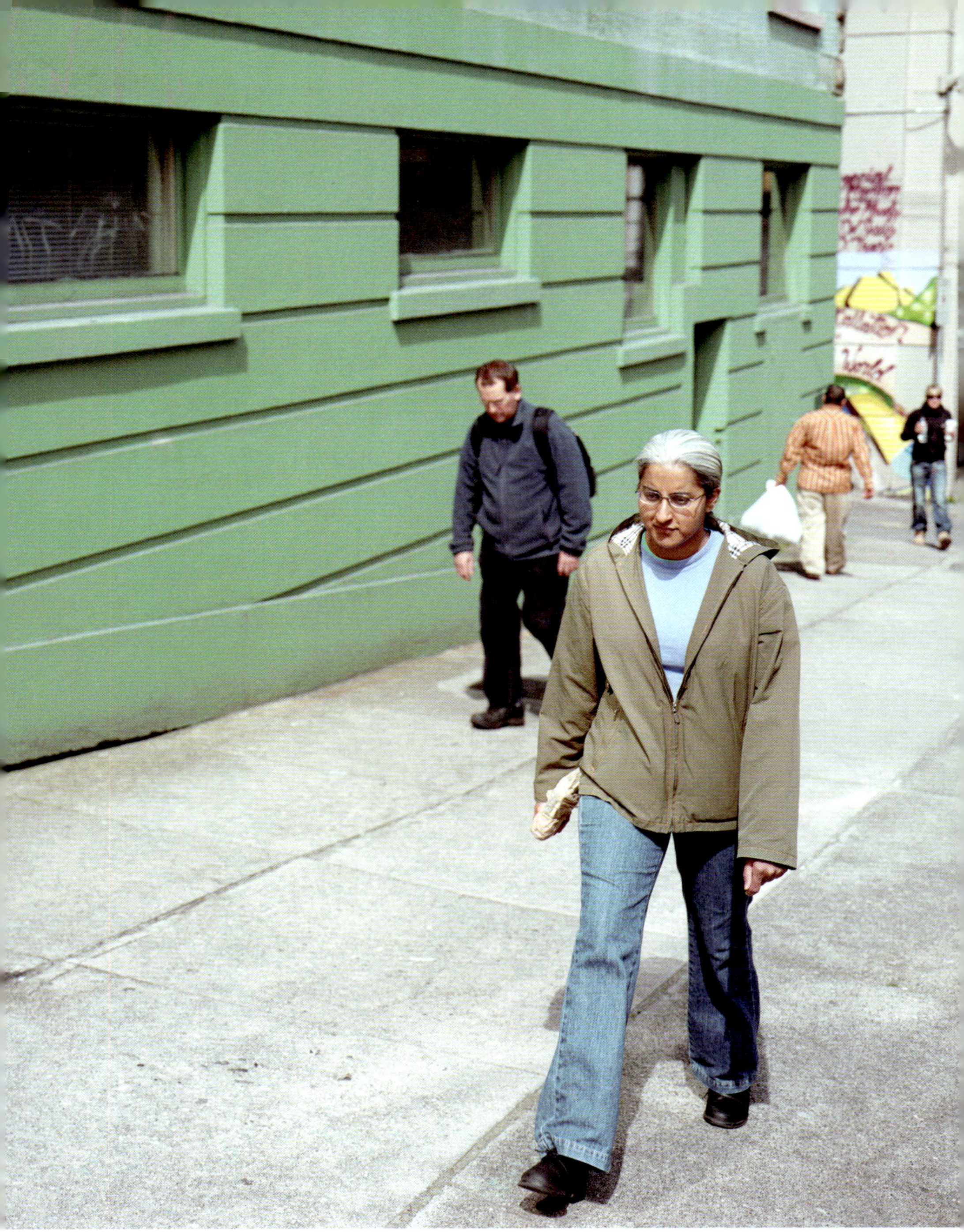

Jeff Wall, Figures on a sidewalk, 2008. Lightjet print, 163 x 132 cm

And then, about the MGBs – there is no way to prevent a viewer from appreciating something shown in a picture more than the picture itself. But it is one of the great qualities of pictures that they can give their beauties even to the viewer who's not looking for them, and who seems unaware of them in the moment of looking. But the beauty has jumped into their awareness nevertheless and abides there waiting to be recognized…maybe waiting forever, but…

There is something very mysterious in the fact that the beauty of certain photographs may work on us without being recognized, and even when it is recognized it may still be incomprehensible. That can happen in any medium of depiction but it's particularly strong in photography because of its document character. But coming back to your earlier point, I agree that the historical avant-gardes had their suspicions of Art and that those suspicions did shape certain attitudes to photography. As we know, even into the 1970s there was great antipathy towards any idea of the tableau form being valid, especially in photography (and there *are* still strong pockets of suspicion!). I agree also that that long moment is over, that there are no rules or criteria. And I agree that the tableau can be a very important resistance to that worrying dissolution into mass culture. But I don't think the photographers I just mentioned were particularly motivated by those avant-garde suspicions. I think they felt that photography simply got energized in extraordinary ways as an art form by that encounter with occurrence, out in the world.
I can see you have your own relation to that energy too, although you mediate and modulate it differently perhaps. I was just looking again at the catalogue of the exhibition held at BOZAR, Brussels (*Jeff Wall: The Crooked Path*, 2012) in which you showed your own work in relation to some of the art you have admired. I notice that the photographers you included mainly come from that "documentary style": Evans, Zille, Brandt, Levitt, Weegee, Winogrand, Shore, Gursky's early work. A few operate in a more constructed, allegorical way (the still lifes of Wols, Christopher Williams and James Well-

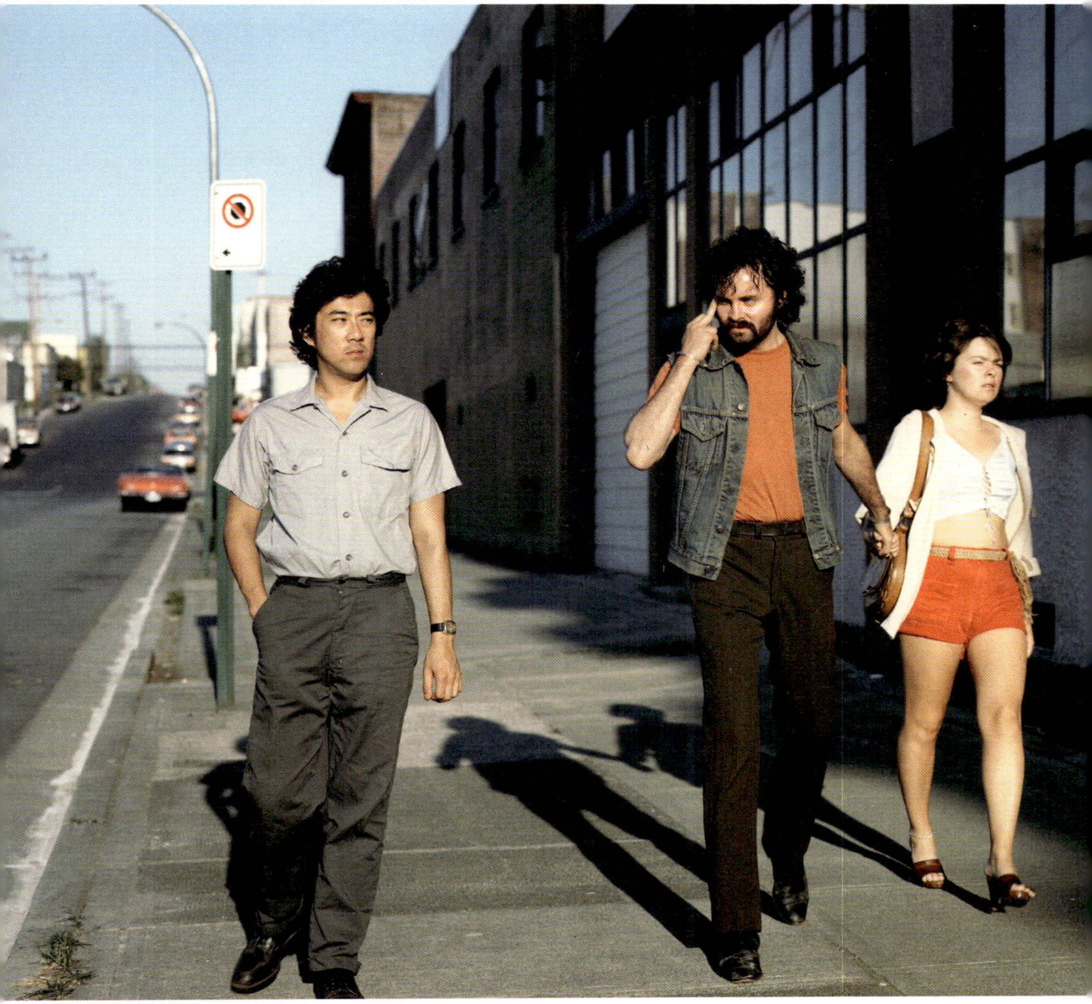

Jeff Wall, Mimic, 1982. Transparency in lightbox, 198 x 228.6 cm

ing). But are there photographs made in your "cinematographic" mode that you admire?
I think they all were motivated by the avant-garde sentiment against "Art", maybe in a somewhat less overt or direct way, but the view is still there. And, right, the documentary project was a very fitting form for that opposition to take, since it had many social, even radical virtues that one could claim that "Art" didn't have, or have any more. But you could also say that everything interesting in the arts between around 1860 and 1960 was motivated by the avant-garde position, because that was the most interesting, compelling and productive one for that long time. Even people who opposed it in some way or other were inspired by it, even if negatively. The whole reduction, or reductive process isn't comprehensible otherwise – and within that process is the project of reducing "Art" to something lighter, quicker, richer, more open to the everyday, not so big and heavy and slow, and grand. When I moved toward photography, though, I had the strong feeling that that process had run its course and that all the virtues of "weak", "small" claim-making had become truisms, not that alive any more.
I always loved Robert Frank and the others and they were an inspiration and model for me since my teenage years, but I just felt that there was nowhere to go with the breaking down and further miniaturizing the notion of art in that avant-garde or neo-avant-garde way. It wasn't about a return to some condition before the reduction – and I've said this many times – I feel it was an authentic reaction or response to the artistic circumstances of that moment somewhere in the early 70s. "Art" was so "out" by then that it just couldn't not become interesting in a new way. My take on the tableau was shaped by my earlier connection to painting and the model of painting as tableau played an important role for me. But I was not attempting to "make paintings by means of photography" or some such cliché of the 80s or 90s. I was making photographs in a way that had existed since the beginnings of photography but that had been eclipsed by the great tide of discovery of the virtues of the documentary mode. That shadow-space was the open space for me. So, for me it's not about some divide between the documentary mode or documentary style and cinematography – photography lives, I think, by means of the infinitely nuanced interplay between those modes. So I don't

think its curious that the photographers that interest me most and to whom I feel closest are those that usually aren't thought of as cinematographic – like Evans or Atget or Zille. And this is not to say I "find traces of the cinematographic within their documentary practice" – that's another cliché by now. I don't find that or need to find it. The inspiration for me is the absence of cinematography in their work.

Around the time of this conversation, the American artist **Lucas Blalock** was coming out of a remarkably prolific period of image making. He showed me more than one hundred and fifty pictures. Most had been shot in his studio and then worked on digitally. They looked to me like very clever fun, taking the protocols of the mainstream still life, portrait and commercial postproduction, and skewing then into some whip-smart and ludic realm. Each new work added something to the mix, a unity in itself but also a stepping-stone in an open-ended improvisation, conducted with enormous creative and intellectual energy.

If you have that kind of energy, photography allows you to move very quickly through a range of related thoughts and possibilities. Lucas was reflecting on this, putting together what would become his extraordinary book *Mirrors, Windows, Tabletops*, eventually published in 2013. He brought me an early dummy for the book. It had an anonymous cream fabric cover, and included a lot more than those one hundred and fifty images. At the front were five pages of typed X's, like an empty placeholder for an essay to come. It was titled "Dressing the Emperor".

"Lucas, are you expecting me to dress the emperor?" I asked.
"Oh no, no. I want a blank essay in the book. But I would also like us to have a conversation that will sit in the pages as a separate pamphlet. If people want to read it they can, or they can just take it out".

Lucas Blalock

Lucas, I'd like to dive in and ask you something about surfaces. It seems to me that photography became modern in the 1920s when it accepted its industrial smoothness. In doing so it made itself available to the expanding inventory of surfaces that proliferate in the modern world – plastics, metals, glass, new fabrics. In denying its own surface it became the supreme recorder of the surfaces of the world (I think of Edward Weston declaring: "The camera should be used for a recording of life, for rendering the very substance and quintessence of the thing itself, whether it be polished steel or palpitating flesh".) Meanwhile modernist painting largely gave up depiction to concentrate on its own surface. Since then of course things have got more complicated both in photography and painting, as artists move back and forth between the surface of their medium and the surfaces they depict. Does this ring true to you?

It does, and it makes me think of the slippage, when describing photographs, between a description of the image content, and one of the physical object. This creates a sort of location problem when talking about photography. I am sympathetic to Weston's insistence on "looking" but my faith in the camera isn't his. For me photography is more an act of drawing than one of index or transparency.

In my own work I think this question of surface has been most shaped thinking about collage, and at what point a photograph moves beyond its threshold into another form. I think another way of saying this might be that part of what is at stake in photography's denial of its surface is a footing in homogeneity and naturalism. I am interested in making pictures that betray these qualities, making heterogeneous or stilted photographs, while at the same time using a consideration of the medium as a boundary.

To that end the title of your book is intriguing. *Mirrors and Windows: photography since 1960* was of course the title of a MoMA show and book put together by John Szarkowski (in 1984). There Szarkowski seemed to wrong-foot his critics by including all manner of heterogeneous or "stilted" photographs. Robert Cumming's sculpture/performance photos. John Divola's theatrical/forensic photos. You've added "Tabletops". It makes me think that the tabletop is the classic location for the still-life (plucking and placing) and for collage (cutting and pasting). Then there's "the desktop" of the computer screen, the location of digital post-production.
The title does refer to Szarkowski's exhibition as well as the table proper in the ways you mentioned. Leo Steinberg's "flatbed picture plane" (which comes from an essay about Rauschenberg's collage techniques) was in the air. WINDOWS MIRRORS TABLETOPS is also the neon that emblazons a Silverlake glass shop which I drove by nearly everyday when I was living in California. I kept, rather absently, thinking about the Szarkowski and what this third term might be. Over the months it started to take on more and more possibilities.

What do you plan and what is improvised?
Almost everything is improvised, though obviously I often set up the initial terms of that improvisation. For me, being in control of the details doesn't seem to me to make very good pictures. I am reading Philip Guston's collected writings and he quotes Paul Valery as saying that bad poetry "vanishes into meaning". I think some analogue of this is true in photography. To be a bit more specific, when I am working I let the momentum carry my decision making. I set objects on the table but the pictures get made trying to figure out how to look at these things rather than composing them. Shooting in the studio is not so different for me from shooting something outside.

Guston had a knack for holding onto remarks that made sense. In an interview from 1960 he recalls something John Cage said to him: "When you start working, everybody is in your studio – the past, your friends, enemies, the art world, and above all, your own ideas – all are there. But as you continue paint-

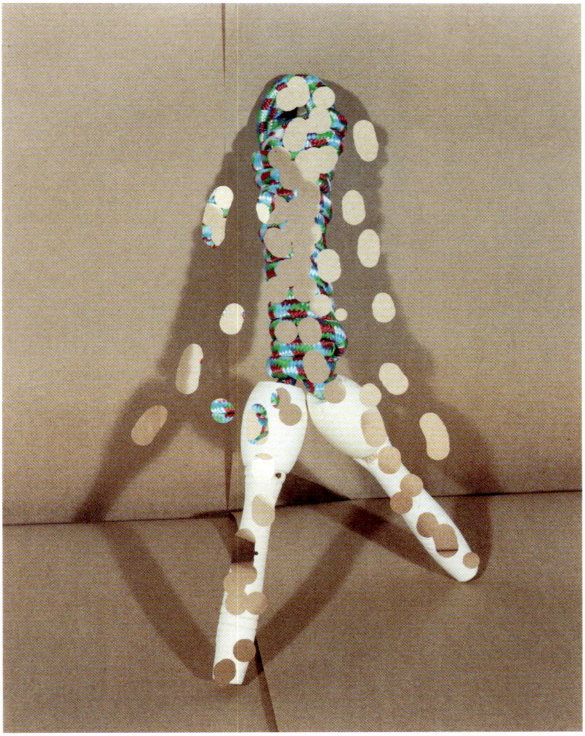

Lucas Blalock, Untitled Figure, 2012

ing, they start leaving, one by one, and you are left completely alone. Then, if you are lucky, even you leave". One can't leave while holding on to every last detail. It's interesting that historically the street was regarded as the space in which control escaped the photographer, while the studio was where it could be regained. That distinction has slowly vanished but what remains is the enigmatic ratio of art, chance and document.

I don't intend to make the claim that the kinds of contingencies at play in the studio are the same as Winogrand's or Friedlander's. I shoot with a large format camera and in the end I think that condition informs the pictures as much as where they are made.

Of course. There's a widespread assumption still that the larger the camera format the less contingency there is. Winogrand the speculative hunter-gatherer embracing all chance on 35mm; the large format studio photographer banishing everything unintended (I notice Jeff Wall gets annoyed when people say there's no chance in his work). Very often I feel the plate camera, sitting there stoically on its tripod, is somehow asking to be entertained, daring you to surprise it.

It just involves a different attitude. I like this thing Godard said about all films being documentaries because the camera was documenting the performance of the actors (Jeff Wall somewhat echoes this with his idea of the "phantom studio"). Maybe with the large camera it becomes a question of limit instead of encounter – or at least limited encounter or cumbersome encounter. I think about the 4x5 less as stoic than slow and clumsy – even though it can be used in very precise ways.

To return to something else you said, I think that the studio is a site of control. Maybe you could say that Winogrand's project was about capturing momentary harmony in a situation of seemingly endless contingency; where the studio is more like a laboratory where contingency can be introduced and made variable. Art historian Svetlana Alpers' book, *The Vexations of Art: Velasquez and Others,* deals with the way that the painter's studio functioned as a site for looking out, or a place for rehearsing how we approach and picture the world. I think that this kind of consideration and picture making invites another set of contingencies, which for me have expanded into the processing capacities of the computer.

I think Godard was quite right. Even the modes, methods and materials of artifice are – or become – documents. It makes me wonder whether the criterion by which all art (but particularly photographic art) survives is primarily documentary. A documentary not just of what was before the camera, but of an attitude towards it. This might be as true of a still life photographer as a street photographer. I look at Winogrand's pictures and I see documents of his world but also documents / examples of particular formal challenges – the stretching of compositional "harmony" until it almost snaps, of becoming "stilted" as you

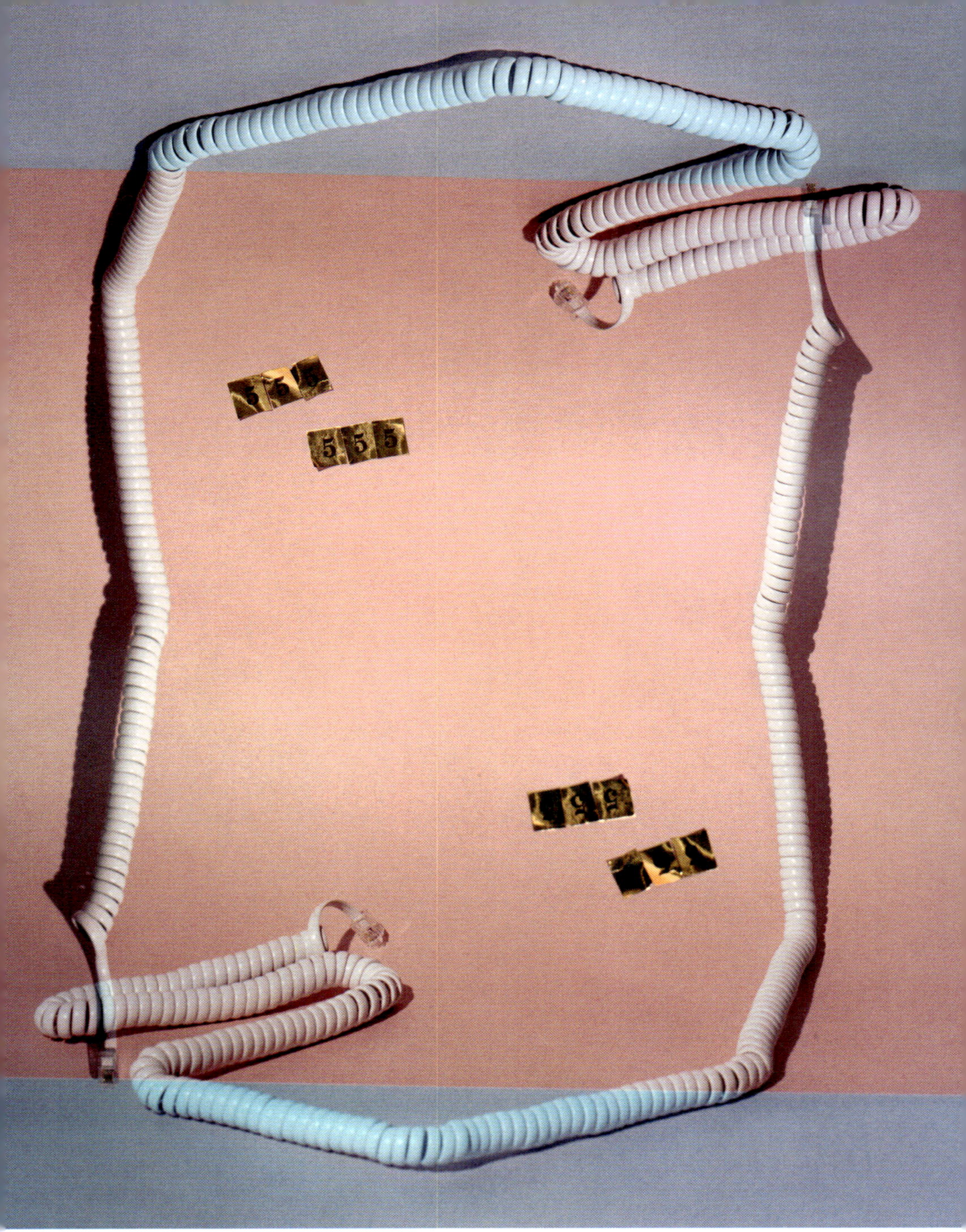

Lucas Blalock, 555 555, 2012

put it. Records of his own undoing, to paraphrase a Scritti Politti lyric. I have that feeling looking through this book too.
I hope so, and this "becoming document" is really close to my own thinking about making photographs. One of the things I have thought a lot about in the last few years is what we as viewers bring to looking at photographs now – how Photoshop, digital, the internet, etc. have altered the terms of that looking.
I have put this idea out there before, that early jazz audiences not only had familiarity with the standards, but, having come up in a culture where it was expected you could play an instrument or carry a tune, that the technical variations were also widely legible. If you played a tune in 5/4 your audience could hear it, and I think photography is in a similar cultural situation now. Not only do a broad range of people understand the camera, but also, increasingly, the tools of the picture's digital processing. Imagining and attempting to re-articulate this ground, putting pressure on these expectations (especially your own), is a big part of what it means to make pictures.

Improvising with materials before the camera is a kind of photographic jazz people understand. That's nice. But improvising with Photoshop seems to be a different matter. Photoshop hasn't reached the "jazz phase" for most people. They use it to standardize, to perfect. A kind of grooming of the image. You don't take that path at all. You take the same attitude to Photoshop as you take to what you do in front of the camera. It's experimental.
It is. Grooming is a great way to describe its more conventional use! And though, from a practitioner's standpoint, I totally agree that the software's possibilities haven't really been explored until recently, I think that apps like Instagram, celebrity-before-and-after-photos, the Iranian missile picture, and others have really primed us in the software's potentialities, and it is this literacy I am (possibly optimistically) assuming.
To respond to another part of what you said, there is definitely a through line from how I begin a picture (with the camera) to the way that the digital file is handled. When I first started making pictures that had been fucked with it took me a long time to understand what constituted their limits. The computer is such a powerful tool and in

the beginning it felt like there were too many possibilities to make these interventions feel specific or necessary. I found a way forward in Cézanne, Courbet, and Manet and also in Brecht's writings on theatre. This opened to thinking about bringing the offstage of photographic production onstage by parroted procedural corrections gone awry. I was interested in the way that I could make these technologies – designed to have a high degree of transparency (the studio, the camera, and Photoshop) – more opaque. An awareness of the computer's invisible hand in its "grooming" capacity had already become part of what it meant to look at photographs, and using these tools in a more forward, evident way felt available. All of this was buttressed by seeing work by other young photographers, particularly Florian Maier-Aichen who was using the computer in really inventive ways.

Beneath all this I do see a grounding in realism in your work. Maybe it's to do with your lighting, which tends to be even, avoiding chiaroscuro or anything expressionistic. From this baseline you are able to foreground the handling of materials and the manipulation of surfaces. It's a bit like close-up magic: one has to allude to transparency if one is then going to subvert it.
Yes, absolutely! A lot of the choices are very direct. I am trying to make a picture "of" something – the thing or situation in front of the camera – and fulfilling this promise of photographs.
It is great that you brought this around to close-up magic. I have been really excited for years about this Adam Gopnik piece from a 2008 *New Yorker* about just that. I read it as I was just beginning to figure out this work and it really clarified something for me. I still give it to students and friends. It is called *The Real Work*.

It's a wonderful essay. When I read it I imagined Gopnik thinking: "I know I can write in a way that could really convey something about close-up magic", maybe because his sentences are so simple and perfect and thus a little mesmerizing. He describes the way one guy works as being "like a man handling cards rather than like a magician handling props". Now, which of those are you, Lucas?
The man with the cards I hope.

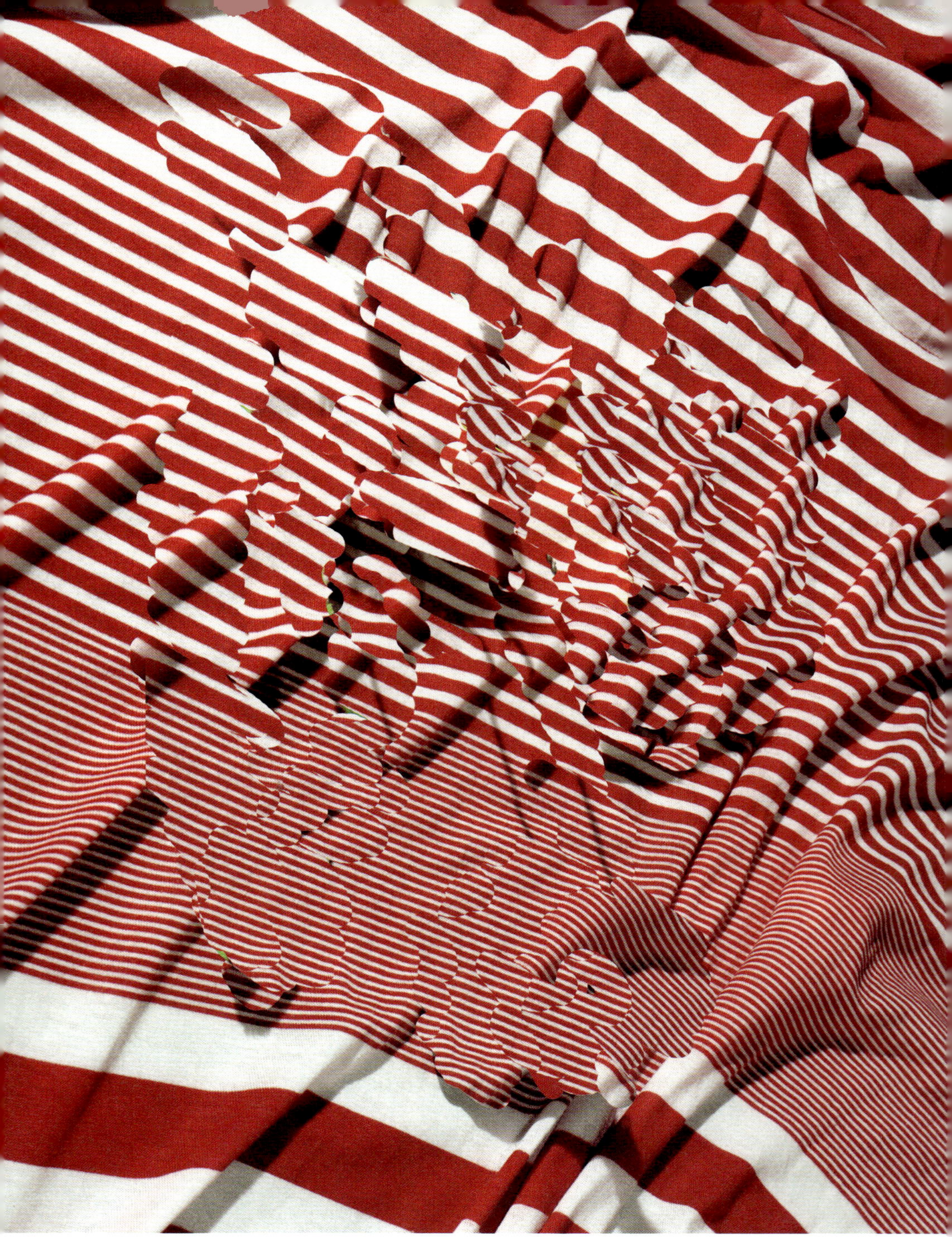

Lucas Blalock, Accurate Walking Style I, 2012

Because looking like a man handling cards makes for a better magician handling props?
I answered that one sort of instinctively… but yes, because it makes for a better magician – or just one of a certain stripe. There is the transcendental strangeness of illusion that is beguiling, but then there is this other strangeness that is much closer at hand. In this latter kind there is a tension between the performance and the work of performing or the prop and its other life off the stage. For me this is where so much takes place.

Mirrors Windows Tabletops **is a big book. You made the work and lots more over an eighteen-month period. You've been going pretty fast. Markets prefer artists to develop slowly and incrementally but photography does allow for rapid work. Huge artistic ground can be covered quickly. I guess most of your thinking is in the doing.**
It is really a book about just that. Having a studio practice has allowed for thinking in pictures, or by picturing, where problems get worked out through putting them in play. The book is a kind of primary text from that practice. It doesn't have the distance of a monograph or a collection – it is more like a notebook. And this kind of accumulation has been very important within the work. I am always looping back to pick up underdeveloped ideas.

That's refreshing to hear, and not so common these days. Perhaps there has been something in photo-art education that has tended to nudge young image-makers into pre-rationalization or post-rationalization, and slightly away from "thinking as making".
That is totally possible, but I think it also rubs up against the desires of the market you mentioned. There is a lot of anxiety. I think ambition is a really complicated thing in this kind of atmosphere. It's a shame it's discouraged (even if just implicitly or internally). For some reason it is really easy to talk yourself out of making a picture… But for me this working method is totally indispensable.

Susan Meiselas has been one of the most innovative practitioners working in the expanded documentary mode. Since her projects in the 1970s, such as *Carnival Strippers* and *Nicaragua*, she has developed her own highly reflexive approach, engaging with people and subjects far from North America, where she lives, but making explicit within her work the terms of those engagements.

Working as a photographer, facilitator, editor and writer, Meiselas has become something of a touchstone for a younger generation of documentarists looking to preserve the potential of the image as witness, while being mindful of the interpretive problems it presents. In some ways, her projects are all ongoing. Meiselas revisits images, places and people; updating, reshaping and extending her work to reflect the changing circumstance of her subjects and her representations of them.

This conversation took place in Susan Meiselas's home in Manhattan. We had met only once before and very briefly. We talked for several hours, as much about our backgrounds as anything. What you read here is an edited version, first published in *Photoworks*, a UK magazine, in 2005. There are two main emphases: Meiselas's interest in keeping all her projects alive and ongoing; and her careful understanding of contexts and formats – books, exhibitions, magazine pages, websites.

Susan Meiselas

Susan, a lot of your work seems to be based very much on process, particularly projects such as *Kurdistan: in the shadow of History* and *Encounters with the Dani*. Do you have a sense of the likely outcome of things, or whether it's important to not consider that at all when you are at the beginning of a project?
That's really interesting, I don't go in with a concept; the concept evolves and becomes self-evident at a certain moment in the process. In time one accumulates ideas of what's possible. With each of my projects I've come to the idea of what they should be in the midst of them. This has been so from early projects like *Carnival Strippers* right up to *Encounters with the Dani* and beyond. And of course very often, between shows and books, they have slightly different forms.

A book has to be finite, although you have reissued books of *Carnival Strippers*, *Kurdistan* and *Nicaragua* in slightly different formats. And making one's way through the book of the Kurdistan project one gets to the final page and realises this is by no means the end either of the project or of the political struggle.
Quite often I find things are inappropriately fixed.

Still, your working process is often so reflexive that the reader knows that the "endings" of your work are pragmatic or highly contingent.
But it does feel definitively arbitrary. And infuriating. Actually with *Kurdistan* I had a concept that I couldn't achieve, looking back on it. At that time, in the early 90s I was thinking less about a book and hoped to make a CD-ROM, which back then was incredibly expensive to produce, around half a million dollars. There was no-one sufficiently interested in Kurdish history to invest at that level. But by 1994-5, just as the web was beginning to shift from being data driven to carrying

images, this notion emerged that a CD-ROM could have a link to the internet. The idea was that there'd be the book, with a fixed nature, a CD-ROM with everything from the out-takes from the research as well as video material and then, through the CD, a link would connect to the internet to tie the reader via active websites to an ongoing history. It was the perfect concept for that project. But I could never get the sponsorship to make it happen. It was a problem of marrying this cutting edge information technology with the story of the Kurds, about whom people cared very little. The Nicaragua project also had a natural parenthesis or point of suspension following the triumph of the insurrection, in that I went back and made a film ten years later, as does my work from El Salvador and Chile. Books and films are by necessity finite and exhibitions are forgotten, so what's the perfect form? I don't know.

Well, one might say that all these formats coexist and they do carry different cultural weight. The book as a physical object in the world which can't be erased simply by wiping a hard drive or unplugging a computer. Plus of course books do have a status, for good or bad, that CDs and the internet don't as yet. So it seems important that a book exists for practical as well as symbolic reasons. It marks a presence where there was once an absence.
Certainly for the Kurdish community. That's critically important. It's important to be aware of the differences of formats in the ways they address you and hold attention, hopefully.

Audiences are faced with certain problems. There is often a moment of hesitation or apprehension when they begin to engage with the archival projects of others that they are getting into something that they'll never be able to get out of in a consensual way. Sometimes the sheer volume is so overwhelming. With Gerhard Richter's monumental *Atlas* project (1962) for example, we marvel at the scale of the enterprise before we engage with any one part.
There is certainly an abyss, an enormity. Many of my projects live in more than one community simultaneously and the challenge becomes slightly different. For the Kurdish community, they are seeing their own representation which means there is less persuasion needed. For another community, the Western audience let's say, one confronts the

question the audience is asking: "Why am I being dragged into this huge, ever growing, complex history?" (Even with the book on Kurdistan I was always pushing for another folio of pages from the publisher to accommodate the constantly gathering material). In many ways that project was trying to find a community. It was a project that overlapped history, photography, cultural studies and politics and I'm not sure it ever really found the nexus of any of them. Perhaps because it was trying to form its own nexus.

That is very much a characteristic of a lot of your work. The process is about constituting, forming audiences. There isn't the comfortable position of making a known, finite project for a known, finite audience. Just as your work wrestles with different forms of address, it wrestles with being in different places in the world and the shifting nature of audiences.
That's very true. Audiences shift across time too. Even when revisiting *Carnival Strippers* I had to think back to the context at the time – the debates in feminism about such women, the idea of giving voice to the women from the inside, and so on.

Many photographers and photojournalists were working with book projects in the 1960s and 70s. In some ways *Carnival Strippers* seems very much of its time, in that it's an experience of photographs that forms a universe in which the reader is immersed. That immersive quality is a characteristic of many of the photo-books of that period. But even at that point you were using extensive texts with images and making sound recordings of places and people you photographed, hinting perhaps that the photograph was not enough even with text. This was at a time of a split in documentary between a classical faith in the descriptive powers of the image and a sense that the image needed to the supplemented.
Yes, supplemented, complemented, undermined. I did have that sense early on in my work. I didn't really come through a pure photographic or documentary background. There were reference points and I'd seen certain works, whether it was Diane Arbus, Garry Winogrand or Robert Frank, but then closer to me were people like Danny Lyon and Larry Clark who had approaches I identified with. Recently I dis-

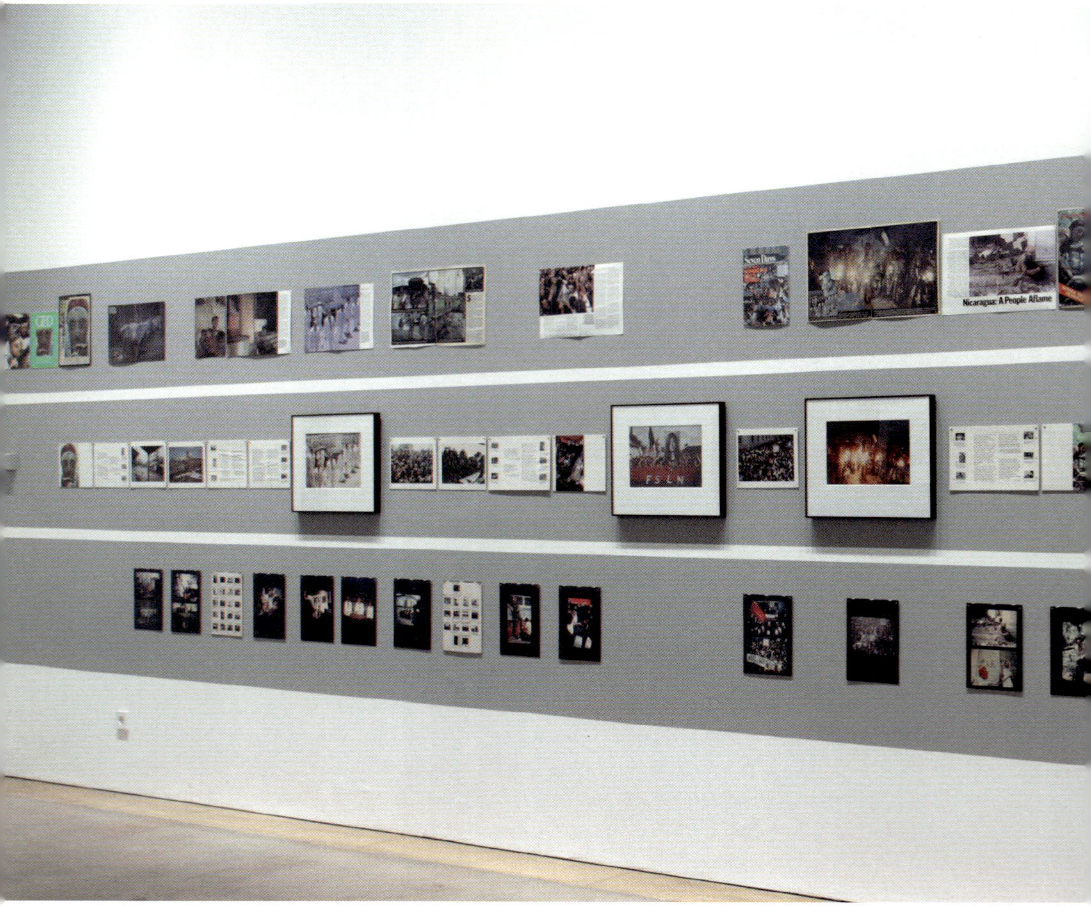

Susan Meiselas, Meditations, 1979, installed at La Virreina, Barcelona, 2011

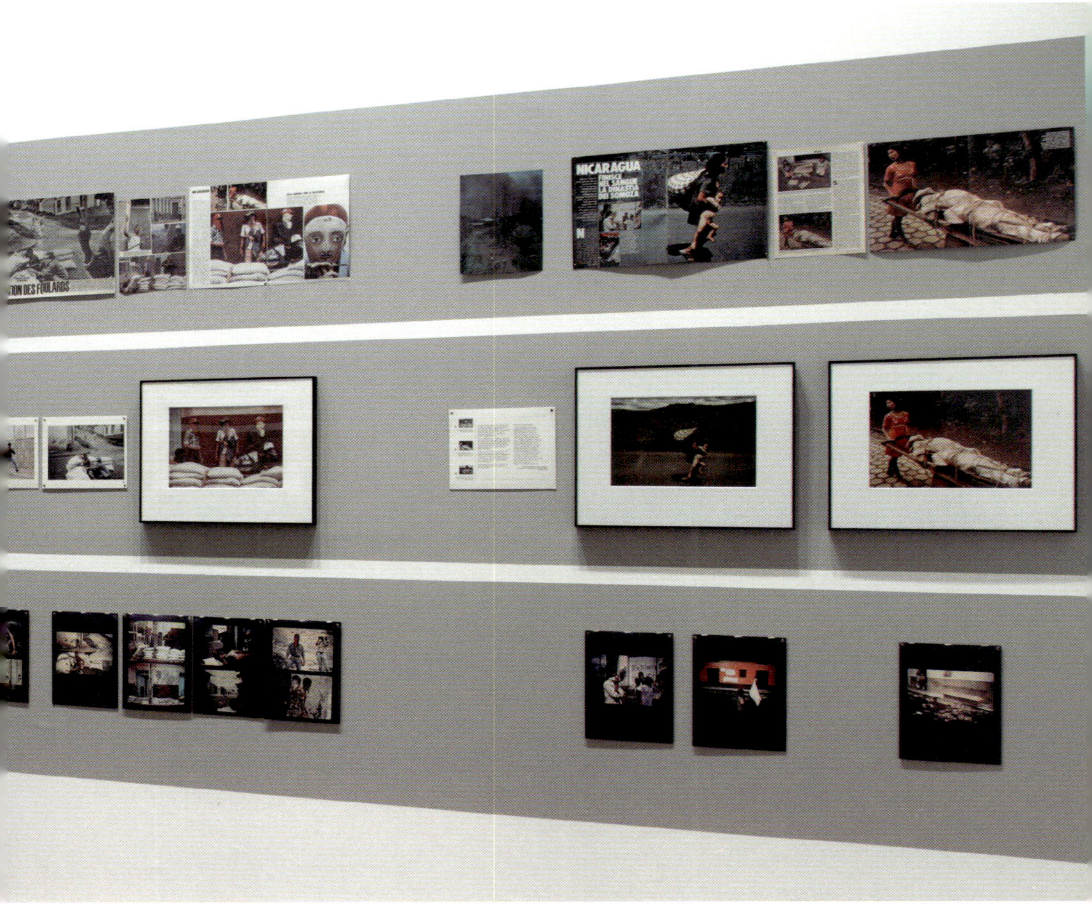
TION DES FOULARDS
NICARAGUA
FINISCE NEL SANGUE LA DINASTIA DEI SOMOZA

covered that Danny Lyon also made sound recordings while working on *The Bikeriders* (1968). Lyon and Clark also moved towards film, as I did, and both preceded me.

In a recent interview the photographer and writer Allan Sekula spoke about the fact that he always found documentary film to be far more willing to engage with radical, experimental practices and formal innovation. Documentary photography has tended to congeal into knowable forms that fit the conventions of conventional magazines.
Yes it's often very static. Although there are ways in which documentary – whatever that is, we're being loose here – has shifted. When I started out I felt there was not much exploration into what to do with the image once you had it. My early work with *Carnival Strippers* was concerned with bringing forth their voices as a part of the overall "picturing". I felt that if I was in someone else's world, they ought to be given the space to participate and collaborate, even though they didn't become partners in the making of it.

Moving through your projects from the 1970s to the present – *Carnival Strippers*, *Nicaragua*, then jumping to *Kurdistan* and the Dani project – it seems your authorial voice becomes less and less evident as the projects become more involved and elaborate. Clearly process for you is very much about collaboration and assembly, giving voice and choreographing. In the book *Encounters with the Dani* you are absolutely there and hardly there. At the same time the Dani themselves are absolutely there and hardly there because the book is structured around those outsiders coming in, their assumptions and expectations of the Dani people.
I'm not sure about this question of the authorial voice. If I were a writer, which I know I'm not, if words came to me the way photographs do, my presence might be different. In all of the projects I am weaving them together so my presence is there. The difference is that it is my primary experience in *Strippers*, let's say. But I didn't live one hundred years in Kurdistan, so I draw from my point of intervention in that history. It's true that other photographers sometimes look at me and wonder why I'm wasting my time on other people's images and other people's histories…

What you do does stand apart from a lot of the ways that the shortcomings of documentary photography have been addressed. I'm thinking of art's deconstructive critique of objectivity on the one hand and the highly, overtly subjective documentary approach on the other. Yours is a third, perhaps more radical position.
Those debates about whether one can speak for or on behalf of the "other" are very important. But I find myself working in areas where not all the pieces of the puzzle, or the argument are there. My projects are authored but I'd like to think they are not authoritative. I feel uncomfortably comfortable acknowledging I am one of those others, who like all others have trespassed and also treasured those experiences and feel that they should be rendered and revealed. In *Kurdistan* one of the many aims was to move the reader into thinking about how I'd come to do the project. I don't do that in the Dani project. I just dive you right in. Whether I can carry a reader through fragmented accounts and fragmented imaginations as if they were there, that's a challenge. It's not a continuous narrative. Much is left out. Can the audience fill in gaps?

This raises complicated questions to do with how a work is received "as a work" or whether it is a less authorially announced occasion for thinking, engaging and reflecting where the question of whether or not one is engaging with "a work" doesn't even surface. Obviously in the context of art the idea of "the work" is inescapable, since the author function regulates so much along with the commodity status of things. Art's audience is attuned to form and structure and method, so art as a context can immediately make a project quite reflexive and quite authored. It is a space in which people think about how things are put together, be it an image, a series of images or a combination of word and image. One could read *Kurdistan* not even perceiving you as a photographer or historian or ethnographer but simply engaging with that material, not even grasping it as a work in an overtly authored sense. It's a little like the film writer Manny Farber's distinction between "white elephant art" – art that aspires to be great art, and "termite art" – art that just gets on with doing its thing and isn't so bothered about being a great or even a work.
That's a really interesting question. Am I preoccupied with whether

my projects will be designated Art with a capital "A" or a small "a"? This reminds me, in 1981-82 I was doing some exhibitions around the Nicaragua project. *Carnival Strippers* had been conceived with images, text and sound. When it was exhibited in a New York Gallery, they only wanted images with captions. It was never published in magazines in America, it went straight to book form. Six months later, I joined Magnum on the basis of a portfolio of images from *Strippers*. "Nicaragua" was a completely different experience as a subject matter and as an approach. I was inside the media in a way I hadn't been, since Magnum distributed the work internationally. It was also a project where I was witnessing history unfold and I was in the thick of it. But as time moved on and the media would come and go, I essentially stayed. Then when I came home I saw how the media chose and dispersed similar images in various territories. I started to become fascinated with the trafficking of those images. I would see the images I had taken come back to me and go out to the world in magazines. At the end of that process I did bring the work together in book form and tried to make sense with multiple kinds of texts in the back – everything from poems to statistics to voices. At the same time I had a show at PS1 in New York of colour Xerox images pinned to the wall. Then in 1982 I had a show first at Side Gallery in Newcastle and then at Camerawork in London. The sense I had for the English exhibitions was to show how I had made selections of images for the book from the mountains of contact sheets and to show the images that I hadn't selected myself but which were used by the media. It was an attempt to de-mask for readers, and for me myself too since I was a reader of my own images as they appeared in the media. Could I reveal to people what they don't usually get to see, rather than just showing a fine print of an image used on the cover of a magazine? Could I show the choices that determine why an image might be reproduced two-by-two inches or as a double spread? Could I show the different cultural resonances of the image choices around the world? Which images are used in Brazil or Germany? So I exhibited tear sheets with my pictures from magazines that paralleled the images I'd chosen for the book (seen as actual book pages) and outtakes of images I had eliminated. The viewer walked into the room and saw three lines, charting out and making the processes of the media and my own mediation visible in a way that it very rarely exposed for us.

If we look at the history of critical writings on culture as they take form in the late 1960s and 1970s along with politicised conceptual art of that time, the critiques were coming from spaces outside of the media. These were slightly removed spaces of criticism. In a sense this led to confusion over your Nicaragua project because it straddles those spaces – the mass media and the critical domain. It is a documentary project that is at the same time a highly reflexive project.
It has always been a problem and a challenge for me. That kind of criticism or risk became more acute when I was working on *Kurdistan*. But that project could only come to me from being in the field working in a certain way, a way based on exploration rather than conceptual assumptions. Even my interest in the repatriation of images of the Kurds – few other even paid mind to it. Who seems to be interested in following what happens to an image over twenty, thirty, a hundred years?

Plus, of course, the history of photography, rather than the history of photographs, is so bound up with print culture that is by its nature ephemeral. Yet, photographs persist, they hang around, to be reused in other ways. So the challenge is twofold: to try and look again at the ephemeral printed matter that has been the basis of visual culture for over a century now, and to track the "careers" of photographic images across time through that ephemeral culture.
I can do that but not as a writer/thinker. If I were, I'd be writing the kinds of important texts Allan Sekula has been writing. I approach it in primarily visual ways. My method is to say "Let's just put it up, or out there and think about it". When I emerged, I was working in a critical vacuum. These questions were just not asked. At least in England you had the beginnings of things with *Camerawork* and *Ten8* magazines. Instead I found myself with colleagues who were galloping off to the next war. I went with them, but then I ended up detouring off from those guys. And they were mainly guys. The whole time I couldn't get this critical, reflexive thinking out of my mind.

This false opposition seems very particular to the way documentary and photojournalism have evolved, which is that either it is reflexive and unmasking or it is "getting on with it"

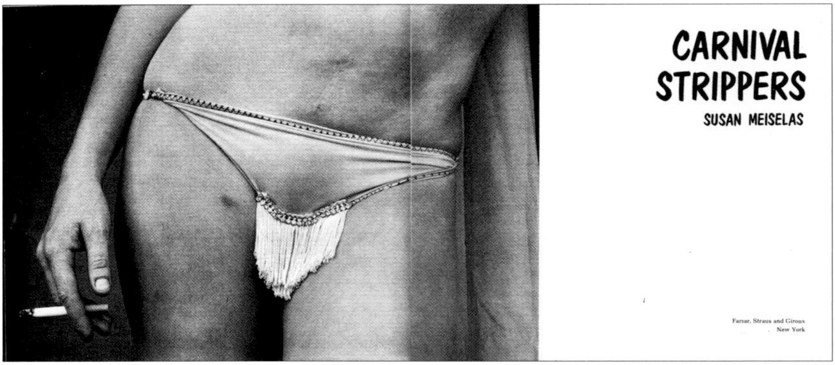

Susan Meiselas, title spread from the book *Carnival Strippers*, 1976, revised and republished by Steidl, 2004

(whatever "it" is). A rigid line is enforced between inside and outside the working practice.
Yes, and sometimes it seems an unbridgeable distance!

But as we said, in documentary film it has been far more acceptable to be both committed and engaged with the world while also being committed and engaged with thinking about representations of the world at the same time, with a certain critical distance or reflexive distance. Somehow, the way the institutions of photography have evolved, it can often seem as if we can't do both. But you are doing both.
I struggle with it, being told one can't do both. I do find that in getting projects done there is always a little erosion. Erosion is a funny thing.

The eroded material turns up somewhere else.
And it keeps my projects churning. Coming back to your point about oppositions between direct commitment and reflexive critique, I think this has a lot to do with form and I'm not sure I've figured out the best forms by any means. I know *Kurdistan* is difficult. I know the Dani project is a little bit more accessible in some ways, but still layered with detours. In neither project do I summarise in an efficient way to get the paraphrased essence.

Because there isn't one. You detour around and around and piece things together. It's like the invisible man – you can't see him straight on, so instead you throw bits of paper and fragments toward and around until something is made manifest.
Yes. With the Dani project, the Dani are largely absent but are revealed and shaped through the "bits of paper", the images and texts made in relation to encounters with them. The few places where Dani voices do come through, they are partial because they are a small community that has done relatively little work on their own oral history, own remembrances. Whereas the Kurds already had Kurdish scholars and archaeologists, and they were a larger community (24 million Kurds dispersed versus 50,000 Dani isolated in a remote village). But more importantly, my going back is still restricted, and to an extent I must live now not knowing how they would receive and perceive that work But if there were to be a second edition of the Dani book it's there in my contract that the book will change, it will not simply be reprinted without the opportunity to update and include recent developments.

This is quite an issue with photographic publishing now since a number of influential books have been recently reprinted.
I thought about this a lot. Robert Frank has made a couple of little changes to *The Americans* that nobody really sees. Well, a big change from the first French publication with all the writing to the American edition with Kerouac's text, but then subtle changes after that. With *Carnival Strippers*, the first change is the printing technology. The original book was printed in halftone. I literally can't reproduce that book now as a facsimile. It's not technically possible. Also the designer determined a number of things I wasn't happy with then. I was in my twenties and had no clout. I didn't have the dialogue I should have had. So this time I thought about whether I should go in a direction that had nothing to do with the original at all. I tried that. I dummied up a vertical book with many double spreads. But I had to pull back. It didn't feel right. I did want to keep the feeling of the period of the original design and do something closer to the book I wanted to do through the sequencing of images.

That impulse may not fit with what we have discussed about accepting that things change. In some respects the most thor-

ough facsimile books seem the oddest. *William Eggleston's Guide* from 1976 has been reissued right down to the corny photo album cover and green paper for John Szarkowski's essay. In fact the printing is now better.
At first I wanted both to return to the book I had envisaged, but to update it as well by following up with the people from the girl shows and adding contemporary essays. I think somebody picking up the book now needs to understand how the book was seen then. It needed to be a book that showed that it was within its time – the time of photographic books as they were then and the time of the carnival strippers as they were then. So one of the book's essays deals with history, while the other discusses women and carnival strippers as they were seen by feminists then. Culture moves on. But it was a huge disappointment not to be able to find the people in the pictures, the people who could report that change best. Two of the key people I was connected with in the making of the book were owners of the shows who had already passed away before I came to reprinting. How do you live with the necessity of closure? For example when the reissue of *Carnival Strippers* was a possibility, I was trying to locate those women I photographed in 72-75, but only found some of them too late, when the book was already on press. I don't know if there'll be a third edition, but in my mind it's ongoing. Along the way there are points where things have to be finite. You let go. I did get to include the original sound recordings collaged on a CD [included in the new edition of the book] and this helps contextualise the images within along with an early interview of me when I had just finished the work.

This is interesting. *Carnival Strippers* originally came out in 1976 and now it reappears within a format that you could never have conceived of: sound within a book.
Yes, the first showing of the work had voices of the participants playing loudly in the space and the pictures without the book's text. The book had no sound, only edited transcriptions, but now the book has the photographs, the text and the sound.

I'm reminded of Chris Marker here, who has been photographing, writing and making essay films for over five decades. Recently he produced the extraordinary CD-ROM, *Immemory*. It is

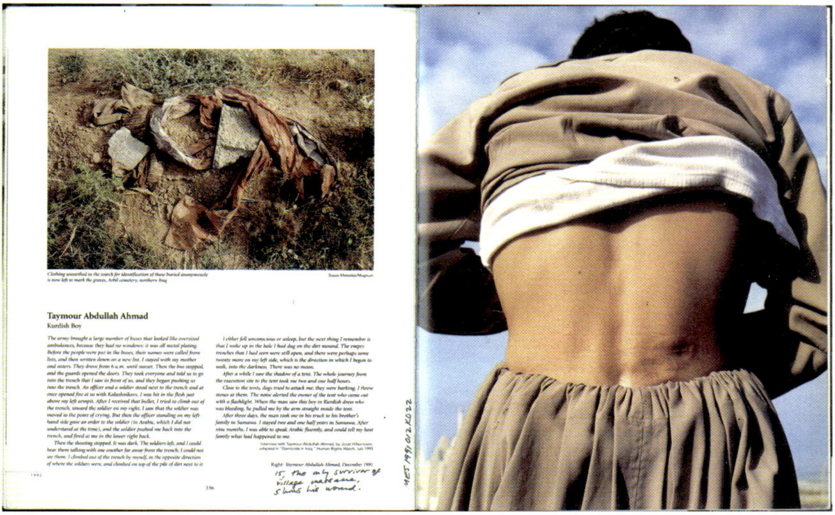

Susan Meiselas, page spread from *Kurdistan: In the Shadow of History*, 1997

a summary in many respects, not just of the work he has done but also of his form of thinking and assembly. It is as if he had been waiting much of his life for a technology that could allow him to map his views about time, history, change, places, politics and images. It seems his life's work was always awaiting a technology to come that would render it all meaningful. You also seem to have made projects that were awaiting technologies.
– that weren't quite there!

I saw your installation of *Encounters with the Dani* at the International Center of Photography show (*Strangers*, 2003): There was a glass cabinet containing many of the archival artefacts – letters, photos, small publications. There were also copies of the book and a Flash sequence of part of the book presented on flat screen monitors. But when I came out of the exhibition, just one or two complex images really stayed with me. One was an image of a group of the Dani counting money earned from posing for photos with tourists. It seemed close to Walter Ben-

jamin's idea of the dialectical image: the image that appears to be an embodiment of the tensions of history, or of power, or of money. Yet I know that this response is the opposite of what such a project is – a reflection on the way all the components mesh together to form our thinking.
You mean the essentialising of a moment or instant from the many? I don't know. I feel something similar about that project. For me there is a moment where a group of older Dani men are sitting looking at photographs of themselves taken thirty years before by the anthropologist Robert Gardner. In the book it's a single image but I present it as a loop of the eight sequenced photos within the Flash sequence as they pass the pictures along to each other and grimace and giggle at themselves. Similarly, there is a moment in *Pictures From a Revolution*, the film I made returning to Nicaragua ten years later to look for the people I had photographed during the popular insurrection. A woman who had been carrying her dead husband in a wheelbarrow turns her head toward me and I photographed her there in the street. In the film I interview her and after the interview I make a Polaroid photograph of her on camera. I give it to her (you only see my hand). She doesn't know which way is up, or what it is. It's the first time she's seen a Polaroid picture develop in front of her eyes. She's mesmerized as she watches her image appear. Especially now, that's such a rare moment to capture in any culture, we're so overexposed to the media.

It's so extraordinary that both of the moments you describe are half way between the condensed, single image and the film sequence. The sequence articulates the photographic. They are also quite uncanny embodiments of Benjamin's highly photographic metaphor of catching history "flash up" before us as moments we can grasp dialectically.
It certainly occured to me to really reduce things, in a conceptual way for the ICP showing of "Encounters with the Dani". I did say to my curators Brian Wallis and Kristin Lubben, "Well let's just have that still animated. Only that. On a screen". That can be enough.

But in a way, such moments have to be found by the viewer in the midst of a larger work. Quite often when such moments are singled out in advance, so overtly staged or presented, they can

lose their effect. There is no discovery. They can become a little too theatrical, no?
That's true, it can be too self-contained in a way that can exclude the viewer's active role. Exactly, all one can do is admire. It goes back to the question of what is "the work"? Is the work the making people work? Hoping people will work?

And so often documentary photographers in league with editors are telling us in advance what resonates. We are given the image and our response to them as one package.
It's the reductive way. It's driven by reductive forces. On the other hand I think we still don't know enough about it. When I think about the Nicaragua work which went from magazines, to book form, then exhibit to film form and so on in different configurations, they all seemed like different audiences and I didn't really know any more about one than another. I could never assume or calculate which images or form will be be the most resonant. I really don't think we know enough about what resonates and why.

I often think this has a great deal to do with whether Photography with a big "P" is being presented as the subject matter, as it is in certain authorial exhibitions or books, or whether attention to the photography itself takes a back seat.
I think of the way, which was brilliant in some respects, that an image lost in a print medium could be used by Benetton. Suddenly attention was forced onto an image in an inescapable way. It is not easy to reinvent new contexts for images and make them matter. Images are generally, still, trapped in limited ghettos. As a consequence, rarely do images have any kind of effect. So, in a quiet way, that's why the Kurdistan project was important. The images were embraced by communities for whom the project was a meaningful process and exchange. In the broader scope this is a small thing, but I do wonder just how much change images can effect. Probably not very much in the end, but enough to matter and want to continue making them.

Victor Burgin is one of the most influential artists and writers working today. He came to prominence as a key figure in the conceptual art of the late 1960s. Turning to photography, he first produced a series of ground-breaking essays and photo-text works that drew on semiotics, psychoanalysis and feminism in order to think through the complex status of representation in art and the mass media. Subsequent work explored photography's place in the understanding of memory, history, subjectivity and space. In the last decade or so, Burgin has explored computer generated imagery and the virtual camera. But rather than proposing a radical divide between so-called "analogue" and "digital" realms, Burgin has maintained that *all* images are essentially mental and thus virtual. They are psychical spaces of fantasy and projection, recognition and misrecognition. Whether on pages, walls or screens, in galleries or online, single perspectival views, or swarms of picture fragments, images are the making and unmaking of our sense of self, and the world around us.

Burgin's work and ideas have shaped my own understanding in profound ways. More accurately, my encounter with his work, when I was an undergraduate, was an extraordinarily exciting affirmation of what I was beginning to intuit about my own fascination with photographic images: they affect us in ways in which we may not even be aware; their role in high art and common culture cannot be separated; the implicit politics of all representation always deserves attention; and grasping the inter-relation of word to image is key to understanding the visual culture in which we find ourselves.

This conversation, recorded at Victor Burgin's home in Somerset, England, was first published in the book *Projective: essays about the work of Victor Burgin*, in 2014, shortly after I had curated a large exhibition of Burgin's work at Ambika P3, London.

Victor Burgin

I have been thinking about what you have said, in recent talks, about the continuities in your work, particularly the panoramic form. Something else has crossed my mind as a continuity in your work and it's to do with what we can call "point-of-view" – in both its narrowly photographic meaning and its subjective meaning. The panoramas in your projection works have a disembodied gaze or impossible point-of-view. But I see it most clearly in *Photopath*, which has a gaze and a "point-of-view" every bit as disembodied as the one deployed in your projection works. Do you think there's a connection between this disembodied gaze without a point-of-view and what you have called the "demotic" space of photography?

First, the disembodied point-of-view. The panoramas in my projection works are not shot with a film or video camera, they are "stitched" together from a sequence of stills and then animated in software. This technique situates the point-of-view at a mathematical point of zero dimensions at the centre of a virtual sphere. The panoramas are therefore "disembodied" in a quite literal sense. There is another sense in which the subject may be said to be absent from my work. Even in my more overtly "political" works of the 1970s, the work of indictment is given over to rhetorical structure – a "process without a subject", to appropriate Julia Kristeva's definition of pregnancy. For example, the panel *St Laurent Demands* [in *UK76*] allocates no place to a judgmental authorial voice – an ego-centred, if not egocentric, "*J'accuse*". There is rather the bringing together in the frame, a staging, of two contemporaneous fragments of reality – the woman worker and the newspaper blurb. It is left to the readers to draw their own conclusion, which of course might not necessarily be a politically progressive one. The "work" is work done by the viewer upon the two fragments using the trope of *antithesis*. The outcome is uncertain, you are not being told what to think, as in the denunciatory mode of address favoured by so much "political" art. Nor is anything "unmasked" in the world, nothing is "revealed" that would not be obvious to anyone who lifted their eyes from the women's page of the *Daily Telegraph* to look at the world of women's labour. Secondly, I should say what I mean by "demotic". In ancient Egypt, hieroglyphics was a writing reserved for the priesthood and the aristocracy. Demotic writing, a cursive form, was the medium of everyday affairs amongst the literate non-elite – for example, merchants. My original turn towards photography, and away from painting and sculpture and their derivatives, is analogous to the adoption of demotic script in preference to hieroglyphics. The first point to be made then is that "demotic", at least in my use of the term, is a form and not a content. To say "demotic" is not necessarily to say "popular", which is measured by audience numbers and/or market share, and even less to say "populist", which is a genre of politics and political address. Photography is demotic in two ways: first, most importantly, by way of its predominance in the mass media where, in association with words, it contributes to the formation of hegemonic popular common sense; secondly, by way of its almost universal use by the general public to exchange meanings amongst themselves. The first demotic aspect of photography determined my early preoccupation with the photo-textuality of advertising, the second contributes to my suspicion of expensive, assistant-intensive, modes of photographic production – my preference for photographic practices distant from those of the film and fashion industries. So what I call "demotic space" is an abstract utopian space of representations, and it's one of the dimensions of the multi-dimensional space in which I work.

You've often worked with a parallax relation to mass media forms. This at first appears to make your work accessible, but because it doesn't serve the ends those familiar image forms lead viewers to expect there is unexpected work to do, and so your work is judged by some to be "inaccessible". For me your work is perfectly accessible – getting into it is easy, it's the getting out that's difficult.
What you mean by that?

Let's take two examples. Your poster *Possession* (1976) borrows the language and imagery of advertising and popular graphics. It's accessible. The studio photo of a glamorous couple embracing is familiar, as are the accompanying texts: "What does Possession Mean to You?" and "7% of our population own 84% of our wealth". It's the relation between the two that's challenging. *A Place to Read* (2010) presents familiar things – ideas, memories, facts, images – but the nexus formed by those is unexpected and demanding. This is common to many of the most interesting artists of the last few decades who acknowledge the fact of the mass media entertainment complex and work through their own relationship with it. What must be refracted in art is a world that is already refracted, structured and otherwise impinged upon by dominant ideas and stupid values. Sorry, that might sound like a rant when it's transcribed.

It's not a rant. It's just about the mildest thing you could say on the matter. I would like to respond – as it were "for the record" – to the charge that my work is too erudite to be "accessible". It's true that my works are thoroughly researched and theoretically thought through, but this is the foundation of the work and not the work as such. I used to live in San Francisco, which as everyone knows is prone to earthquakes. I remember an architect there who had built himself a modest but beautiful house. On being complimented on it, he complained that 70 % of his budget and design thinking had gone into the foundation, which was never seen. The foundation is not where you live, it's not the part of the construction you actually *use*. I try to make a work as well as I can, which means the structure has to have a firm foundation, which for me includes a sound theoretical basis. But once I have "built" the work, I walk away from it and leave it to others to inhabit as they will – and I certainly don't expect them to dig up the foundations. For me, "accessible" means "free". As a working-class child, with nothing of "high culture" at home, I had access to well-stocked free public libraries. No one patronised me, no one condescended to provide me with books or paintings they thought I would "understand" – after all, what does "understand" mean if not a perfect match between the message emitted and the message received? This understanding is for traffic signs, not art.

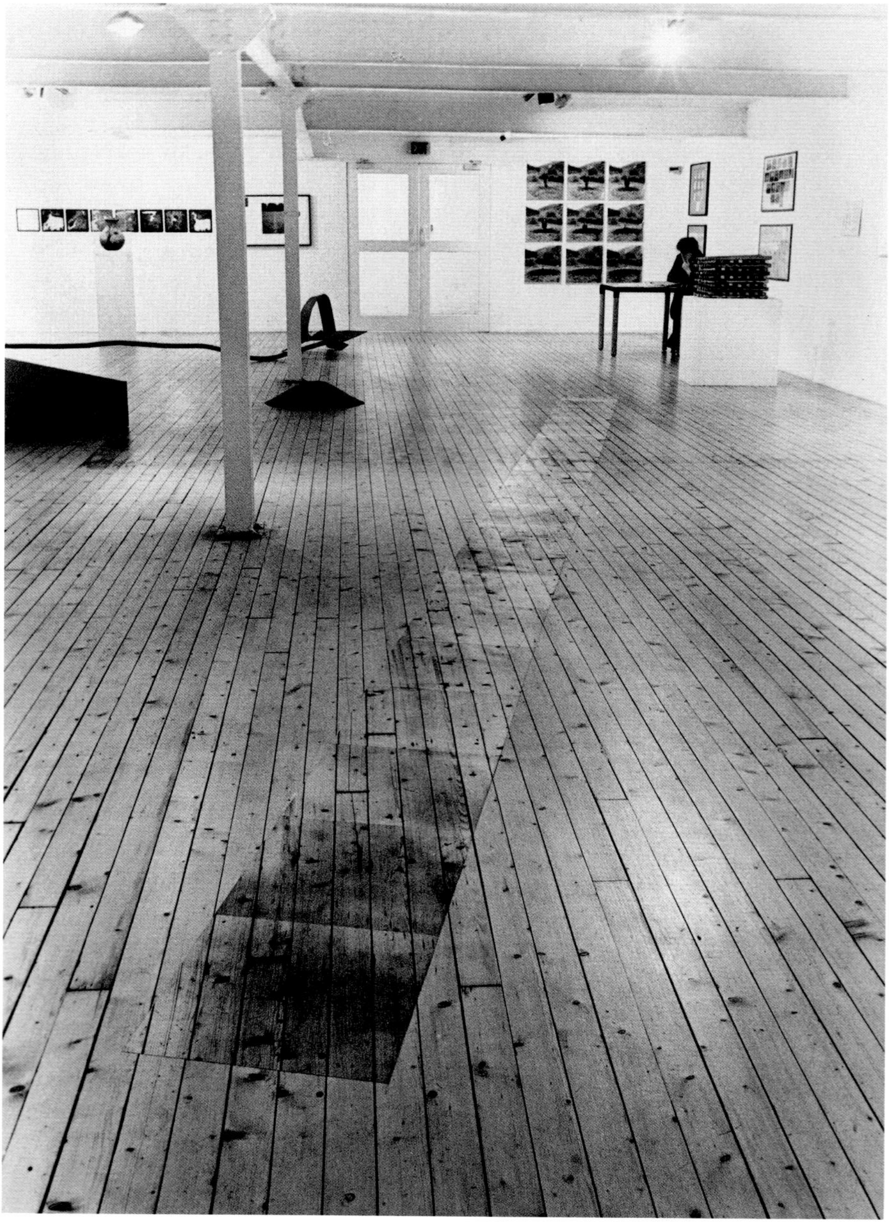

Victor Burgin, Photopath, 1967-1969, installation view,
When Attitudes Became Form, Kettles Yard, Cambridge, 1986

The departure point for a recent project is the Seth Peterson Cottage of 1958, designed by Frank Lloyd Wright, in Mirror Lake State Park, Wisconsin. I understand you're using computer modeling for this, rather than photography. These programmes are extremely complex. Why not work with specialists?
I trained as a painter and I'm very aware that a lot of what happens in painting comes out of a struggle with the medium. It will never quite do what you want or expect. Later, using photography was a struggle. And I always found the dialectic between what you think you want to do and what the medium will let you do is an aspect that keeps things alive. That's not to say that the result is going to be any more or less appealing or interesting to an audience. Now, if somebody works in the directorial mode with assistants and technicians…

They're not struggling with the medium, not benefitting from the dialectic. But two art forms that have been most significant for you are architecture and cinema. Architects don't build their own buildings and cinema is usually collaborative.
Even more basically, playing Devil's advocate, I might say to myself: "Well, you've just spent eighteen months learning the rudiments or four very difficult 3D modelling applications, but you didn't write the software. Whatever you do is predetermined by decisions that the programmers have made.

Yes, I've noticed that the idea that the camera has a built-in doxa is widespread now, particularly via the writings of Vilém Flusser: the idea that photographic technology is ideologically preprogrammed to replicate a consensus complicit with the dominant capitalist/technocratic order that produced it.
I haven't read Flusser, but that sounds like an idea that was prevalent in film theory in the 1970s – where the monocular system of perspective was seen as essentially a support for the sovereign gaze of the bourgeois individual. There's a difference, of course, between ideological constraint and technological constraint, even though the former may be implied by the latter. Anything you do is by definition constrained by the medium. Kant spoke of the dove that dreams of how high it might fly if it were free of the resistance of the air – but

no resistance, no flight. Painters in the Renaissance, photographers in the nineteenth century, 3D modellers today are all constrained by the technology available to them.

The question then is how constrained ?
I think there are two issues. One is the constraint of the medium. While we accept that we are born into a language we didn't invent, we also accept that there is sufficient leeway between Saussure's *langue* and *parole*, between what Chomsky calls "competence" and "performance", for individual creative expression to take place. Is this the case with a computer programme ? I believe it can be. Some applications have become so complex that even programmers can't predict what they're going to do. I can give the example of the software I'm using now to model a desert for the Seth Petersen project. It's a programme that's been used to create scenery for mainstream movies like *Pirates of the Caribbean* and *Avatar*, so it's industrial strength. In more recent versions of the programme the modelling can also be done by fractal algorithms derived from observations of nature. They can mathematically simulate the way rocks are stratified, the way erosion takes place, the way the atmosphere affects the appearance of an object, and so on. I am completely in awe of the minds that convert the natural world into algorithms – or rather, demonstrate by computer simulation that matter may already be organised in algorithmic terms. Now, you can deploy the algorithms built into such programmes without necessarily knowing how to write them, but they interact in such complex ways that the outcome is unpredictable even to the programmer. The unpredictable result, welcome or not, demands a creative response; one finds oneself "pushing the results around" until one intuitively recognises when to stop. Moreover, as in natural language, there are a variety of ways to express the "same" thought, represent the image one may have in mind, not all of them found in the technical manuals. Hence the dialectic I spoke of.

And the other issue, didn't you say there are two?
The other issue is the already mentioned "directorial attitude". Here, the issue for me is not simply the creative independence of this or that individual artist, it's more the possibility of the universal emancipation that artistic autonomy often serves to represent. If we think,

for example, of the expression "popular culture", it's a long time since popular culture has actually been popular, it has been replaced by populist *industrial* culture, the self-styled "creative industries" – which together produce an economically globalised orthodoxy of the aesthetic which has largely erased the former distinctions between mass-market entertainment, grass-roots popular culture and "high" art. I'm an advocate of "popular art" in the sense of individuals making art as part of the exercise of autonomy and creativity that I think is fundamental to any truly democratic political system. And I see a progressive erosion of that capacity for individual autonomy under the onslaught of the "creative industries" – which are rarely as creative as they are trumpeted to be. In fact there is a general dearth of real innovation, and not least in politics. We are all more or less unavoidably conscripted to the "creativity" of market capitalism – to "wealth creation" – the chanelling of common wealth to the rich. I'm interested in the extent to which people can exercise autonomous creativity outside of that daily routine of collaboration – which is why I'm interested in the ways in which, using digital tools, "ordinary" people – non-specialists – can make "films": video mashups, machinema and so on. Of course, it was photography, historically, that did most to open up this "demotic" space of popular creative practice. I think of my own work as situated in this same common space.

Video mashups can have a lot in common with art we can find in galleries. I suppose you would say that what matters most is not where we find the work, but is the individual's creative relation to the quoted or appropriated material.
Yes, I can accept a collage of found clips as a creative work of art if it is more than the sum of its parts, if it's structured in a way that takes me by surprise or causes me to think otherwise. We have seen a lot of artworks composed of clips taken from Hollywood films. Although I can enjoy them, I find that my enjoyment is derived almost entirely from the original materials – like the pleasure one can take in watching a sequence of trailers. What has been added to them is generally rather slight, very little real transformation has taken place. I'm left with almost no sense that the work was the product of critical self-reflection.

This can be my cue for a citation I have here, in a recent online interview you say:
"I think that the most important work that art can attempt is to provide alternatives to the hegemonic popular common sense created by industrialized mass culture and propagated by the media. That is to say, to support the exercise of one's own intellectual and sensual faculties, without ceding to pressures from outside".
I agree, and see photography education facing the same challenge. What do you think?
Art practices and education in general are in pretty much the same boat. In Britain this state of affairs originated about forty years ago when Thatcherism first promoted business and commerce from the status of mere occupations to that of transcendental values. The progressive withdrawal of public funding for arts and education that began under Thatcher pitched museums and educational institutions alike into the marketplace to survive as best they can, with the result that a whole range of intellectual and cultural activities that were once valued according to their own criteria now have to look for their legitimation in market terms – in terms of "contribution to economic growth" and "impact on society", in terms of money and mass audiences. This has produced the widespread tendency in contemporary art to address much the same range of interests, forms of attention and reading competences that the mass media typically assumes in its audiences. For most of modern history the role of the arts has been to accommodate non-consensual thought and provide a space for intellectual and formal diversity and complexity, but this role has declined dramatically over past decades.

One salutary effect of the present recession is that it has clarified for many the situation you describe. In a recession a palpable gap opens up between the mass media image regime around us and our own lived experience. Is this a source of hope? Optimism, even?
History does not encourage optimism. Nevertheless there are periods of respite, "parentheses in history" as a friend of mine calls them. The immediate post-war Labour government, in a time of great economic hardship, introduced the National Health Service, unemploy-

ment insurance, public pensions and free higher education for working-class children. It was a parenthesis in history that closed with Thatcher-Blair and is now being walled off from memory by Cameron/Clegg. Although I was always an opponent of the vulgar-marxist argument that culture is nothing other than a superstructural projection of the economic base, it's more difficult to argue against it when you look at what happened to the art world during the years of unrestrained finance capitalism. As the saying goes: "We get the art we deserve". A whole generation has grown up knowing nothing different. I just read a piece in *The Guardian Weekly* about the artist Jeremy Deller. He refers to Chris Burden's 1971 performance, which consisted of Burden being shot in the arm by an assistant. Deller says: "I doubt if he made much money out of that but as an idea they don't come much stronger, and you will never forget that I've told you that". Here are those terrible twins again – "money" and "impact". They speak equally through the mouths of artists and government White Papers on education. Back in 1969 I ended an essay in *Studio International* magazine by citing Bertolt Brecht's suggestion that rather than judging a work by its suitability to the apparatus, we should judge the apparatus by its suitability to the work. I was writing then from within another parenthesis in history. My limited optimism now is for the opening of another clearing in history, but there first has to be widespread recognition of the possibility of an *outside* to the currently dominant apparatus, and the value-system it enshrines.

Much of your artwork since the late 1960s has taken up this problem at a formal level: *Photopath* (1967-69) eluded easy commodification just as the art market for photography was getting going; your photo-text pieces of the 1970s and 80s reworked and revealed the conventions of reportage and advertising; and you have talked of your projection works as "uncinematic", ignoring spectacle to open up other relations to the moving image.
Photopath was one of the first works I made after graduating from Yale School of Art, where I met questions about the limits of mark-making and what can count as sculpture. Underlying these questions was a historical shift of attitude towards the frame, iconi-

cally represented in Hans Namuth's photographs from 1950 of Jackson Pollock at work. You can see these images as background to that 1971 Burden piece – the performance of a body making a mark, the performance of a mark made on a body. The breaking of the frame, in both physical and discursive terms, broke the historical pact with commodification, as the art object – now reconceived as "work" – entered into more complex negotiations with its outside. The apparent anti-commodity stance of the late 1960s and early 1970s was more often an unintentional by-product of working through these historical questions than it was a conscious intention on the part of the artist. The market eventually adapted, as it always does, and work from that period has now been commodified. Anything can be commodified. The distinction is not between work that can be commodified and work that cannot, it is between work conceived from the outset as commodity and work where the conception is indifferent to commodity status. The reportage, advertising and street poster works you mention were also in part a continuation of work on crossing the frame – the architectural frame of the gallery walls, the discursive frames of advertising rhetoric and documentary conventions. My projection works are continuous with the earlier work in their attention to the "demotic" as I defined it earlier. What I might call the "demotic attitude" differs from aesthetic populism in that its focus is not on actual mass cultural forms and contents but rather on virtual possibilities, alternative configurations and outcomes, inherent in contemporary technologies and extant languages.

One of the ways in which the relation between actual and virtual has played out in your work has been in the tension between real, exterior space and psychological, interior space. *Room* (1969) is a series of sentences asking the viewer/reader to consider their immediate perceptions and memories. *UK76*, *US77* and *Zoo 78* play the supposed "immediacy" of street photography against the fantasies of desire and ideology. *A Place to Read* (2010) includes a computer modelled virtual environment of an ideal Turkish coffee house that was demolished by the forces of corporate real estate speculation.

To have an interest in the relation between real exterior space and psychological space is quite simply to be interested in the *image*. The "image" is neither a material entity nor simply an optical event, an imprint of light on the retina, it also is a complex psychological process. It is in this sense that the image is defined as essentially "virtual" in the phenomenological perspective that Gilles Deleuze derives from Henri Bergson. The "image-for-commerce" is something that can be propped on an easel beside an auctioneer, something that can sit easily on the cover of a magazine, something that lends itself to becoming logo or brand. But the image is a different thing outside the circulation of commodities, outside the order of the spectacle – which is to say, outside of modern Western history. For example, in the Western tradition there are *things* – objects, "images", whatever – and then there is the space between them, which is empty. In a certain Japanese tradition the space between – "*ma*" – is as tangible as any material thing and is as charged with sense. This is the place and the substance of the "image" as I understand the term.

Your moving image works make use of contemporary image technology but often their "subjects" are moments from the past – a building, a symbolic site, a film, a social formation that were all short-lived gestures of resistance, extinguished by commercialization. These are brought into the present and suspended for the viewer as scrolling panoramas of digitally stitched still photographs. In this suspension, both the hybrid technological "form" and the historical "content" can be re-thought, opened up. This, too, seems to be a counter-model to the commodification of the past exemplified by Hollywood's mobilizing of techno-spectacle to "make history come alive".
A historical event is a complex of fragmentary and often contradictory representations – archival, fictional, psychical, and so on. Hollywood film depictions of historical events tend to coat such representational complexes in a sticky layer of unifying ideology, a mix of consensual categories, stereotypical crises and predictable narrative resolutions. To show the event "as it really was" is not an alternative. It never "really was" any one thing – past and present alike are sites of contestation where radically different perspectives collide. I mentioned Bergson, for whom the "image" is a process in which memory is invested with the experiential force of present perception – an idea famously given extended literary exposition by Marcel Proust. There is

something of this idea in Walter Benjamin's notion that our access to history is a matter of the activation of a memory in a moment of crisis. One way I understand that moment of crisis is as the experience of affect, or even the lack of it, in our first encounter with a place. You earlier mentioned my work *A Place to Read*, which was the outcome of an invitation to make a work in response to Istanbul. After several visits to the city, I found myself preoccupied by the ongoing process of destruction of some of the most beautiful public aspects of Istanbul in the pursuit of private profit. What came to metonymically represent this present process for me was the past destruction of an architecturally significant coffee house and public garden, on a beautiful site overlooking the Bosphorus, to make way for a hideous orientalist luxury hotel. The completed work was then installed in the Istanbul Archeological Museum. I am responding to you now having just replied to a question about this same work put to me by the editors of a cultural theory journal. They raised the much debated issue of photographic "indexicality" in the age of digital simulation, and consequently of the status of my "site specific" Istanbul work to its historical referent. I told them that I have been unable to share in the excitement over the question of "indexicality" in relation to digital photography – or computer simulation – because I never considered traditional photography to be indexical in any epistemologically fundamental way. I gave the example of news reports that refer to images of a massacre but with the caution that the veracity of the images "cannot yet be confirmed". This has become a familiar refrain throughout the reporting of the recent and ongoing conflicts in the Arab world. The image is never enough, at some point someone has to step forward and say: "I was there, I saw this" – and then even this statement has to be interrogated and either substantiated or denied by others. It makes no difference to this process whether the image is digital or was shot on film. The most epistemologically profound register of the indexical is discursive and affective, the optical is quite literally superficial. A woman at the opening of the installation at the Archeological Museum in Istanbul was in tears – she had known the original coffee house as a child. In retrospect, it is most striking to me that there was absolutely no reference in Istanbul, either in what that woman and others said to me at the time of the exhibition or in the response of the audience when I later screened the work at a conference, to the *difference* between the actual building and the computer simulation of it – the "indexicality" of the work in this sense seemed not to be an issue, suggesting that we need to broaden the definition of indexicality beyond the tacit empiricism of the discussions to date.

The idea that a computer-generated work may produce an image that is as "indexical" as any other also raises interesting questions about "virtual cameras".
Strictly speaking, the camera has never been anything other than virtual. There is a *New Yorker* cartoon that shows two people in medieval dress walking through an architectural environment of crazily incompatible vanishing points. One of them is saying: "I won't be sorry when they have this perspective thing worked out". The perspective thing was worked out in the West centuries ago, and has framed our view of the world ever since. When photography replaced perspective drawing as the principle means by which the West represents itself and its others it was consistent with the central impulse of the industrial revolution: the delegation of previously time-consuming and skilled manual tasks to the automatic operation of machines. Where photography represents a shift from manual to mechanical execution, computer imaging effects a shift from mechanical to electronic execution. However, where photography *represents* a particular aspect of the object in front of the camera, the computer *simulates* the object in its entirety. I see no difference in kind between the virtual camera and the lump of metal with "Nikon" or "Canon" stamped on it, but rather see them as different implementations of the same geometrical and optical knowledge. The prevailing criterion of realism in computer modelling is not the world as such, it is rather the world as it appears to the camera – an index of insecurity in a period of historical transition, like the trace of a potter's fingers in the design of a moulded plastic bowl. In time we may forget how physical cameras once showed the world, and accommodate our supposedly "natural" vision to the new conventions.

Can you say a little more about the different registers of "specificity" that inform your work? In the past, you have talked and written about discursive and institutional specificities

(for example in your book *Components of a Practice*, Skira 2007), and your artistic career got going at a point at the close of the 1960s when notions of the specificity of media were joined or eclipsed by overt concerns about the institutions of art and the media.
At first, the idea that specificity should be a "criterion", something we should pay attention to, certainly came from Clement Greenberg – from essays he wrote beginning in the 1940s, but which were perhaps most influential in the 1960s. My early education was "modernist" in the Greenbergian sense. What Greenberg means by "specificity" is that which differentiates an artistic practice from the other art practices around it. He was interested primarily in painting. For Greenberg, what distinguishes painting from other arts is paint itself, applied to a plane surface, and so he condemned figurative painting for compromising the flatness of the canvas. Greenberg's idea of specificity, which actually has its origins in Lessing, is simple but can be quite powerful. Ultimately, though, it remains formalist, and deeply conservative – in that Greenberg never questioned the position from which he himself spoke. I never abandoned Greenberg's version of specificity, but I became more aware of ideological and institutional specificities. There was a transition from a formalist notion of specificity to a more political one, which for me came out of Louis Althusser's writings. So, I had Greenberg's specificity and Althusser's specificity. And, of course, feminism made its own contributions to that. So although I still find the concept useful to think with, it is now subsumed under a more general concept of *apparatus* – in the sense that Foucault, and before him Brecht, have given to the term.

By which you mean...?
For Foucault the "apparatus" is a complex of interrelated discourses and institutions – ways of speaking, architectural forms, minor regulatory systems and so on – articulated within overall systems of power to produce what counts as legitimate knowledge in a particular society at a particular time. If we take "art" as our example, then under "discourses" we might list the various bodies of speech and writing that take "art" as their object: historical, sociological, technical, philosophical, curatorial, critical, journalistic and so on. Under "institutions" we would list such entities as the Royal Academy, The

Metropolitan Museum of Art, Art Departments in art schools and universities, as well as such instruments of legitimation as Documenta and the Turner Prize. Foucault's notion of apparatus would also take in the various types of physical structures within which artworks are presented: art museums and galleries certainly, but also magazines and newspapers and the Internet. It is obvious to commonsense that art discourses, institutions, and so on, all face upon the singular common object that has given rise to them all: "art". But this apparent singularity is in fact the reification of a mutating complex of disparate practices incapable of presenting a coherent picture without discursive framing. The art apparatus does not serve up something that pre-exists it – "art". It is the apparatus itself that defines, produces and legitimates art. Brecht effects a comparable reversal of entrenched habits of thought. For Brecht, "apparatus" means every aspect of the means of cultural production – from technologies, through publicity and promotion, to the financial and political elites that bankroll and control the various cultural institutions. Brecht's fundamental point is that the apparatus embodies the interests of the dominant class in the society of the day – accepting art that rejuvenates the values of that class and rejecting work that does not. He speaks of what he calls the "muddled thinking" of artists and critics alike in that they imagine they control an apparatus which in fact controls *them*, and which moreover is an apparatus which is itself out of control. Brecht's analysis is perfectly apposite to the past three decades of an artworld fuelled by finance capitalism and driven by fashion, a "world" in which voluntary amnesia has allowed novelty to replace innovation, where those who ignore history feel entitled to repeat it.

As you've just described it, "apparatus" is a much more all-embracing concept than the idea of "specificity" you began with – which after all concerns the particular rather than the general. So may I bring you back now to say a little more about "specificity" in relation to the particular nature of your own work, and how does it relate to the apparatus?

To use a photographic analogy, moving between considerations of "specificity" and "apparatus" is like shifting focus between foreground and background – everything is in the same picture, but the attention is differently weighted. While I'm actually working, considerations of apparatus tend to be relegated to the background. As an example of when issues of specificity in the Greenbergian sense come to the foreground in my work, I can think of the act of projecting moving images on the walls of galleries. What is the specificity of that setting, defined in its *difference* from the setting of the movie theatre, or the domestic space of television? Perhaps the most obvious difference from cinema is that works made for the gallery are usually viewed by people who come and go at unpredictable intervals. The convention of the loop begins to take account of this, but there is much more to consider. For example, the fact that any image on the screen may be the "first" image for the peripatetic spectator, just as any sentence may be the first sentence, makes specific demands on the form of the work. The structure of a projection work specific to a gallery setting is in principle closer to that of a psychoanalytic session than to a narrative film. No part or detail of the material produced in an analysis is considered a priori more significant than any other, all elements equally are potential points of departure for chains of associations. This has led me to make projection works that typically take the form of fragmentary, circular and repetitive short sequences – analogous to the structure of daydreams and fantasies. No less significant is that, in galleries and museums, the conditions of spectatorship are analogous to those once associated with painting, where the relation to a work is one of repetition, or more accurately reprise, and where the ideal viewer is one who accumulates her or his knowledge of the work, as it were, in "layers" – much as a painting may be created – and in acts of contemplation. The word "contemplative" today tends to be associated with passivity, but it formerly implied active interpretation. The etymology of the word "contemplate" is in the Latin verb *contemplari* – "to look attentively, thoughtfully" – and the Latin noun *templum*, a "place for observation". As Marcel Duchamp famously remarked: "paintings are made by those who look at them". Today, we have become familiar with paintings that solicit forms of attention closer to those we give, for example, to publicity or jokes. For me, the specificity of painting today has got nothing to do with paint on a flat surface, as Greenberg once defined it, it is rather with the *temporality* once characteristic of the reception of painting – a time of *contemplation*. There's a specificity to spectatorial behaviour in museums and galleries, and a corresponding specificity of spectatorial address to that viewer. The only substantive specificity "painting" has now is in a spectatorial address framed by considerations of repetition, contemplation and interpretation – regardless of whether one happens to be using pigment or projected light to form the image on the wall.

The "spectator" of course can in fact be any number of very different people. To what extent can you take account of that individuality ?

I can have no idea who the viewer will be as an individual. The viewer is an asbtraction, and is in a sense part of the work – in that she or he is *presupposed* by the form of address. A good question to ask in front of an advert is "who does this ad think I am?" You can ask the same question in the cinema. Producers of publicity and entertainment, often the same thing, construct their audience address mainly through market research aimed at determining what content their audience is looking for. In Althusser's expression, they "interpellate" the viewer as a subject of the signified. I myself interpellate a subject of the *signifier*, a subject of interpretation, of contemplation. This is not to say, however, that I never take the most likely audience into account if circumstances warrant this. For example, when in 2013 I made a work as a commission for the Geneva Wagner Festival, I thought it reasonable to assume that a substantial proportion of the audience for the work would be familiar with Wagner's life and work. There can be a specificity to the *event* of the exhibition that has to be taken into account, which may modulate the more general "considerations of spectatorship". A more complex example would be the work I made for a 1999 cultural festival in Weimar. I was allocated a space in the Schloss Ettersburg – which has historical connections with Goethe and is also close by the site of the former Buchenwald concentration camp. My work is "site specific" in that the work was conceived of as inseparable from the house and surroundings that appear in the work – but then there are further considerations of specificity that determined the form as well as the content of the work. First, I knew that the work would be seen by a "general audience" of visitors to the Schloss, people largely unaccustomed to encountering moving image works in galleries, and so I structured the work to accommodate what I believed would be their "reading habits". Although *Lichtung* loops, therefore, it nevertheless has a clear beginning, middle and end. The beginning is unambiguously announced by a frame of solid red and an orchestral fanfare – the opening bars of the overture to *The Magic Flute*, a choice determined by Goethe's admiration for this opera. The end is announced by a crescendo of train noise and what follows the *coup de théâtre* of the child's party favour that resolves into a swastika. The whole work moreover has a linear structure marked by the passage of the woman through the woods from the Schloss to the remains of the camp. In this case, therefore, the points at which the material repeats are clearly marked, and its "narrative" structure may be easily reconstructed no matter where the visitor may enter and leave, assuming he or she stays long enough for the reaction "this is where I came in". I conceived of *Lichtung* as a component in a larger *de facto* installation that included the Schloss and the path through the woods to Buchenwald. Apart from the figure of the woman in early nineteenth-century dress, there is little in the content of the work that cannot be replicated in the visitor's actual experience of the place where the work is situated. The work was intended to give the visitor something to think about, prospectively or retrospectively, on her or his walk between the two sites. This imposed a further consideration of specificity, in that the work raised the question: "Can the Holocaust be represented?" Whatever position we take on this we all know the arguments. Since its original installation in the Schloss Ettersburg I haven't shown *Lichtung* publicly as I am reluctant to be seen as attempting to make a work "about" Buchenwald – even though I do not believe that this is what I have done – and because it was only ever conceived of as a part of a larger whole. It cannot be moved, so in purely formal terms it has something of *Photopath* in it.

***Lichtung* has a strong relation to the built environment, particularly to the history enshrined in it. Architecture has remained a persistent and recurring object of attention in your work, perhaps especially in the more recent projection work. Could you say something about where this interest began?**
I became interested in going to Yale after the Royal College of Art because the Art Department there was part of Yale School of Art and

Architecture. During my time in New Haven, most of the people I hung out with were architects, not artists. I seemed always to have had an interest in architecture even though I was never quite sure what it was. I didn't reflect on it, it was just there. But a lot of it was to do with the building as an object. I'd worked my way through late-modernist painting, then through the minimalist rejection of painting in favour of sculpture, and then come to the conclusion that sculpture was completely redundant, for me at least, because any formal interest I could take in sculpture I could take in architecture – but architecture had the added virtue of being socially useful.

But might we say that the moment architecture is usable it ceases to be an object?
Well I think it can be both. Certainly at that time I thought it could be both appreciated as an object, for its sculptural qualities, but also inhabited and used. So out of my admiration for architecture I developed a loathing for sculpture, at least modern sculpture, and most especially in its public forms – those lumps and sheets of stuff through which puffed up egos parade in public space, the visual equivalent of someone playing "their" music on a ghetto blaster in a park. It was while I was at Yale that I came across Bernard Rudofsky's books *Architecture Without Architects* (1964) and *The Kimono Mind* (1965), which had just been published, and which I read with great interest. Rudofsky visited Yale while I was there and I took part in his class. His approach to architecture had nothing at all to do with the formal appreciation of objects, and I can see in retrospect that I was coming to subscribe to diametrically opposed views of architecture without ever having had to think through the contradictions. But today the aversion I feel for sculpture I now feel for a lot of architecture – the large scale, spectacular architecture that seems made primarily to be publicized, that is itself a form of publicity. So I have a consciously critical relation to architecture now that wasn't there previously. I have "come out" as a critic of architecture, which is not at all the same as being an architectural critic.

That tendency towards the spectacular in architecture starts early in twentieth-century modernism, in no small part due to the increasingly intimate relation of architecture to photogra-

phy. Buildings were increasingly designed to look great in photos, and became complicit with their own image as publicity, or propaganda.

The political opportunism of canonical modernist architects like Le Corbusier and Mies van der Rohe used to be routinely swept under the carpet. The readiness of today's architects to become state apparatchiks seems no longer to be a cause of embarrassment. I was doing some reading in preparation for a talk I was asked to give at the Royal Danish Academy of Architecture – trying to inform myself about the current state of debate between contemporary architects – and I came across the transcript of a conversation between Rem Koolhaas and Peter Eisenman. Eisenman was talking about Koolhaas's building in Beijing, for China Central Television.

Known as the CCTV.

Appropriately, that's right. CCTV is directly answerable to the Propaganda Department of the Chinese Communist Party. Whole neighbourhoods of people were expropriated and evicted to make way for the new headquarters. Eisenman calls the building a "spectacular success" and says that after Koolhaas's CCTV building the critical question for architects is "how do we make a great skyscraper now?" I found this staggering. I thought: "This is supposed to be *the* architect-intellectual of the Western world and *that's* what he sees as the critical question?!" Max Weber noted how the evolution of the design of pianos, and even of the music written for them, was intimately complicit with the evolution of the bourgeois domestic interior and middle-class mores. The CCTV building is a monstrous concert grand, custom built to express a ruthless and brutal form of totalitarian state capitalism.

Whatever else they do, your "architectural" works invoke context, and they dramatize the unoccupied space and encourage an imaginative projection, of either living in or being in those spaces. Some of your works centre on examples of architecture that were always intended to be seen as objects. For example, Ludwig Mies van der Rohe's Barcelona Pavilion of 1929, which you explored in *Elective Affinities* (2001) was/is a structure not to be inhabited but "visited" and "experienced",

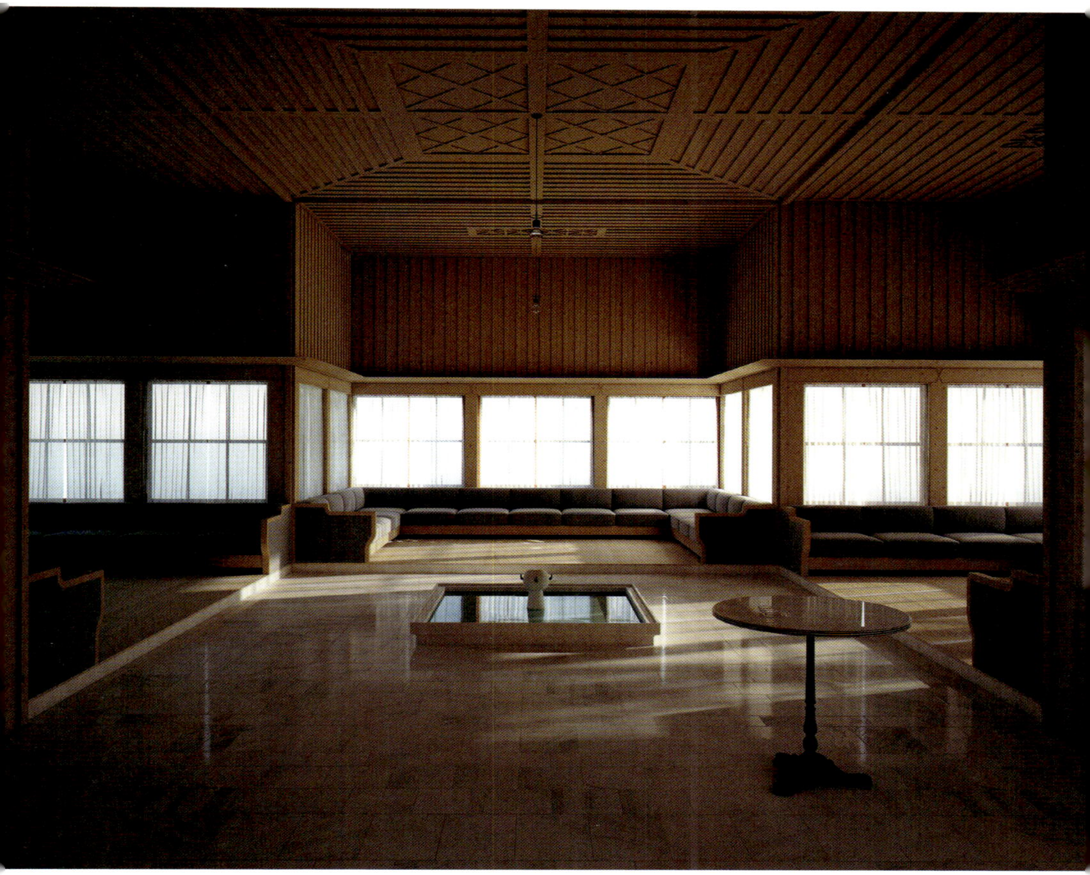

Victor Burgin, image from *A Place to Read*, 2010. Video projection

but ultimately understood as an object in itself. Whereas Rudolph Schindler's 1922 Kings Road House in West Hollywood, which you photographed for *The Little House* (2007), was once occupied but is now preserved as an object to visit.
They're diametrically opposed examples. In the Barcelona Pavillion I found myself preoccupied with the question of what it meant to design an object like that in the time of emergent fascism. The building unavoidably raises the question of the complicity of modernism with fascism, not least if one has seen the project sketches by Mies in which he has the swastika flying from the pavilion flagpoles. I was thinking of the Civil War shortly to come, and Michel Serres" remark that Picasso's *Guernica* was not a response to fascism but a symptom of fascism. So as my body turned in that play of real and virtual spaces, my mind was projected outside. In the Schindler House my associations stayed mainly inside. When I was researching the history of the Kings Road House I became interested in the socialism and gender politics of its first occupants, and their efforts to find alternative ways of living together as friends and as lovers. Schindler referred to it as an exercise in "cooperative dwelling". I found myself thinking of the early experiments in domestic communalism described in Nikolai Chernyshevsky's pre-revolutionary novel *What is to be Done*, where the question of the partition and disposition of spaces is inseparable from questions of communism and relations between the sexes.

Perhaps this is the opportunity to observe that just as the city and architecture figure prominently in your work, so do women. Why this consistent presence of women in your work?
I remember the last time I was asked that question – in 2007, by a French graduate student at a film summer school in Italy, a man actually. It came as a complete surprise. After all, why ask *me* that question, in *that* context, given the prominence of women in mainstream cinema? So I can try to answer the question, but we should also question the question. There are no women in my early work. Women first appear in my work when I "appropriate" advertising images, and then later when I start taking photographs in the street. But women only move to the centre of my work when I start to take feminism on board. I remember that back then, in the mid-1970s, the

film-maker Peter Gidal said he had stopped showing women in his work in response to feminism. My own response to feminism was to *start* making images of women. At that time there was a great deal of very interesting feminist theoretical work on the construction of feminine sexuality, which was being described in all its complexity. Masculine sexuality, however, received no comparable attention; by implication there was nothing much to say, masculine sexuality was self-evidently simple. It seemed to me that this again made sexuality a "woman's problem". So I tried in my work to represent masculine sexuality as no less an uncertain and precarious construct than that of women, albeit of course differently so. It wasn't a question of making "images of women" as such, albeit that's the way it was seen by many feminists at the time, but rather of trying to make a mise-en-scène of a heterosexual male relation to the image of the woman that would admit the component of desire without denying the woman her difference and autonomy. For example, the *Office at Night* series was self-consciously, even programmatically, a *détournement* of Hopper's picture that represented the woman as not only the object but the *subject* of voyeurism and epistemophilia. I've spoken at length in the past about the sexual politics of my work, mainly in psychoanalytic terms, but I don't believe that the issues of "sexuality and representation" that were predominant during the 1970s and 80s were necessarily implied in that question put to me in 2007. We live, in the post-Enlightenment secular West, in a largely sexually integrated society, albeit not yet in a sexually egalitarian society. We are largely emancipated from the duality of barracks and gynaeceum to which, to give the most obvious contemporary example, militant Islamism would have us return. This means that negotiations of sexual difference are constantly present in almost every aspect of everyday life. I used to read a lot of science fiction, and I've never got over a perhaps somewhat adolescent sense of wonder that things are as they are and not otherwise. Imagine that life based on sexual difference is only one of many other forms of existence. Imagine growing up in a world in which everything was the same as our own world apart from the fact of sexual difference. Now imagine the intellectual and emotional shock and wonder of passing from that world into our own. We have all, in fact, already made that passage between worlds as very small children – a passage that psychoanalysis describes in great detail. In response to feminism I was once most concerned to intellectualise the experience of sexual difference, to consider its political implications and expression. I am perhaps today more inclined simply to wonder – to bracket out what I know, in what Husserl calls the *phenomenological epoché* – and simply try to represent the experience. Imagine that Baudelaire, in *A Une Passante*, had given his desire for the passing woman no more or less weight than his experience of the light on the pavement or his passing recollection of a newspaper article. The *epoché* is of course an aspiration rather than something actually achieved. "Experience" is already a set of representations – a totally unmediated relation to the real would be pure psychosis. We're back with Althusser's observation that one can only work on ideology from within ideology. As for the question of the question itself, I can only suppose it to be prompted by the fact that the figure of the woman in my work has more to do with the history of painting than with the history of cinema. In mainstream cinema our relation to a woman on the screen is usually to a personality – an amalgam of the fictional character and the actress playing her. Outside of portraiture a woman in a painting is first of all an element in a formal composition, after which she may be the personification of an abstraction, the embodiment of an ideal, the illustration of a condition, or whatever else. The anonymity and stasis of the painted figure privileges the formal and intellectual over the anecdotal and personal, the general over the particular. I would suppose that this "painterly" condition of the women in my work prompted the question from the student of cinema – as they appear differently from the way he is used to seeing women in films. Another difference is that there are apparently no men alongside the women in my work, which is extremely rare in cinema. I say "apparently" because the man is there in the very subject position from which the work issues, the position looking towards the woman in the image. This in no way prevents a woman from occupying that position, but she will occupy it differently. I might suppose that it was this difference – relativising the representations to which he was accustomed, and his own relations to them – that prompted the young man's question. His question therefore was not simply a question put to me, it was a question to *himself*, and to the world in which he finds himself – it is at base the question of *difference* itself. The naïve sense of wonder that inhabits the *epoché* I might have posited as an "alternative" to the intellectualisations of psychoanalysis turns out to be the very *object* of psychoanalytic enquiry.

I think I understand what you mean when you describe your work in terms of a phenomenology, but could you say more about how a work evolves in terms of image and text? Does a piece come to you as a set of images that will then be interspersed with text, or is it the other way around, or does that relationship vary ?
The work begins in an encounter with the real. Most of my work is in response to an invitation to go somewhere, to respond to ... *something*. I go to a place, may go back to the place a number of times, and the work emerges from that encounter with the real of a place. By "real" in this context I mean just everything that's there – you can never describe it fully, there are never enough words, never enough images, there's no *outside* to it from which you might compare it to anything else. So that first encounter with the real is just *everything*. Then in returning to the place, in thinking about the place, in doing research about the place, in reading about the place, having fantasies about the place, maybe even in dreaming about the place, gradually, over a period of time, certain elements, certain aspects seem to become disengaged, and privileged, as if somehow they become "brighter" and all the rest starts to dim. So then I'm left with various bits and pieces, it could be an image, a story, a historical fact, it could be anything, and these fragments start to coalesce into what will eventually become the work. As an analogy, by way of illustration, I think of a scene from an early movie version of *The Invisible Man*. The obvious problem for the film-maker is that you can't *see* the invisible man, so a variety of devices have to be used to show the audience where the invisible man is, and what he's doing. In the scene I'm thinking of, the invisible man is in the street, there's a lot of litter in the street and suddenly a wind whips up and stuff gets blown about and starts to stick to him – so you can see his form, although you still can't see the invisible man as such. Analogously, I can't show you the *je ne sais quoi* in my encounter with the real, but there are these fragments that "stick" to this *je ne sais quoi* and then serve to represent the unrepresentable. It's not the real, but it's a representation of

it, and of course there could have been a different representation of it. So that's how the work starts, but it can't just be a random assembly of associations because it has to be a work of art, has to satisfy certain formal criteria, and that again make it more complex – so it then takes on a life of its own, independently of the encounter that prompted it.

To come back to something we touched upon earlier, most of your career you've worked with image forms that are "out there" in the mass media, for example cinema, and yet have a way of putting them together in a way that separates them from our experience of the mass media – it might be a question of tempo, it might be the quality of the prose or the care with which the image is made, or the relation between the elements.
If I say that a work begins in an encounter with the real, then that "real" includes mass media productions. I could decide to exclude them entirely, but then they would be present by exclusion – as what Althusser calls a "structuring absence", or as the repressed – so I feel that I have to account for what is there in my encounter with the real of mass media production, but then the media fragment has to undergo, as it were, a "sea change" in order to be brought into the work. For example, that passage down a ruined street in *Parzival* (2013) was suggested by an association to the opening title sequence of Rossellini's *Germany Year Zero*, where a camera on a vehicle moves down a ruined street in Berlin. But I very much doubt that anyone would recognize the Rossellini sequence from my 3D modelled representation of my memory of it. On the other hand, someone with a knowledge of Rossellini's films might conceivably recognize the boy who occasionally briefly appears in the work, as the boy is extracted directly from the film. The "sea change" in this case, however, is in the total recontextualisation of the image, in its complete disengagement from the original narrative setting.

I recently watched a clip, online, of Alain Robbe-Grillet talking about Antonioni. At one point Robbe-Grillet says that it's not only the condition of the modern artwork, but the necessity of the modern artist, to keep the door of meaning open, because we have a mania for meaning delivered up on a plate.

But then, later, Robbe-Grillet refers to a remark Albert Camus made, to the effect that every artist is trying to find, return to, the two or three images that first "opened their heart". So you have two very different ideas of what might motivate an artist, one might be a response to an encounter with the real, trying to open up another space outside the consensual categories of the media, but then you have something much more explicitly psychoanalytic.
Yes, there's "the real of the unconscious", as Lacan put it. If you say that the real is that which cannot be represented, that which cannot be known as a totality – before you even get to psychoanalysis – in psychoanalysis the real is also the real of the unconscious, which is also by definition that which cannot be known, which cannot be represented in its totality, that which is only known *through* its representations – but again, in the manner of the invisible man, through certain privileged signifiers, those that "stick". Clearly there is something *at work* while I'm working that is the work of the unconscious. So there are things in my work that I myself don't understand. Why is that there? I don't know, I felt it had to be there, even though it may be implausible. For example, in *Mirror Lake*, why the man under the rock? It's implausible and it's not *explained*. The job, if you like, the "art job", is to make what is implausible at the level of everyday reality irrefutable at the level of form.

Photographer, film-maker, painter, writer, graphic designer, maker of books... **William Klein** has had one of the most remarkably creative careers. Born in New York in 1928, he came to Paris in 1948 and never left. He could have been an abstract painter, but instead reinvented street photography, produced some of the most celebrated and influential photobooks, turned fashion photography on its head, made innovative documentary and fiction films, always on his own uncompromising terms.

I had admired Klein's work since I had seen it as a teenager. We first met in his apartment overlooking Paris's Jardin du Luxembourg. This was in advance of his retrospective at Tate Modern in 2012. I ended up writing the text of the catalogue for that show, and essays for a couple more of his books (*Paintings Etc.*, 2012; *Black & Light*, 2014).

This conversation is a partial transcript of a public talk William and I had later in 2013, at the Museum of Art and Design, New York. For him it was an unexpected homecoming of sorts. The place was packed with young photographers a quarter of his age, art world luminaries, and the great and the good of the fashion scene. New York was the city Klein had left in order to become the artist we know. Although he has photographed and filmed there over the years, that was the night that America re-embraced him.

William Klein

It's very rare for an artist to make a mark in one field, but to make a mark in six or seven and turn them on their heads is something else. So we're not going to be able to cover everything here. Your early works date back to 1948, that's 65 years of activity. It really is an extraordinary career. You were born here in New York but then moved to Paris in 1948. Was it a painter you really wanted to be at the beginning?
It's nobody's business. When I was in the army, I won the war. We soldiers at that time would get the equivalent of the time we wasted in the army as a salary, a sum of money to make up the years lost in the army, and go to school or pick up work done elsewhere. When I was in Paris, I had the choice of going to an art school or working in somebody's studio. So in Paris, there was L'Ecole des Beaux-Arts, and then there was the studio of Fernand Léger… in France they say *y'a pas photo*, that means "the choice was very easy", everyone wanted to go to Fernand Léger. We all admired him and we had never met a real artist, a great artist. Half of us were soldiers with this G.I. Bill of Rights, another half were Romanians, German or Italians who came to Paris just to be at the Léger studio. And Léger had a kind of studio, it was like a traditional studio. He would put a still life in the middle of a big table and there would be easels all around this table. Everybody sat there and did versions of the still life in the style of Léger. We found the atmosphere of the atelier was kind of depressing and I only stayed there about three weeks. I arranged to work at home and then to come in on Fridays which were the days when he would come and criticize and give us advice. I would get there on Friday with what I had done. Léger was a big muscular guy like Lee Marvin, he would talk in a very simple way. He would not use that complicated bullshit that these critics' essays would use. He would say "that's strong, keep it up" and shit like that. We would look at him like an uncle, like a father and we'd ask

him all these questions like… "You were in New York during the war and you've been in Moscow, what would you prefer? Life in Moscow or in NewYork?" And he'd say "I'm more in tune with what's going on in Moscow but NewYork is more fun". That would ring a hundred bells for us. And we'd ask him all these questions like children. And he answered in a very simple Normandy way. He was a Normandy peasant and he would say "that's good", "that's tough", "that's strong", and that's it, no references to Heidegger or to Kant. But he did have a reference to culture, and a culture that we didn't know. He talked about the *Quattrocento* and what the painters in Italy were doing during the 15th Century, and the thing was to work with architects. He said, all you pseudo geniuses, you're trying to find a gallery, trying to meet collectors, trying to sell your stuff, but all that is bullshit.What you have to do is work with architects, and work in the city. At that time there were big tableaux outside of movie houses, where a guy would take one photograph to advertise the films and make big murals of the scene from the movie. And he said, these guys are working in the city and what they're doing is much more important and relevant than what you're doing jerking off in the studio here. So check it out, learn about Masaccio, Cimabue, Piero della Francesca.

There's already something of your visual style in your early paintings, with the kind of all over characters in the composition.
Yeah, so that's a light bulb, and that's a guy in a blue suit, and these are guys playing cogs… so I'd show something like this to Léger and he'd say ok, keep it up. And we did. We were all influenced by Léger of course, otherwise we wouldn't be there. And we were all trying to get out of the influence of Léger and we would find little things that we thought were versions of another take on his kind of work and we could see that the things we were doing were very different. But somebody would look and say *C'est du Léger*, you're in Léger's studio, right? And we would say no, it's a departure really. That's the way it is. And so these things… we were thinking as he said, working with architects, we were thinking of mural projects, and so I did things without people, but with geometrical patterns. So that's the kind of work I did at the time.

There is an installation shot from a show in Milan, with a little invitation card for that show.

That's a painting that I had done for that exhibition, which was used in the invitation for the gallery, a kind of a big time Milano gallery. I had the opportunity of doing a show in the lobby of a theatre called Il Piccolo Teatro, which was run by an experimental director called Giorgio Strehler. He was really one of the top directors of modern theatre in Europe, and specially in Italy. I had the show in the theatre, and somebody from this gallery Del Milione came by and said how come you're exhibiting in these crappy corridors, come to our gallery, we have a spot for you in three months. So I took all this stuff that was in the theatre and exhibited in the Galleria Del Milione. Evidently it was quite a big deal. So I did these painting at that time and I thought an architect would come along and say "I have a project". Of course that was a million to one shot. But fortunately there was this young architect who was looking for young painters to go along with him. And he had an idea for a room divider, which would be made of four panels, and then six panels. They had to be painted on both sides. I had never done anything that big or that ambitious. He said, "can you do this? You have to paint on both sides". I said "of course", I was 23, you know? I thought I could do anything, so I did it. I painted these things. They are in a very big Milanese apartment now.

This was also the passage into photography for you, wasn't it?
This was curiously enough a backwards way into photography and into creation because these panels were painted and you see the rails on the top of the ceiling… there were tubes that fit into the rails.You could move them in the middle of the room to make the separation or you could put them on a railway track, you could put them on the wall and make different combinations because there were four, six of them and you had both sides… They were published in *Domus* magazine. And then I photographed the set-up and had somebody turned the panels so that the geometric lines blurred in the long exposure. Then I realized that there was something that could be done with blurriness in photography. And I wouldn't need big panels, I could go into the dark room, take a piece of paper, cut holes in black paper, put the enlarger light on the paper and get blur. And I thought maybe this is a way out of the rut of geometrical forms, curves, straight lines, triangles and whatever. So, as I said, they were reproduced in the magazine *Domus*. And *Domus* was a magazine that had a big reputation, it was done by

two people – Lisa Licitra Ponti, the daughter of Gió Ponti who was a big time architect, and her friend Enrichetta Ritter. They said "how would you like to do some covers for the magazine?" I said "sure", so I did a whole bunch of them. A couple of years later I cut out the word *Domus* and I made a multiple exposure with filters changing the colours, so that was one of the covers of the magazine. I did about 20 covers. I used one of the covers of *Domus* to make the New York book. I cut out the words "NewYork" and then my wife held the flashlight behind them and I would change the filter on the camera, and make multiple exposures. And so what you have is "NewYork, New York, NewYork", and that was the cover of the New York book.

Nobody wanted to publish it in America.
I did the book, and it was considered a breakthrough for a lot of reasons: for the layout, for the way the photographs were treated, and the writing. I didn't want any text in the book. I republished the book and there was a little brochure that was attached with a cord to the book. A lot of people came into the bookstores with a pair of scissors and they cut off the little magazines of the text and they had to send it back to the editor to get new brochures, otherwise they couldn't sell the books.
So then I did the first film, and I thought I would do a film which would be the contrary of the New York book – in colour, beautiful and at the same time about brain washing. One of the most beautiful things in New York was the most accessible: Times Square, the lights. Everybody who came to New York, the first thing they would photograph or film would be Times Square, which is still true today. So I treated Times Square commercials, the cycles of the ads like Duchamp would call ready-mades. For me, these cycles of films on Kleenex and Coca-Cola were like ready-mades.
So I did a book on New York and I showed it to Fellini, whom I met in Paris, and he said "listen I like this book I have it already. It came out in Italy, why don't you come to Rome and be my assistant?" I had no idea how movies were made. And I asked "what does an assistant do?" And Fellini said, "no problem. If I'm sick you shoot". And I said "no problem I can do that". So I came to Rome. I had a friend who had an apartment, and we settled in Rome with my wife.Then I discovered Fellini who's a terrific bullshit artist. He had about 8 assistants, he really didn't need

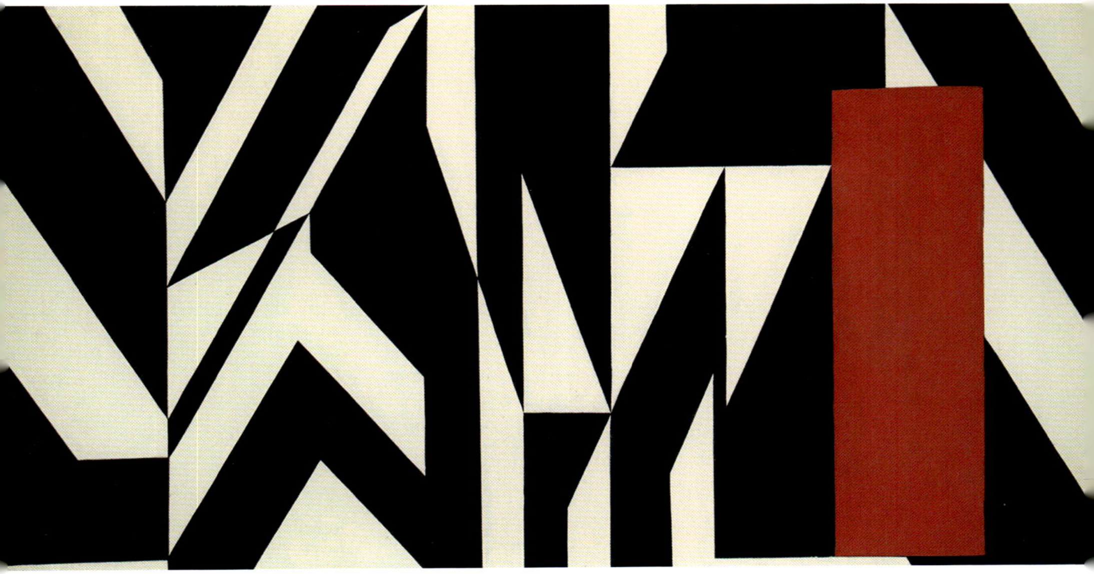

William Klein, Painting, Mural Project, 1952-54

didn't need me. But at the time he was doing the casting for *Nights of Cabiria*, and as you know it was all about a bunch of whores.There are a lot of whores hanging out near the monuments in Rome. And these whores were very loud-mouthed and tough and guys would stop and try to bullshit them and the whores would curse them out. But with Fellini, they were like little girls. They would say "Federico" – they called him by his first name – "how about me? I'd like to be in your film". And he was like one of the boys and he'd slap them on the ass and say "you come to my office". And they all came to his office and brought photographs taken 15 years before. You saw these big-busted women – looking like Vivien Romance, who was a French movie star – with a lot of make-up and big tits. And they would bring their pimps, who would come with them. One of them was hanging around and Federico would say to me in English "this guy is the biggest crook and bastard in Rome" and the guy was smiling and saying *Sì, signore*, then he would follow me out in the corridor and he'd say "can you do something for me with my stuff?" And I said "I'll try". Anyhow, that was the atmosphere. Then the film was delayed so I thought maybe I can do a book – I did one on New York, maybe I try something on Rome – so I did that.
I had the opportunity of doing a couple of other books… in Tokyo and Moscow… Rome came out in 1960. The other books were finished in 1961 and published later.

***Hairdressers' School*, from *Tokyo* (1964), is my favorite spread from all your books.**
This happens to be one of my favorite photographs. A funny story, because I was invited to Tokyo by big corporations – by Fuji, by the Museum of Modern Art and so on.You have to have sponsors when you go to Japan and I had all the sponsors. We had a meeting and all the sponsors were there and they said "what can we do for you?" And one of the sponsors was a big newspaper and I said "you have a baseball team and I'd like to be invited to hang out with some of your star players". They said "we can arrange that". Except that in Tokyo – in Japan – people don't do things like that, they don't call up and say "I've got someone who'd like to do this and that". They have to manage, to arrange sending a present to a guy to ask for a favour and then the guy sends back a present… this takes forever. And I discovered it and said, "well, fuck that. I'll just walk around and do what I want". And I saw this hairdressing

school and so I just walked in, and they saw a big American with a camera, as if I belonged there. And I started walking around taking photographs. So this is an example of the kind of photograph I'd take without anybody's permission, without anybody setting it up. So, then there is the series I did for *Vogue*. I actually was very amused taking fashion photographs because first of all, I was doing photographs which you could call *fotografia povera*. I had one camera and two lenses, while for fashion you had assistants, you had lights, cameras, all kinds of things.

You went back into painting at a later point. How did this happen?
I was always painting. I was doing a period of painting with letters, it was 1963 and 1964. I was still working for *Vogue* at the time. I hadn't been fired yet. But I was fired soon afterwards because I did a film which caricatured Diana Vreeland, the boss at *Vogue*.
It was *Who Are You, Polly Maggoo?* And Polly Maggoo was not this great beauty, but she was a great model, played by Dorothy McGowan. Dorothy was not like Kate Middleton or people like that, a great beauty, but she was the greatest model ever. I realized that she could be an actress, she wasn't really very fluent in French – it was a French film – but she learned the lines. She was able to play opposite really top French actors like Philippe Noiret and she was terrific. There's a scene – she's looking in the mirror, and I drew different versions of what Polly could become and she could become anything. Nowadays she is as beautiful as ever and she deserves a 20-pages spread in *Harper's Bazaar*, because she was maybe the greatest model-actress ever.

Then there was the Cassius Clay film, *Muhammad Ali – The Greatest*. Was it shot in Florida?
Florida, yeah.

How did that come about?
You know, I'm American and like all Americans I was obsessed with sports. I followed boxing like everybody else. I followed Joe Lewis. Here's Cassius, we called him Cassius at that time. I ran into Malcolm X in a plane and we talked for three hours going from New York to Miami and we became more or less friends because I was curious about the black Muslims, about Malcolm himself. He was curious about a

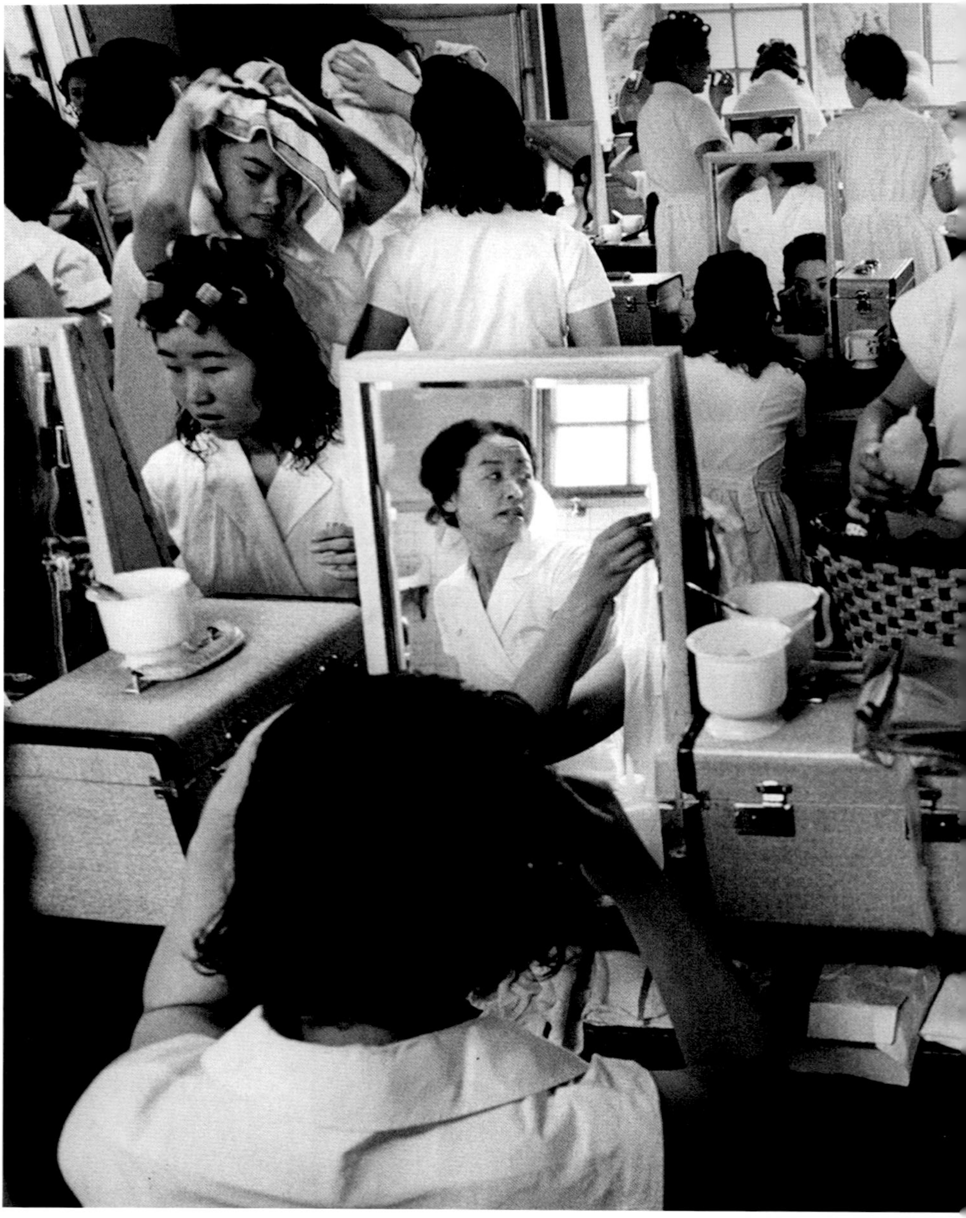

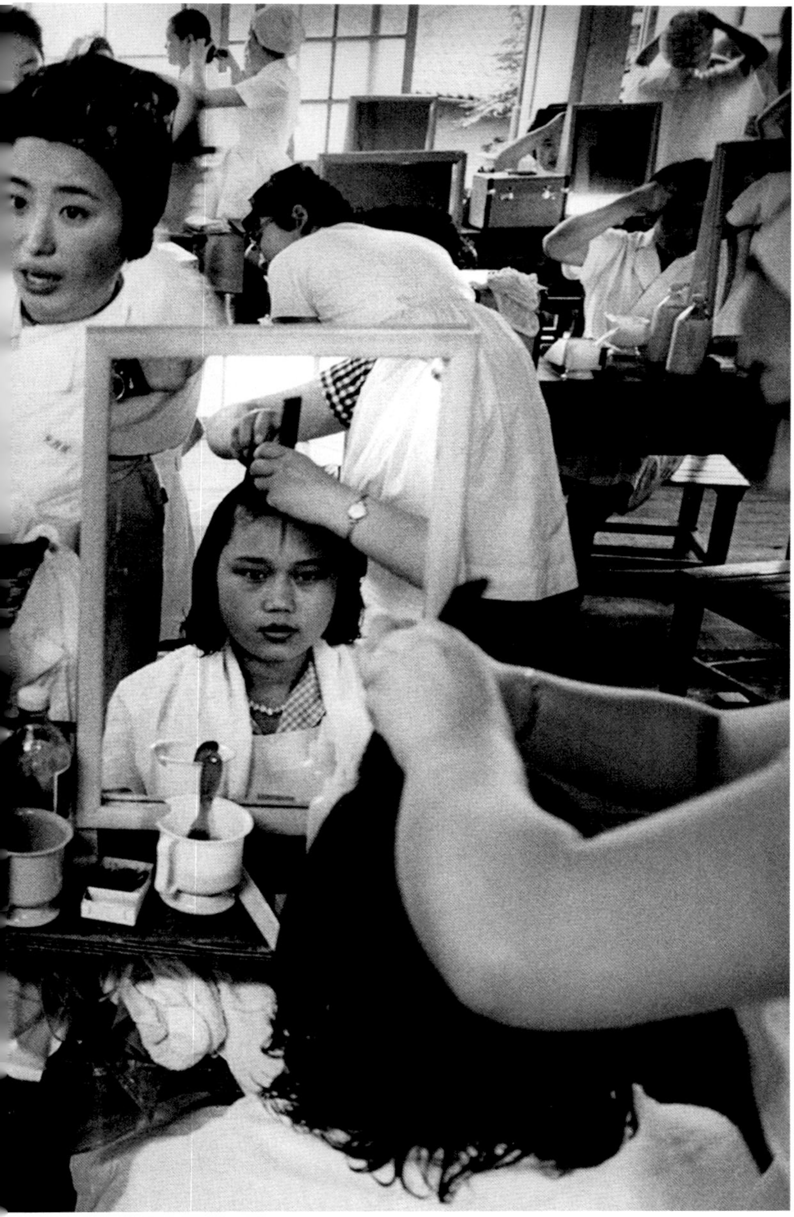

William Klein,
Hairdressers'
School,
Tokyo, 1961

Jewish film-maker coming from New York, living in Paris, coming to Miami to film a championship fight between Ali and Sonny Liston and he spread the word that I was ok. And when I came to the camp, I was accepted in the circle around Cassius and I could do anything.
There was a film at the time that got me separated from *Vogue*. Chris Marker organized a film which was called *Far from Vietnam*.The students had these meetings against the war, and they wanted to show a film, but most of the films that were done at the time were done by people who didn't know how to do movies, they were out of focus and grainy and crappy. The kids in college for example, if they had the chance to see *Far From Vietnam* or *Love Story*, they would go see *Love Story*. Chris Marker said, "no I won't do the film, but I'll get some friends to do it". So he called up Alain Resnais, Godard, Ivens, Varda, Lelouch…
They all agreed to do work on the film for nothing. And we didn't know that much about the war in Vietnam, it was horrible, but we didn't know too much what the Americans were figuring. What they were figuring was the domino effect. If Vietnam fell, all of Southeast Asia would fall into the hands of the communists. That was the preoccupation.
So *Far From Vietnam* was more or less a documentary and it didn't really go over that big in Paris and in France because people didn't really go see documentaries that much. So I thought if I wanted to do a film saying the same things denouncing American imperialism and intervention in places like Vietnam, I would have to do something that would be more accessible, and I thought I'd do a kind of a circus… and so I did a film like a comic strip. My idea for *Mr. Freedom* was of a super hero, but I would show who is behind the man, a right wing John Birch Society or whatever and Donald Pleasence played the role of a John Birch character. *Mr. Freedom* was very obviously a fascist meddler into international affairs.
Since there were a lot of demonstrations in the film against *Mr. Freedom*, the French censorship people thought it was a film about May '68, while the film was actually done in May '67. It was censored for a year and it came out in 1969. The French were convinced that it was all about May '68 and they were very preoccupied with May '68… and what can you do?

You made lots of raw and colourful sketches for the film design, and the final movie really retains that cartoon-like feeling.

We had no money to make sets and this place was an abandoned gas factory and we painted all the walls red, white and blue, and so it became like the drawing in the beginning. The costumes were made from industrial outfits and cricket clothing and baseball and football and everything. Freedom is dressed up in what is actually a baseball catcher's protection outfit. My friend, the painter Jack Youngerman, married this incredibly beautiful lovely young actress, Delphine Seyrig, who won the first prize in the Venice Film Festival with the film Last Y*ear in Marienbad* with Alain Resnais. And how come she did this film? She was considered an intellectual actress, very reserved and high class. She was having tea in our apartment and she saw the drawings of the scenario for *Mr. Freedom* and she said "what's this?" I said "well, it's a film I wanna do" and she said "who's this *bimbo* on the cover?" and I said – "I'm looking for some pop star who has a great body and who could play the role of Mr. Freedom's girlfriend, who is actually a traitor" and she said " I can do it". I said "what do you mean, you can do it?, she said "yeah, I can do it!".

She's kind of like the prototype for Madonna and Lady Gaga.
Yeah, Lady Gaga picked up on her. Actually if there was Madonna around, I would've asked Madonna to do it. That's the kind of person I wanted. Who could imagine that Delphine Seyrig, high class, Katharine Hepburn sort of actress would do that? But she did it.

The film *The Model Couple* came out after you had a period of making commercials and adverts.
I had done many commercials to finance everything. This is a film which is like a tele-realité, reality TV. And this is a program that the French government and I invented to find what the needs of the Frenchmen of the future would be. So this couple was chosen as a typical French couple, the film was called *The Model Couple*, like the model apartment. They were put in an atmosphere where they had all the gadgets they wanted, being spied on all night by sociologists and psychologists to find out more or less, according to the Ministry of the Future, what the Frenchmen of the future would need.
The aim of the film was to question what will the citizen of 2000 be? Because 2000 was a figure of fantasy. Nobody thought we'd ever live until 2000 and here we are in 2013.

Stephen Shore is one of the most remarkable photographers of this generation. For over five decades he has been pushing pictorial possibilities and exploring the medium in all its complexity. Although he has become well-known for his colour work made on road trips in the 1970s, the breadth of his work is unusual. He is always testing new ideas, new techniques, new ways of presenting his work, be it on the wall, page or screen.

I first met Stephen in 2003, on the occasion of Tate Modern's inaugural exhibition of photography, *Cruel + Tender: the real in the twentieth century photograph*. When Stephen had a retrospective show in Europe in 2014, I was asked to write a text for the catalogue. I suggested a conversation instead. So, Stephen came to London and we talked for most of the day.

In conversation, Stephen is just like his photographs: precise, articulate, informed and playful. He switches easily from philosophical reflection to disarmingly simple statements. This has a lot to do with his temperament, but I suspect it's also the result of having been a teacher for many years. When you teach you have to choose your words very, very carefully. Transcribing this from the recording was a revelation to me. No repetition, no false starts, no hesitation. Just careful thoughts expressed in careful sentences. The original conversation was very long, so what you read here is a series of extracts.

Stephen Shore

I know you had a precociously early start in photography. Where did the affection for photography come from in the first place?
I feel, in retrospect, I was just very lucky. When I was a little kid, I had a chemistry set. I also had an uncle who was an engineer in the U.S. Navy and who thought, Well, maybe if this little guy is interested in chemistry, he'd like to try photography. And so he gave me, for my sixth birthday, this little package made by Kodak that had hard rubber trays, a developing tank and reel, foil packets of chemicals, and an instruction book.

So, the chemistry came before the picture making? It's unusual.
Yes, I wasn't making the pictures. My family just had a Brownie Hawkeye, and I would develop and print their snapshots. And then, by the time I was eight, after two years of darkroom work, it was a natural progression that I would want to take pictures. About three months before my ninth birthday, I got a 35mm camera – a Ricoh Rangefinder.

Did you have any kind of artistic background at school?
No. Well, I was going to what in those days was called a "progressive school", and so we had art classes, but I don't think there was much of a relationship to my interest in photography.

That can be an advantage – to arrive at a medium without any baggage, or history, weighing you down.
Yes, if you have ambition.

By beginning in the darkroom with other people's images, did you have a more analytical attitude?
If I'd been twenty, I would have, but I was six, seven, eight and just having fun making prints! But I know I was thinking analytically about the prints, because the one surviving example is of a snapshot

of me with an older cousin, and I'd printed it inside of a heart-shaped cardboard mask. So, I was thinking about visual possibilities and possibilities of printing.

But within a few years you'd developed some kind of artistic sensibility.
The influences at the time were largely terrible! The photography magazines were just showing the most banal stuff.

Kitsch.
Yes, mainly. Even at the Museum of Modern Art at the time. I wouldn't want to speak ill of Edward Steichen, but *The Family of Man* (1955)… it had some good photographs in it, but they lost those qualities in that context of sentimentality. A Garry Winogrand image in there gets drowned out. I didn't see the show, but I had the book.

So, where did your cultural ambition come from?
We lived in an apartment house, and the man upstairs was very cultured – the head of a music publishing company. He knew my interest in photography, and for my tenth birthday he gave me a copy of Walker Evans's *American Photographs*.

Wow, starting at the top! It's a difficult book, in lots of ways.
Oh yeah, and I'd never heard of Evans. But I feel very grateful that my neighbour had that kind of insight. He could have given me a lot of other books and my life might have turned out very differently! [laughs]

Such early exposure is amazing, but it's a while before one realizes just how high and how permanent those standards are. You couldn't have known Evans's photography would become a lifelong relationship. He seems to be one of your guiding lights…
Absolutely. And I don't even think of it as simply an influence. Maybe I could bring in an analogy from left field: in homeopathy, there are what they call "constitutional types", and I feel he and I are the same constitutional type.

Made of the same stuff.
Yes. It feels much deeper than just an influence. When I saw his work

I recognized someone who thought the way I would think if I were mature enough to think that way. I didn't think that way about it when I was twelve, looking at his work. But as I've lived with it over the years, I've recognized the kinship – but, in a way, the kinship predated any influence.

And within a few years, you approached Edward Steichen, who was head of photography at the MoMA. How old were you?
Fourteen. I think I didn't know any better, but it was a different world then. He probably had very little to do all day. There weren't a lot of photographers coming to see him. If I were forty and not fourteen, it might have been a different answer.

But there is an understanding that promise and talent, and accomplishment, can show themselves very early in photography. Maybe it's because the basic craft complex of the medium can be grasped pretty quickly.
It couldn't be easier.

And that allows for very rapid artistic development.
I look at the work of some of my students: some struggle along, and then they make a breakthrough, but others have something right from the start. But one of the indicators of success is *ambition*. With some students, I *know* they have more talent than they think they have, but they have little ambition. And I know that soon there will be so many other influences – the demands of life, having a job, having a love life – and they drift away from photography. It's very easy to find that you don't have time to do your art. I think I answered the ambition question when I called up Steichen at fourteen!

What did he say?
I don't remember. I have some visual memory. It was early days at the Modern. There was a series of townhouses on the street that had been joined together (this was several renovations ago). So, there was a warren of alleys to get to Steichen's office. He was very gracious and bought three prints there and then for what was called the Study Collection.

And soon after, you met his successor, John Szarkowski...

Yes, John was more interested in curating and writing than he was in collecting, which was a problem that Peter Galassi then had to deal with later. John did his great thing with the Atget collection but was more interested in other aspects. Anyway, he traded two of the prints Steichen had bought for two of my new ones; it's baffling to me why he did that. He saved the museum thirty dollars (fifteen dollars a piece), but the clerical time involved – de-acquisition, acquisition – it was so complicated! He could have just bought the new prints.

But did you get on with Szarkowski?
Oh, yes. Szarkowski arrived in 1962. In 1965 I started photographing Warhol and the Factory. I would go to John and ask to show him the work I was doing. The thing is, anyone could have walked into MoMA, but there were so few of us. I'd never been published at all – I wasn't a known "name" – but I just called up and asked to see him. And as time went on, I would show him work regularly. I feel that, more than anyone, he was my teacher. Whenever I had a new body of work, I'd bring it to him. But that relationship came later. In 1965 I think he saw me because there were very few photographers asking to see him. It was a different world. Even in the early seventies, when Harold Jones opened Light Gallery in New York, anyone could come in off the street, sit down, and show Harold their portfolio and talk with him. But by the end of the seventies, the position of photography had changed and gallerists couldn't do that. I think there was also a change in attitude. Joel Sternfeld refers to the early time of colour as its "early Christian era". But in the seventies, we also felt like initiates. As a parallel, in the eighties, the photography scene in Italy was somewhat like it was in America in the sixties – as primitive and unrecognized. A group of photographers there called themselves I Fratelli del Deserto [the brothers of the desert]! That was the feeling: we were brothers in this arcane craft.

Let's talk about your time with Warhol at the Factory. I remember in the 1990s, when a book of the photos you had made there was published [*The Velvet Years*], many people were surprised that those diaristic, informal images had been made by the same photographer who later became well known for his sober and formal colour work. It seemed to come from a very different

attitude to the medium. People so often talked about "photographers" and "artists using photography", and it seemed you moved position. People wondered how come the guy who made *Uncommon Places* had been at the Factory.
I understand the distinction they're making, although I look at the Factory work I made and I see a formality to it that I feel is just ingrained in me.

How often were you at the Factory?
It varied over three years. For a while I would go every day.

A large selection of your Factory photos appeared in Warhol's 1968 Moderna Museet catalogue. "Photographs by Stephen Eric Shore", it says.
Yes, that's the place to see them.

Did you consider yourself a chronicler of the place? Were you thinking anecdotally? Some of the pictures are quite formal, but others definitely have the looseness of an ongoing diary.
Well, I was there so long that there are different answers. I first went there simply because it was the Factory; it was exciting, and I was documenting what was going on. But then these people became my friends, and so that changed the work. And then there was a period where Andy let me put up a sheet of seamless paper and I did a series of portraits of people who came in. There's actually a photo of me in that catalogue.

In the folio of photos by Billy Name?
Yes, a portrait of me with Ivy Nicholson.

Dandy suit, big floppy hat – is that how you were dressing at the time?!
Yes. Well, not always. I think I was dressing up a little there!

Did you feel like you fit in at the Factory? People now see you as this urbane, formal, analytical, slightly detached guy, and they find it hard to picture you in that bohemian maelstrom.
Are you suggesting Andy *wasn't* urbane and detached?

Sure, he was urbane and detached, but the impression people have of that environment is very different.

Well, different people were there for different reasons, but Andy worked every day. He was not a morning person, but he came in every afternoon and he had a 4-by-8-foot sheet of plywood as a table, and he would *work*. He always had something going on. There were other people who came, and there was a famous couch at the Factory, and they would sit and stare into space all day. And I remember at the time finding this just baffling, while Andy was so industrious. They would sit there waiting for the evening, when Andy would be invited to some party, and whoever was in the Factory went along. But I think I fitted in, and, as I say, a number of people there were my friends. Even when I went through periods of not going to the Factory, these were the same people I was spending time with.There was a crowd at the Factory from Cambridge, Massachusetts, who were the people around Edie Sedgwick. Most of them were friends of mine. I think Edie herself thought she was too sophisticated to deal with a seventeen-year-old kid photographer, and I don't think we ever had a conversation. When the Velvet Underground came, I never really got on with Lou [Reed], but John Cale and I became good friends. And Sterling Morrison. And Billy Name. Then there were people who were more peripheral – friends of the Cambridge people. I felt I fit in.

Were you taking drugs?

Not as much as some others. There was a lot of speed, but that was about it. There wasn't a wild drug scene. And also I was straight, which was maybe a little different from some of the people there.

You've spoken of picking up a real work ethic from Warhol and an attitude to artistic problem solving.

Yes. I didn't realize this at the time, but in retrospect I see Andy was very open about his process. What I saw every day was someone making aesthetic decisions. He would try different colour combinations, different printing techniques, and he'd say, "Oh, Stephen, what do you think of this colour?" And it wasn't that he actually cared what I thought or [that] he was insecure; I think it was because some people like to work not in solitude but with people around them. It gave Andy energy to focus, and he would ask them questions to draw their energy into him.

Are you like that as an artist?
No, I work alone. Although, through doing commercial work, I learned to work in a collaborative way.

Did your affection [for] everyday things and scenes come from Warhol? Obviously, photography has a disposition toward that.
I think photography has a disposition toward it. And I think this is something maybe a little bit like Walker Evans – I'm not sure I learned it from Andy, but I was attracted to his vision or attitude because there was some similarity. Andy may have been more…cynical than I am. But he took pleasure in the culture. He was just amazed at how things just are. It struck a chord that may have already existed in me. And as you suggested, this may have been why I was drawn to photography. It's what photography deals with.

You made a series of pieces that have come to be known as your "Conceptual work". These include *Circle* (1969) and *General Semantics* (1970). These works are systematic, analytical, serial.
That's how I was thinking just after I left the Factory. Andy's work wasn't really Conceptual, but he was dealing with serial imagery. And, for me, a very influential book at the time was John Coplans's *Serial Imagery*. I started hanging out at John Gibson Gallery that showed – on the less Conceptual end – Christo and Richard Long, and – on the more conceptual end – Peter Hutchinson and Dennis Oppenheim. In fact, there were a number of conceptual artists who saw photography as a graphic element or documentary element. A number of them became friends of mine.

Artists identified as "conceptual" are either regarded as seeing photography as a means to an end or they have a very testy, suspicious attitude to it, not so much an affectionate one.
Well, I wrote a text on the work of Bernd and Hilla Becher [*Festschrift Erasmuspreis*, 2002] in which I suggested that although they are talked about as conceptual artists, they are *photographers*, and the ultimate meaning of their work is not the concept. The "concept" of photographing six hundred water towers is not a very complex concept. In fact, it's not a concept; it is a *framework*. I know they achieved a certain status within Conceptual art, but they clearly transcended that. John

Szarkowski had his blindnesses, and this was one of them. When the Bechers were first shown at MoMA, it was in the sculpture department.

Well, a lot of photographic work first got shown that way at MoMA. In 1970, when Szarkowski was putting on the big Evans retrospective, Kynaston McShine was organizing the big Conceptual show *Information* in the sculpture department.
The meaning of the Bechers' work is visual, and that separated them from figures like Douglas Huebler. Huebler always had a plan, a system, like many conceptual artists, and a lot of the photos they made were dumb intentionally.

Perfunctory.
Yes, they wanted to deflect critical attention away from the work as photography and keep the image simply as a documentation of the idea. In a way the Bechers were doing the opposite, and that's where I went.

The Bechers really loved those water towers. They knew a lot about them and wanted the viewer to see them.
Yes. So, coming out of a photographic background, I thought I could bring something visual to a concept. And so, for example, I did a series on Sixth Avenue in Manhattan, where I'm starting on 42nd Street and walking up to 59th Street. And at the beginning of each block, I'm facing due north and take a photo – but I do it with infrared film and the sunlight glares off these people walking by, and its highly visual.

It's systematic but not mindlessly so.
I'm trying to remove a certain amount of subjectivity from the decision making.

You're still choosing when to press the shutter.
Sure. I once talked with the artist John Baldessari about the idea of trying to arrive at a less mediated photograph. If some of the decisions were made by a Conceptual framework, it would take out some of the personal influence, some of the personal conditioning. I did a series photographing a friend of mine over twenty-four hours. I'm still choosing where to stand, how to frame, focus, and so on – but I'm taking the photos exactly on the hour and half hour.

But you didn't work in that way for very long.
I realized I wasn't really addressing the issue and that's when I began *American Surfaces*. I was still after a less mediated photography, a less mediated experience; it's still about making a photo that is less the product of visual and artistic convention. So, as a mental experiment, I would try to take a mental snapshot of my field of vision – what does this look like now? How am I looking at something? I'd do this without a camera, but I would use this experience as a guide to structuring the pictures.

So, this is why so many of the photos in that series feel like hyperlucid stares at the world.
Exactly. But in the translation of seeing to photographing, certain conventions are entering.

That's inevitable, no?
Some snapshots are clearly very conventional, and there are many different conventions. But every now and then, there is a snapshot or a postcard that just shows what the Hi-Lo Motel *looks like*.

It's usually in the middle of the frame.
Yes, that's how people see. In art there is the "rule of thirds", but if I put you in the lower left-hand third of my field of vision when we are talking to each other, it is disconcerting to both of us. It's just not how people look.

But if we think of the visual field as being made up of "things" and "scenes", I can see that *American Surfaces* was largely about things, while the next project, *Uncommon Places*, was mainly concerned with scenes. There are overlaps, but as a general rule you go from surfaces to places.
Yes, but I should say *American Surfaces* was called that in my mind while I was taking those pictures; I had that in my head. *Uncommon Places* was a title I came up with in 1982 for the book of that work.

It might have been a disaster if you'd had that as a working title! When did you first start thinking about photographing beyond New York?

It came out of experiences in Amarillo, Texas, where I had friends. It was actually through one of the Cambridge people at the Factory, who had a younger sister who was dating a young man from Amarillo named Michael Marsh. Michael became one of my closest friends. He appears in some of my work. In the Conceptual "twenty-four-hour" piece, he's the guy. The first photograph in *American Surfaces* is also of Michael. He lives in New York, and every three months we still have lunch together. Anyway, through him I met a number of other people from Amarillo who were all living in New York. And in 1969 I went to Amarillo with them. I had been to Europe every year of my life – London, Paris, Madrid, Seville, Rome – but I'd seen very little of America. I'd been to LA once, but really New York was the western edge of my travel and Rome was the eastern edge.

New York is very European in many ways. Did you photograph in London?
I went once for a month and once for three months. I was friendly with John Chamberlain, who was making a film. I hung out and took pictures. But when I began to photograph America, I was also in many ways a foreigner. And I *loved* it, immediately.

Did you drive to Amarillo?
No, I flew. I didn't drive at the time. If you grow up in New York, there is no reason to even have a car. In fact, it's a burden to have a car. I loved Amarillo, not just what it looked like but the way people hung out – the pace of the life, the car culture, the barbeque joints.

It was exotic?
It was exotic but familiar, too. I didn't love it like a tourist; I got *into* it. I would go there for a month.

The light must have been a big source of attraction.
Oh, yeah. Just to digress a little: recently, I have been one of twelve photographers commissioned to photograph for a big project in Israel. I have had an assistant who has also been assisting the German photographer Thomas Struth. It's a desert country, Israel, with clear skies most of the time. The assistant told me that Thomas would wait hours for one tiny cloud to block the sun and then he would take his photograph.

He's used to overcast Northern European light.
Right. He's from Germany; I'm from America. And I love sunny days. I would photograph from Texas to Arizona, going to places where I knew I could have a sunny day every day. This morning, I was showing a magazine editor here in London some recent photographs from Winslow, Arizona, and she remarked on the blue skies; an American wouldn't even comment on the blue skies.

For you the blue is also compositional.
It's a weight that balances the tonality of the bottom. A white sky wouldn't do it. Last week, when I was in Ukraine, half the time it was overcast and I would have to construct pictures differently to deal with not having that weight on the top of the picture.

Many photographers see a problem in bright light and blue skies, and the drama of shadows, but this is exactly what you prefer.
For me, that Southwestern light communicates a mental clarity, so there is a psychological attraction. It isn't simply a symbol of it, but a representation of it. Also, if you work in that light for long enough, you have to work out how to integrate a shadow pictorially so that it is not about the shadow, it's about the physical object – but, structurally, the picture has to take the shadow into account.

If those scenes in bright light are striking you as potential pictures, is it partly physiological? In bright light, our pupils are small, and so everything appears in focus from foreground to background.
This is something I've been thinking about this past month. I've been reading a book by a Nobel Laureate named Daniel Kahneman [*Thinking, Fast and Slow*]. He talks about psychological experiments in which people have to concentrate hard, like a mathematics problem. When they do this, their pupils dilate. I realized this is a problem for photographers.

Because with dilated pupils, the depth of field is smaller?
Yes. When I'm concentrating on making a picture, I understand three-dimensional space is being collapsed onto a picture plane. With dilated

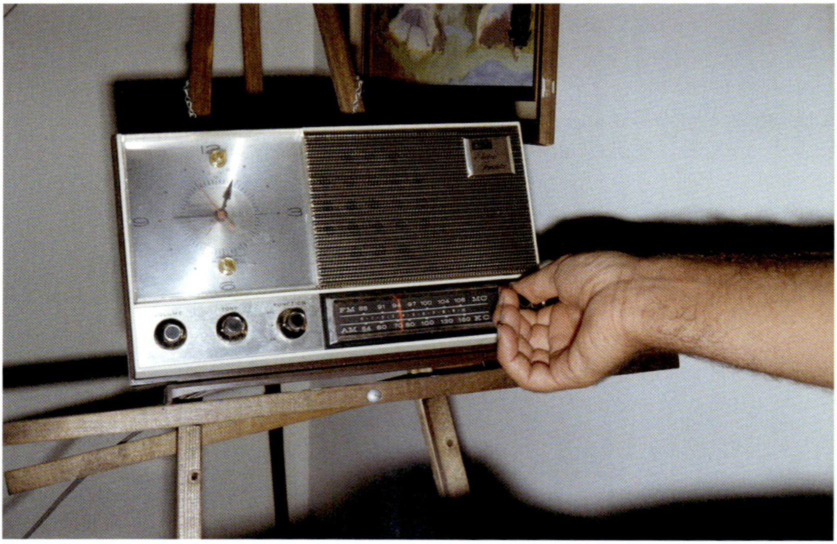

Stephen Shore, West Palm Beach, Florida, April-May 1973,
from the series "American Surfaces"

pupils, I'm not able to see the relation of foreground to background. I have to become so familiar with this that it's no longer a mental strain.

So, bright light helps with this problem. Concentration and pupil dilation is offset against bright light and pupil constriction! I can see a whole theory of European civilization being built on this! The more overcast the light, the more dilated the pupils, and the easier it is to concentrate on things in close proximity – reading, writing, painting still lifes and portraits!
I'd never thought of it that way. Maybe that's why I went to the bright light! Also I didn't need to wear glasses until about twenty years ago.

Coming back to the transition between *American Surfaces* and what came to be called *Uncommon Places*, can you talk about how much and how often you were shooting?
Well, in 1972 I didn't have a clear idea about what I wanted to do. But

I knew a couple of things. I'd gotten a little camera, a Rollei 35mm. It was a 1972 version of a good "point and shoot" camera. I liked this because it was unintimidating. I could go up to someone on the street and say, "Can I take your picture?" and they wouldn't be anxious. I had other cameras – Nikons, Leicas, a Hasselblad – but I liked the Rollei a lot. It was innocuous-looking. Secondly, I had this idea of the "natural photograph", and I knew I was going to print the results as small snapshots.

Drugstore prints?
Yes, in those days Kodak actually made the prints. They had a lab in Fairlawn, New Jersey, and your film would be sent to them. A few days later, your prints would come back. Now, the year before I'd made a series of photographs using the Mick-a-Matic.

The camera in the shape of the face of Mickey Mouse?
Yes. Those pictures were a homage to the snapshot, the unmediated photo. At the same time, the Mick-a-Matic played against this because everyone smiles at that camera! You can't avoid smiling. But still, I was hoping for a kind of spontaneity that some snapshots occasionally contain. After a while, I wanted a camera with better optics, and the Rollei was perfect.

Tiny and beautiful, but extremely high-quality, camera.
The flash unit was mounted on the bottom, not on the top, and this was a godsend.

People often can't put their finger on the source of the oddness of those flash-lit pictures.
Yes, it's the fact that the shadow is cast upward. It has this weird, almost cubistic quality.

Your photo of the hand reaching out to the transistor radio on an easel is very strange.
The shadow separates the hand from the background. Still, today if I'm using flash, I'll hold it under the camera or turn the camera upside down so the flash is underneath. But I can rarely get the result as good as the Rollei. I don't even know if the designers thought it out or

whether there was only space for the flash underneath. Maybe there just wasn't enough room on the top for an accessory shoe.

The closer the subject to the camera, the more pronounced the effect. And most of the flash-lit shots in *American Surfaces* are close range.
It was a small flash that wouldn't work beyond fifteen feet.

You were shooting like that for a year or so?
Roughly eighteen months. It was very exploratory. Within two days of beginning the trip, I noticed I was photographing the food I was eating, the beds I was sleeping in – I was making a diary. I'd made all that Conceptual and system-related work, or work with ideational frameworks. I was thinking about the work of Bernd and Hilla Becher. So, here was a way of deconstructing the experience of America through a series of repeated motifs. Well, what if I kept up this diary? Every single meal I ate? Every bed I slept in? I was gone two or three months, and you can get a lot of work done in that time.

And what if America is a series of repeated motifs?
Exactly. It wasn't a picture of life but a picture of life on the road. Then I would come back to New York.

Were you seeing any of the results as you went along?
I know that I was sending my film in packages back to New York, and they would arrive processed and printed all with the same date stamp: 7/12/72 A, B, C, D, E. That was my filing system. I know when I started using 4-by-5 film, I was getting it sent back to me so I could see what I was doing. When I returned to New York, I thought I could do this for the rest of my life, or at least the following year.

When was work from *American Surfaces* first exhibited?
In the fall of 1972, at Light Gallery – a little over two hundred unframed Kodak snapshots with white borders, covering three walls of the room in a grid three-rows high, attached to the wall with double-sided tape.

How was that received?

Not particularly well. One review thought it was just terrible. I think people had many problems with it. I'll list them. There was the "fine art photography" tradition; the other people being shown by the gallery were André Kertész, Paul Strand, and Frederick Sommer, although also Winogrand and Friedlander, and Emmet Gowin. Then there were Robert Fichter and Robert Heinecken. A great range, but there was an overriding sense of *craft*. I wasn't making these prints myself and I didn't frame or mount them – there was no reverence in the presentation. Plus, the grid made them hard to see as individual images.

And the subject matter was not "acceptable"?
I don't think [the reviewers] even got to the subject matter! Also, the prints were in colour. A year later, I had lunch with Paul Strand, who – as a polite older gentleman talking to a young aspiring artist – told me that higher emotions could not be communicated in colour.

That was such an entrenched position back then.
I remember thinking, What would Kandinsky think of this statement? Higher emotions could not be communicated in colour?!?

Even when photographers were not being adamant about colour in that way, many were equivocal. Walker Evans had been publishing colour since 1945, but still in 1969 he's writing that it's vulgar and only artistically viable if the subject is the vulgarity of man-made objects and surfaces.
Ah, well, I understand that. When I got to the 1980s, I realized that photographing nature untouched by man, in colour, is very difficult. It can be done, and I believe I've done it, but it raises lots of problems. My wife Ginger was a picture researcher at *Fortune,* and I would ask her to find back issues containing Evans' photo essays, many of which were in colour. Anyway, people would come into my show and just see it as a kind of coloured wallpaper. It was up for at least two months, and after a while I remember some of the people working at the gallery would tell me they had begun to really look at the pictures in a way that was very different from their first impression. I showed the series much more recently at PS1 in New York. I made the prints very slightly larger, I kept them high-gloss and in a grid but had them framed. I understood this was taking away the "snapshot-ness" of them – par-

ticularly the materiality – but it was giving the viewer the space to look carefully at each one individually *and* at the series as a whole.

I remember when you were part of the group exhibition *Cruel + Tender* at Tate Modern in 2003, Martin Parr showed *Common Sense*, his grid of ring-flashed close-ups printed and pasted in a grid directly to the wall. It had taken nearly thirty years for audiences to come around to that way of doing things.
The one person who was actually very supportive of the Light Gallery show was Weston Naef, who was at the Metropolitan Museum of Art at the time. He bought the show. You couldn't buy the prints individually; it was only for sale as an entire show.

All two-hundred-and-something prints?
Yes, and it sold for two-hundred-and-something dollars! It wasn't shown at the Metropolitan Museum until much later.

What was Weston Naef responding to?
We'd become good friends. He had curated the Met's show of my Conceptual work the year before, 1971. He was prepared to spend time looking closely at *American Surfaces*.

At what point did the 4-by-5 view camera begin to interest you?
In 1973 I was still continuing with 35mm, but after the show I became less interested in my pictures as snapshots and more interested in other visual qualities – and in what the content was. This was becoming an exploration of America. In fact, the "snapshot-ness" began to interfere with people's understanding of the content; it was presenting a barrier. I wanted to make larger prints and found that I couldn't because the 35mm film was just too grainy (I can make slightly larger prints today because I can boost the saturation to match the saturation of the smaller prints, but if I go much larger, I'll have sharpness problems). I needed a larger negative. I wasn't aware of any medium-format cameras that weren't two-and-a-quarter square. I don't think the Plaubel was around or the medium-format Pentax. So, I got a Crown Graphic, a press camera, and thought I'd use it hand-held to continue with *American Surfaces*. Then I realized the flash was nowhere near as good as the Rollei 35. Also, if you look at *American Surfaces,* half the pictures are architectur-

al. So, if I'm photographing a building, there's good reason to put the camera on a tripod. And totally to my surprise, I found I loved working with a tripod. And I loved looking at the ground-glass screen of the 4-by-5 camera. The next year, I got a 4-by-5 studio camera because I wanted to use lens movements. I never hand held it; it was always on a tripod.

It slowed you down; you couldn't take as many pictures. The noticing, the observation of the world around you, becomes very different.

Yes. To use an analogy, we learn to walk when we're one year old, roughly. By the age of three, we can do it automatically. By the time we're twenty-five, we walk into a room and notice everyone is looking at us – we become awkward and, suddenly, we don't know how to walk again. If you were an actor, you'd have to learn how to walk with a conscious mind. You'd have to walk consciously across a stage – being observed while trying to look natural. It's a skill you have to relearn consciously. I'm convinced that a good actor, having gone through that process, can go on the stage looking completely natural. There is an essential difference between that actor looking natural and the stagehand who walks naturally onto the stage after the performance. Because of the actor's conscious practice, he or she will move with stage presence. And I'm convinced there's something equivalent to this in photography. With the 4-by-5, and later the 8-by-10, shooting *Uncommon Places*, I was starting with structurally fairly simple pictures, but they soon became more and more structurally dense. And at the point that they become the densest, I made an abrupt switch, and they started becoming simpler again, almost returning to pictures like those in *American Surfaces*. But I've gone through this process of completely taking apart an image structurally, playing with it, seeing how much I can pack into it, playing with every element I can think of, with every variation, and coming back to something simple.

But your photographs are so assured from the beginning of this process; that's what I find remarkable. Let's continue with the acting analogy: an actor can act clever, or act stupid, or learn to walk "naturally". But if that actor has to play the part of a juggler, then he or she really does have to be able to juggle – there's no acting about it. When you see an actor juggle on screen, the

acting falls away and you're just seeing the person juggling. That's a human competence you're watching, you can't fake it.
That's a wonderful point!

Well, you were able to "juggle" very well pretty much from the beginning. I know you'd been thinking about pictures since you were six, so it's not as if it were completely new to you when you picked up the 4-by-5 and the 8-by-10. But whatever the achievement of *American Surfaces*, it was partly a form of photography that downplayed deliberately the skills of picture making in pursuit of that snapshot feel. And a photographer can hide behind that kind of dumbed-down borrowed language (as Warhol was doing, as Ed Ruscha was, in part, doing). But when you pick up the 4-by-5, you now plunge yourself very rapidly into the very highest standards of complex composition, and you are able to do it. You're making virtuoso photographs within a matter of months. The standards are high almost immediately.
I can't explain it. It would be awfully self-congratulatory to agree with you, but I understand what you're saying.

A few years ago, you emailed me having read something I'd written about Eggleston's photography. I was pointing out how assured his pictures were from very early on. There's something in the medium that allows for that. But life goes on, and, as you say, an artist moves in and out of self-consciousness. I remember reading your book *The Nature of Photographs* (1998) and thinking, "Are these the writings of an artist who is now able to reflect carefully and put into words what was beyond words for him back in the seventies"? How intuitively were you working back then?
There are several aspects to the answer. Firstly, there is a difference between working intuitively and working analytically; then, there's a difference between working analytically and being able to write about it. I wouldn't have been able to write about what I was doing in the seventies. When I wrote *The Nature of Photographs,* I had been teaching for over a decade, and it had taught me about speaking about photographs. I had found some ways of talking about some things that other people were doing intuitively or unconsciously.

Can you describe what you had been doing?
In making *Uncommon Places,* I was walking down the street and watching all the relationships changing – watching objects in the foreground change in relation to the background, thinking about how space is going to be seen in monocular vision on a picture plane. What happened for me was that, right away and throughout the work, structural issues and questions came to my mind. I had to solve those questions, and in the process of solving them other questions would arise. But it wasn't as if I was sitting around thinking about them.

The thinking was in the doing.
Right. It was organic. And it began almost as soon as I began using the 4-by-5. How is the frame different if I lower it slightly and the bottom of that pole is in shot? What happens when it's cut off? How does it change the space of the picture? How do people read these little changes? I liked intersections because they gave you real pictorial challenges. How do you organize that three-dimensional space as a picture? As I'm answering this, another question would arise, then another. This went on for five years. And it was totally conscious.

I have heard you describe what you were doing in those terms before, and I can see clearly what you are getting at. But in some ways, that formal language you use seems to suggest that the world or the picture is only made of forms that you're trying to handle. What do your formal decisions then do for the viewer of the picture as communicating something about, for example, America? Or "the everyday"?
I think I was convinced at the time that the psychological tenor of a picture is partially communicated through structural means – that the structure was not just a way of beautifying something that was there but was integral to the whole physical aspect of the experience of seeing the picture. I remember driving in New Jersey on some of the highways and in the distance you'd see the World Trade Center, and from certain angles it seemed to me the towers were too far apart and the proportions were wrong. But there were certain angles where the towers were closer together, and it seemed right. And I realized that I would stop at this point, and if you were driving you might stop at another point. It's not that one is right and one is wrong but that there is

some physical, emotional, psychological connection that I have with a certain proportion that might be different from what you might have. I think that kind of thing happens in these little decisions I am making. On the other hand, I'm not in any way suggesting this takes precedence over the fact that, for example, in one of my photographs there is a sign for a restaurant called Sambo's, which is clearly racist.

Yes. If we go back to the avant-gardes of the 20s and 30s we might say there were two aims: to show beauty where there was thought to be no beauty, and to point out what was wrong with the world. In the postwar decades, serious photography begins to take everyday life as its primary subject matter. It's not that the world is redeemed by being turned into a picture, but there is a discovery of extraordinary beauty in things or scenes that were barely designed with an aesthetic in mind – the ad hoc occurrence of different things in a space, a street, an interior. When I look at *Uncommon Places*, I fall in and out of formal judgment.
One of the things I was reading a lot at the time were the – I guess now disgraced – Austrian economists: people like Eugen von Böhm Bawerk and his book *Value and Price*, and Ludwig von Mises. One of the things that comes from an economic study of society is a sense of complexity. I think that's something that attracted me. So, my photograph that contains the Sambo's sign is not merely a condemnation of racism; I saw the situation as complex. I was interested in *what was*. Jumping ahead to 1993, I was commissioned to photograph Luzzara in Italy, exactly forty years after Paul Strand was there (although I wasn't asked to do a "rephotographic project"). The Italian photo historian Paolo Costantini sent me a copy of a letter that Strand had written from Luzzara saying it was difficult to photograph there because there were no buildings of architectural interest! What struck me was how differently Strand and I would have understood "architectural interest". Strand was looking for a building that was either "fine architecture" or something edifying of the human spirit. Whereas Evans might look for the beauty in simple architecture, seen through modernist eyes, I was fascinated with architecture as a physical expression of cultural forces. You can't photograph cultural forces until they have a physical expression – that's what I'm always looking for. A picture can *contain* conflict, like the photo with the Sambo's sign, but that's not all the picture is about.

That's interesting. Many commentators see Jeff Wall's picture *Mimic* (1982) as a denunciation of racism. But Wall has responded by saying, "Yes well, maybe. But it's easy to denounce racism; you simply say racism is bad. But this has nothing much to do with the pictorial experience". You're interested in the fact that the Sambo's restaurant is there as one irrefutable presence in a complex world and a complex picture.
Right. And in physical terms, that sign isn't even the centre of the picture; it is part of a larger structure.

Most of your pictures are about a world that is unplanned, and the complexity comes from an accretion of these unplanned elements. That's the milieu in which you work best, no? Part of the problem of resolving a scene as a picture is coming into a relation with an unplanned world.
Yes, that's where the cultural forces show themselves. How do these forces interact with each other? That's what I'm looking for.

In total, do you have an idea of how many pictures you took for the *Uncommon Places* project?
I don't, but I know that the number of pictures I find interesting is close to seven hundred.

That's a lot. And when you first published it as a book in 1982, how many were included?
Forty-nine.

In retrospect, it's a strange selection in that book. So many great images were not included.
I think there were a number of reasons for that. The size was small because it was the first colour book the publisher, Aperture, had done. For them, it was a very expensive book to do. Even though the book came out in 1982 – and there were a couple of pictures at the end from the late seventies and early eighties – the book really began in the mid-seventies. In 1976 I had a show at MoMA, and Ansel Adams saw it and liked it and brought his publisher to it – a man named Tim Hill. He was the editor at the New York Graphic Society. He contacted me and asked if I'd like to do a book. But Tim left and went to Aperture. Well, we had to raise

money and apply for a National Endowment for the Arts publishing grant. Then he left Aperture, and Carol Kismaric took it over. So, by the time it was finally printed in 1982, a lot of the editing was a long time in the past. One thing I'd say in retrospect is that it's very dangerous to let an artist edit past work when they're still in the midst of it. There were certain visual problems on my mind in the late seventies that meant that pictures I'd done in, say, 1973 were irrelevant to me.

But with hindsight...
Now I look at those pictures and I can see them on their own merit. Anyway, that influenced the edit. I should say the title, *Uncommon Places*, was my idea but that wound up in a way influencing the edit and the book so it became mostly pictures of places. Three pictures were kind of "stuck in" that didn't fit with the edit – a close-up portrait of my wife Ginger (because she just looked so beautiful); a portrait of my friends Michael Marsh and his then wife Sandy lying on a couch; and a picture of pancakes – all because they meant a lot to me. I fought for them to be included, and it may have been a mistake. Rather than thinking of the book as a summation of my work of the seventies, maybe it should have been just a book of places, or intersections even, and more conceptually coherent as a result.

But the project you shot was very diverse.
Yes, it was. As with *American Surfaces,* I was doing portraits, still lifes, townscapes, landscapes. The *Uncommon Places* book was not designed to be a reflection of the whole body of work, but it came from it.

I know you understand photography as a matter of problem solving. Do you think you know at the time when the problem has been solved and you can move on?
My experience at the time was that I didn't have to make those decisions; it happened almost automatically. There came a time when the problems stopped arising. It took me a couple of years to realize I had, in fact, solved all the structural problems I'd set myself. I had, in fact, "mastered" those formal issues – maybe not all of them, but the ones that were in me that needed to be dealt with. It confused me at first when the questions stopped coming up. I didn't know what to do.

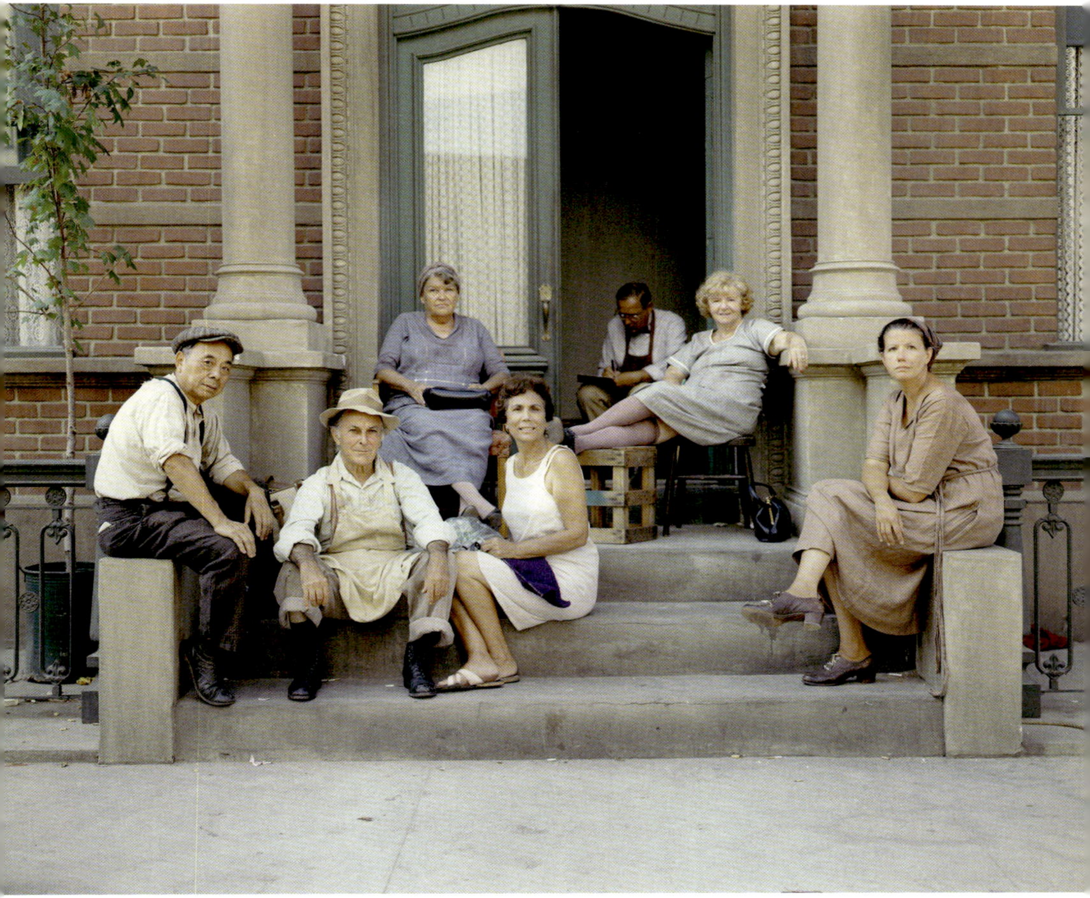

Stephen Shore, Burbank, California, August 10, 1981

American Surfaces **was a large project, as was *Uncommon Places*. I see that there is a difference between the widespread compulsion to repeat that photography seems to invite and your approach, which is more teleological – this problem, then this one, then this one. A project comes to an end and you clear the decks a little. And over the years, you've had a lot of changes in direction. Those changes might be to do with motif or camera choice, or pictorial challenge. That has stood you in good stead. I see a parallel with the way Paul Graham has worked: once something has been achieved, he changes completely – the camera, the subject, the way of noticing or observing – even though the photography world would like him to continue and repeat. This way of going about things is fascinating. It implies that for all the unwavering commitment to photography, you keep open the question of what the medium is, what it's for, what it's best at doing. Historically, most photographers have not done that. The medium has been something specific for them, whatever it is, and they have stuck to it as a kind of mantra.**
There is a lot to think about there. I have begun my recent lectures with a story of having dinner at Weston Naef's loft in the mid-seventies with Adams. We got on really well and Ansel has been a great inspiration, but during this dinner I saw him drink six large tumblers of straight vodka. And then at some point in the discussion, he said, "I had a creative hot streak in the 1940s, and since then I've been potboiling". He didn't say it with anguish but just out of recognition of the nature of his achievement and his situation. I thought to myself, Gee, when I'm eighty-five and talking to a twenty-five-year-old, I don't want to look at my life and say that. Think about Timothy O'Sullivan's understanding of the medium: barely twenty years after the medium is invented, he and several others – George Barnard's work from the Civil War stands out – are making work that's almost as good as it gets. But they have a different historical understanding of their medium than we do today. I knew by the time I was twenty that O'Sullivan had an active life of maybe ten years. I knew all the Walker Evans pictures I loved were made in an eighteen-month period.

Evans did other great things pictorially, but he never surpassed his "hot streak".

Robert Frank, too. And coming to photography in the late twentieth century, it's impossible to not know all this. And these aren't minor photographers; these are the *best*. These are the people who have changed the medium. Frank and Evans are not lesser because their creative hot streak was a couple of years. There are people who had forty-year careers and are well respected but [who] didn't change the medium. The people who have had long careers that I respect fall into two categories. There are those who had monomaniacal visions that propelled them, like Atget or the Bechers. Then there are people who kept looking at new things, new ways of doing things. They kept changing, like Alfred Stieglitz and Harry Callahan, or in a slightly different way, Lee Friedlander. I know that I'm in this second category. I can't spend my whole career doing one thing, because, as you say, it's to do with problem solving. So, there I was in the early eighties feeling shocked because I might have "lost it", and then I come to realize I have maybe moved beyond it and need to begin a new phase.

All that time you were shooting *American Surfaces* and *Uncommon Places*, were you also working commercially? How did you pay your bills?
At the time of *American Surfaces* and the beginning of *Uncommon Places,* I was living off a little family money. By the end of 1974, that had gone. I was fortunate in that, in 1975, I got a National Endowment for the Arts grant. I also got a commission from Robert Venturi, which really paid for the cross-country trip that year.

I've seen a few installation shots of the Venturi project – an exhibition in which some of your photos were used mural-size.
Yes, 16-by-20 feet.

What was the nature of that project?
Venturi was commissioned to do a bicentennial show on American architecture, for the Smithsonian Institution. It was called *Signs of Life: Symbols of the American City*. It had a number of different parts. There were neon signs that he'd collected. There were rooms of photographs of different styles of American architecture. There was a suite of three rooms, each including a 16-by-20-foot facade of a different style of house, a 16-by-20-foot photograph of a view down the street, and

then behind the facade was an actual furnished room. The furniture would have cartoon speech balloons around it, pointing out the historical sources in the styles. So, he was deconstructing American culture and taste. I shot some things that he wanted. They had to be on 8-by-10 transparency. Through a Japanese process called Neko, the image was airbrushed automatically onto three-foot-wide sheets of paper and hung as wallpaper. Essentially, this was a 1975 version of scanning and inkjet printing two decades before it became common practice. Beyond that, I had a rough list of things that interested him, but it was clear that our sensibilities were so similar that he was essentially asking me to carry on doing what I was doing. I started in Los Angeles, and I drove to New York.

Were there other commissions?
A few. The next year, I got a Guggenheim grant. Also a commission from the Forth Worth art museum. Lee Friedlander and I were invited to Fort Worth, so I have a lot of work from that part of the world that year. And then, the following year, there was a very interesting commission for AT&T. I was one of twenty photographers invited to do whatever they wanted. It was a completely open brief; AT&T were just seeing what might happen. Firstly, I went to Florida and made some good pictures there, including the one of my wife Ginger standing in a swimming pool with her back to me. There were others, too. The group on that commission was very good, including Harry Callahan, John Gossage, Lewis Baltz, Frank Gohlke, Mary Ellen Mark, and Richard Misrach. The final work was published as a book called *American Images* (1979). My pictures of the Yankees were also made as part of a commission. So, there were several invitations. In 1976 I was one of the photographers on the courthouse commission from Seagram's.

That was a huge survey of America's courthouses.
Yes, very big. I did a lot of work on that and got some work done for myself at the same time. Around 1977 I got a commission from the Metropolitan Museum to photograph Monet's gardens. It was to coincide with the museum's show of Monet's years painting at Giverny. My photographs were in a room showing what the gardens looked like after a big renovation. The woman who was the main backer of the renovation, called Lila Acheson Wallace, asked me to go back about

five years later, when the gardens were more established, to photograph them again. That's how the book of those photographs came about.

The matter of how photographers survived before the art market is not often discussed. When asked how he had made ends meet, Walker Evans said there were only four options: you are either independently wealthy to begin with; you are paid to take pictures ("commercial work"); you are paid for your pictures (as an artist); or you do something else for money and your photography is your serious pastime. It's kind of sobering but useful to see it in those terms. And, of course, good work can come out of a hybrid circumstance – working commercially but exploring one's own interests along the way. Arguably, much of the great work of the last century got made that way.
Commissions can bring a challenge that you weren't expecting. Well, for me, some did and some didn't. I got a commission from Fuji in 1978 or 1979 to use their new 8-by-10 film and their lenses. Among others, my shot of Merced River in Yosemite was shot on Fuji. But the company was so disappointed: it wasn't what they were expecting a Stephen Shore photograph to look like. In fact, for their advertising campaign, they just used one of my older pictures. They even put the Fuji notches on the edge of the film to make it look like it was Fuji film!

Were you selling many prints in the 1970s?
Yes, but at $150 each. The gallery got half, and then you paid taxes. So, it was commissions that paid the bills. I got occasional editorial pieces for magazines. There just seemed to be enough each year to keep me afloat.

For all the continuity in your work, there are lots of anomalies that I find very interesting.
What are you thinking of?

Well, one of my favorite photography books is *Annie on Camera*. You were one of several photographers, including Eggleston, Meyerowitz, Winogrand, and Epstein, who were invited to photograph on the set of the movie *Annie*, directed by John Huston.
It came about because someone at the production company liked pho-

tography and wanted to have the making of the film photographed by a range of different people. I went to Burbank in California, where they had built a huge set of a 1930s New York City street. The first decision to make was whether I was going to do it in black and white or colour. I hadn't done black and white in ages, but I considered it. I could make pictures that could be pretty convincing as 1930s documents. But I went with colour. It was the first time I'd got to see a great Hollywood set – how they made it look old through distressing, the oil stains on the street, the dust on windows, the fake condensation on glass. It was amazing to see. So, I embraced the reality that I was photographing a set.

But even in that strange world, you were definitely making "Stephen Shore" pictures: intersections, shop fronts.
That's true. Most of the pictures do have little indications that it's a movie set. A contemporary car in the background or some scaffolding. But even the decision to shoot in colour meant that I was making photographs that couldn't have been made in the period setting of the movie. It's an anachronism. There are streets in New York that still look like those streets, but the decor and dressing are anachronistic, too. It was great fun.

You had not photographed in Italy at this point, but you made a group portrait of extras that seems to be a homage to Paul Strand's famous image from his study of Luzzara.
Yes, that's what I was thinking about. I think I was shooting there for a week. I'm going back to a number of different little projects I have done, to scan the negatives before they fade beyond salvage. In the process, I've come across lots of work that somehow got neglected, perhaps because I'm a bad editor or it just got sidelined. There's one group of pictures from 1976 that I'm looking at. I got a commission from *Fortune* magazine to photograph decaying steel towns. This came about because *Fortune* was changing its format, reducing the trim size, going from a monthly to a fortnightly magazine – they weren't going to have long articles and big, classic photo essays. Hedley Donovan, editor in chief of Time Inc., which owned *Fortune*, had come up through the ranks at *Fortune* and was familiar with the great Evans photo essays. He wanted one of the last, large monthly issues to have one last, big picture story.

I believe he requested me. So, I did this work on steel towns in Buffalo, New York, and several paces in Ohio. I shot with a 4-by-5, at a time when I was shooting *Uncommon Places* on 8-by-10. So, it was a blip, and as time went by I forgot the work, but I like it very much. Some of them should really have been included in *Uncommon Places*.

How was the layout in *Fortune*?
Not great. A number of small images with larger ones printed across the gutter.

You're not a gutter man.
I'm not. It was one of the first editorial jobs I had. I had a fit and said, "You cannot gutter my pictures". But that kind of magazine work was coming to an end anyway.

You began teaching around 1982, when *Uncommon Places* was published. Has teaching changed your relation to photography?
When they are working, a photographer is thinking visually and there aren't really words attached to it; that's not useful to students. So, I had to put into words things I'd been doing silently.

You'd achieved a lot photographically by that point, but you yourself had not studied photography at school or college. Did that make teaching slightly equivocal?
Oh, I think that helped because I didn't have to pretend that college study was the only route. But I'd been interested in education for a long time. I went through a period of reading a lot of educational theorists. I once spent a month at an experimental school in Cuernavaca, Mexico, run by a man named Ivan Illich. There were seminars by various American educators, and I was fascinated by how people learned things. I'd been through enough with my own work, done it long enough, that I had a sense of a path an artist can take. So, I've seen my role at Bard [College] as helping each of the students to find their voice, which sometimes means letting them reach a dead end on their own or discovering something on their own. I've felt I could guide them.

Around 1982 you also moved out of New York.
Yes, to Montana. For various reasons, my wife and I loved fly-fishing.

We'd spent two summers in Montana and just didn't want to leave. There was this landscape. And I began to ask myself: "How do you take a picture of a place that isn't man-made without it looking like a calendar picture or a postcard?". I had got to a point where I could walk into any town in America and have an understanding of the forces at play and come to a sense of what to photograph. But when I walked out into the land in Montana, I was just a New Yorker in paradise: "Oh gosh, isn't this beautiful!" I knew if I took a picture of that, it wouldn't have a deeper perception of the land. So, what I did was just live there without taking pictures of it for two years – just walking on the land, cross-country skiing on it, seeing it in different light until I felt I was at a point where I had something to communicate about it other than its beauty.

And that led to a decade of doing landscape work.
Yes. At some point in the middle of the 1980s, for me the last essential formal question arose, or returned. Sometimes I would come across a photograph that had a convincing illusion of three-dimensional space.

What does that mean "a convincing illusion of three-dimensional space"?
I use those words because I understand I'm looking at a flat piece of paper. So, it is an illusion; I'm not looking through a little window at a miniature world. I say "illusion" because it is an illusion.

And yet nobody actually mistakes a photograph for a window. They don't mistake flatness for depth, so what does "convincing illusion" really mean here?
I'm convinced there are some pictures that feel three-dimensional. One question that really began to preoccupy me was how it is that some photographs give you a convincing illusion of three-dimensional space. I tried to work on that in formal terms.

That's a challenge in the Montana landscape.
Exactly. An open space is not differentiated like an intersection. That became a real challenge: how to articulate three-dimensionality in a photograph of that kind of landscape. It's difficult to explain, so here's an analogy: I love the movie *The Departed*. I've seen it four or five

times. Recently, I've been focusing on Mark Wahlberg's performance. He's not one of the three main actors [Jack Nicholson, Matt Damon, and Leonardo DiCaprio]. I watch Mark Wahlberg, and I begin to forget this is Mark Wahlberg. There is something magical about him. He is almost physically transformed.

Yes, he's reminiscent there of what used to be called a "character actor" – not a star performance, but one that adds to the "reality effect" of the milieu in which the "stars" operate. Although, Wahlberg usually is a star.
You get so involved, you don't see him as an actor. You've crossed into this other world. Coming back to photography, sometimes you buy into the illusion. Every now and again, you see a photograph where that illusion is really strong. In the seventies, I tried to work on it structurally. How does one little compositional detail – perhaps a post or a curb meeting the edge of the frame, or a telegraph pole – how do these things change the perception of space?

The strange thing about the illusion of transparency is that the more successful it is, the more disarming it is, which leads the viewer to reflect upon the illusion and, thus, it ceases being an illusion. I have this feeling really strongly when I look at your picture of the green car (p. 242). It's the most illusory photograph I've ever seen. It's quite unnerving. But that feeling produces an attention, a scrutiny of the image that undercuts the illusion. I'm brought up to its surface as a flat picture. It's too good.
Are you saying you can't win?

Yes, the more successful the illusion...
...the more you are aware of it being an illusion.

With that picture, I'm guessing, the illusion is not just a result of formal and technical qualities, like the light and focus being different in the background while the greens are continuous. It might also have to do with the repose of the car in that quiet social setting and what that might mean for me as a viewer. Often when photographers want to see what the world will

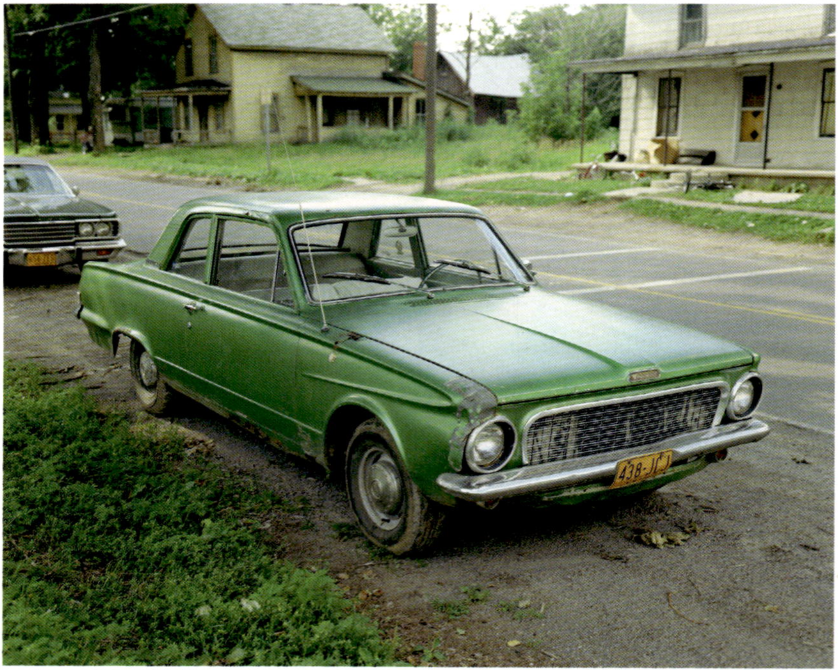

Stephen Shore, Natural Bridge, New York, July 31, 1974;
from the series "Uncommon Places"

look like as a picture, they close one eye. But if you want to see what a picture might look like as a three-dimensional world, you can do the same. Look at it with one eye and let your brain fill in what's missing. That picture needs to be reproduced well. Interestingly, some photographs are difficult to reproduce well, but that one always seems to reproduce well. I think there's another aspect to this, and it gets to what I was working on in the 1980s in the landscape pictures. It has to do with the state of mind and perception of the photographer. Let's say a person has spent a decade mastering the formal tools; that's not all that difficult. But then the photographer's perception of the scene obviously influences their photographic decisions. If I have become highly attuned to the three-dimensionality of space, I'm going to make slightly different decisions. It sounds almost tautological, but it's true. And then what if a photographer is feeling the silence or stillness of a place? Maybe that affects the decisions also. It's not like I am consciously figuring it out; it's almost inevitable that it will come into the picture.

It's interesting, your mentioning sound and silence. All photographs are mute, but I think of you as a silent photographer. Your photographs don't appear to be cutting off any sound. It's not just that you are photographing quiet places; it's to do with what you are seeing, your perception of the place, and how that translates into a photograph. I look at Winogrand's work, and I often think of the noise that must have been around him. It's not just that he photographs in noisy places; it's to do with how he photographs. One can make a quiet photograph in a busy street.
Most of my pictures are made in a state of mind where there is some centre of quietness. I'm not tuning out the sound, but I'm hearing it in a place within me that is quiet. I'm quiet inside.

If photography for you is a matter of moving through a series of problems, what would be "mature work"? If extraordinary standards can be reached very early in life, what is the kind of photography that you now feel could only be made at the age you are now?
That's a fascinating question. I want to go back to the matter of three-dimensional space because it will lead me to answering you. You asked me a while back how I give a feeling of depth in a picture when all there is before me is a field of grass. It's one thing to do that at an intersection of two roads, where I have one-point perspective and curbs and telephone wire all delineating space. It's quite another to do it in a field of grass or the Texas desert. Can I do it? That was the question I was working on in the second half of the 1980s, and I felt like I answered it. I think now I can speak as a sixty-six-year-old man who started photography literally sixty years ago. I feel there are different levels of mastery. First, there is technical mastery, which doesn't mean how to set f-stops but is about understanding the meaning of technical decisions. In photography that can come quite easily, I think – more easily than almost any other medium. Then I found

there was a process of formal mastery, and for me that arrived when certain formal questions stopped arising. That came at the end of the 1970s. Then in the 1980s, I'd say I was involved in a kind of psychological mastery. I remember reading a Chinese story called *Prince Hui's Cook*. The Prince marvels at the easy way his cook is butchering a piece of meat. He asks the butcher how he does it. The butcher tells him, "An ordinary cook hacks at the meat and has to change his blade once a month. A good cook slices the meat and changes his blade once a year. But I cut with my mind. I find interstices and simply insert the blade there. I have had this blade for twenty years, and I've never had to sharpen it". I remember reading this and thinking, Oh, that's just a kind of precious Chinese wisdom, and I forgot about it. And then in the eighties, as I'm working on this issue of space in the picture, this came back to me. I realized that's what I'm aiming for. After all the controls – the physical and structural controls have been dealt with – what I'm doing is changing my mind. The way I create depth in a landscape picture with no formal elements that seem to allow it, really is, for me, to have a three-dimensional mental image and trust that I've had enough experience as a photographer that I will make very slight decisions that will put that into play. I don't try for it; all I'm doing is changing my mind, altering my perception. I'm not saying that alone is doing it, but that along with years of practice, technical and formal. In most sports coaching at a professional level, imagining is used. A basketball player is taught to imagine the ball going in the basket, and the reason is that to shoot from the foul line, muscles are used from the toes to the fingertips, and you cannot consciously control every muscular activity. But if you practice a couple of hours a day, five days a week, and have natural talent, maybe you could do it 60 percent of the time. In the imagining, you build up a muscular knowledge, muscular memory. Your muscles know if the throw feels right. The imagining becomes the coordinating factor. I'm proposing that something similar can happen in photography if you've mastered the technical craft and the structural craft.

Are the things that you photograph a consequence of the pictorial problems that you decide to put before yourself?
Yes. And at a certain point I thought, Okay, I want to go to a place that's more extreme. So, I picked west Texas and Scotland because I

wanted places with no trees. I felt I'd hit on a way of controlling the medium in a very subtle way, but for me to really practice and hone this mental craft I had to go to a place where I have almost nothing to work with. I'd been to these Texas landscapes in 1975, and they made an impression on me. I'm not picking places just for formal reasons, because those reasons can't be separated from your feeling for the place. I was *connecting* with those landscapes, feeling what it was like to be there. Scotland… I don't know how that happened. I wanted open land that was lush, not dry, and I'd never been there. I looked at a topographic map and picked a place in the highlands. I lucked out and spent a good month there. It was just what I wanted. I found it emotionally a very strong place. For *years* I had dreams of those landscapes of Scotland. The place has to mean something to me on a level beyond the formal.

That's quite an extreme motivation. What does the beholder of your Scottish pictures feel?
Well, they don't know my feelings or motivations.

You don't set things up, so on one level the observed world remains primary for you. By contrast, a photographer like Jeff Wall may also be setting himself pictorial problems but is also setting up a scene in order to solve them. When people look at your photographs, they don't necessarily know that the subject has been chosen in an attempt to work through a mental or formal problem you have set for yourself; they may just see a highly descriptive image of a place or thing – organized as a picture, certainly – but the subject matter is forcefully there in front of them, just as it was in front of you. It's a world the viewer may not have visited, but your pictures invite them to visit it imaginatively. This relates to the documentary dimension of the medium, which you accept. Your pictures don't fight photography's worldly description at all. Can we ever know how our pictures are viewed? I can see Walker Evans was a pictorial problem solver. I can also see he was interested in making statements about America in the 1930s.
Right. If I think back to the seventies, when I'm attempting to gain formal mastery, whenever I had a question in mind, I explored it not

just in my work but in looking at other people's work – by doing it and by studying the past work of others, including Evans. I was looking at how conscious photographers of the past had dealt with the same issues. I felt I was apprenticing myself to a tradition, a tradition that may have started with – oh, I don't know – George Washington Wilson via Francis Frith and Timothy O'Sullivan, Carleton Watkins, and Charles Marville and Atget, and obviously Evans. It was particularly people who used the view camera. There were others who I felt had consciously dealt with these problems. They were leaving traces for me to learn from.

In that tradition those photographers are not only rising to pictorial challenges, they are also trying to communicate things, often very subtle things, about their world.
Yes. I think both can happen at the same time. Maybe they *have* to happen at the same time. The formal decisions have to grow out of what you want to show. Otherwise, it feels as if there's a structure imposed on what is shown, overlaid on the world, in such a way that it loses the transparency and becomes only about the "composition". But two of the essential problems or challenges that this tradition is dealing with are "What do you want to show of the world?" and "What formal means do you have in order to resolve that?" I flew three thousand miles to rural Scotland so I can be on that open land, but I'm going to a place that presents the physical situation for me to work in. It's not that I'm imposing something on the place; I'm going to a place where the problem is inherent in the place itself.

That's very neatly put! How did you end up photographing in Yucatan?
It was another place that had meaning for me. I had been there a number of times before and had strong memories of it. I was also interested in it because of a sense of a traditional culture in a land that is finely balanced in terms of natural forces – the climate, the geology. A few centimetres more of rain or a few more hours of sunshine leads to very different vegetation patterns and, therefore, a different way of life. Other places are irrigated and have a very different feeling. I was taking what I'd learned about the control of space while also being sensitive to the meaningfulness of a place – the culture, the patterns of land use.

That's also there in your work in Luzzara.
It is. Although it may be regarded in Western terms as a more sophisticated culture than that of the Yucatan, it's still traditional in many ways. I'm photographing people going down to the river, for example.

In 2001 you made a series of panoramic street photographs in New York. It was quite a big jump from what you'd been doing before. What was the challenge there?
Well, in the landscape work I'd had this idea of honing a mental craft. I felt I'd really been able to put that into play in a number of series. And when I finished that, around 1991, I realized I'd spent twenty years working only in colour. I was looking for a new way forward, and a couple of things came together. I'd been teaching for a decade nearly, and that included teaching black-and-white printing. In explaining it to students, I'd become a much better black-and-white printer than I'd ever been in the 1960s. I got really pretty good. Back in 1971, the only people using colour, it seemed, were myself, William Eggleston, William Christenberry, Joel Meyerowitz, Luigi Ghirri, and a handful of others. The art photographic world was black and white. By 1991, *nobody* was working in black and white anymore, and so I thought, What's this? This is another convention. Colour has become a convention.
So, I decided that for the next decade I would work in black and white.

It was as clear-cut as that?
Yes. It was that clear-cut.

Can you see in black and white, the way Lee Friedlander seems to be able to see in black and white?
Yes. I couldn't now, but at the time I could get right into it. Anyway, the black-and-white New York pictures came at the end of that period. But also, I was never really able to come to grips with New York street photography for myself. Garry Winogrand has always been one of my favorite photographers. I don't have a lot of work hanging in my home, and none of my own pictures, but the photographer [whose work] I have the most of is Winogrand. I have the park bench photograph [*World's Fair*, 1964], which I look at all the time. He and I were friends, but his was just another world, not the world I dealt with. I had done some photographs of archaeological digs in the 1990s, and one of the projects

was in Italy on the Adriatic coast. I went there with Guido Guidi. We were both using Deardorff 8-by-10 cameras. Guido gave me a present, which was a wooden slide that popped into the back of the Deardorff, and it covers up half the frame. You can take two 4-by-10 pictures on one piece of 8-by-10 film. I had this for a couple of years and didn't know what to do with it, but it was in the back of my mind. And then at Bard College, we got a new Hewlett Packard digital printer – this was the late 1990s – and you could print on a 44-inch roll paper, any length you like. I thought, Okay, what if I make 4-by-10 negatives and printed them with this digital printer? What could I do? The first thing I did was photograph the trunk of a tree. But I thought this was so stupid, so obvious. Then I realized that because the diagonal measurement of 4-by-10 is a lot smaller than an 8-by-10, the normal lens is smaller. I could put a 180 mm lens on my 8-by-10, and the image would cover the film area and have more depth of field. Through my darkroom alchemy, I had found a better way of pushing film development. One Kodak developer, HC110, decreased in contrast the more dilute you used it; this allowed me to push the film and keep the contrast normal. The problem of shooting 8-by-10 in the street is the small depth of field and the low shutter speed. Even in bright sunlight with 400 ISO film, you need to be shooting at least a 250th. But I could shoot in sunlight and push the film to 1600 ISO and shoot at a 400th or a 500th, and with the shorter lens I could get a good depth of field and stop the action.

But the problem is how to actually shoot the pictures, no?
Exactly. So, what I was trying to do was the most complicated photograph under those conditions: how do I take Winogrand-esque street pictures with an 8-by-10, without being able to look through the camera and refocus?!? It's a ridiculous challenge, really, to make charged New York street pictures that way. But the crux of it was a belief that I can set up a camera on 57th [Street] and 5th [Avenue] or 77nd and Broadway, focus on empty space, and wait.

It's New York. Something is bound to happen. You can lock the camera off on a tripod, preset your focus...
Things always happen in New York. You don't have to notice something and then quickly whip out your Leica. If you stand in one spot and wait, something will happen.

That's a little like Walker Evans's series *Labor Anonymous* (1946), where he waits with his Rolleiflex on a street corner in Detroit. But you are sensing that if you can do it, you'll be catching a kind of photographic seeing we've not seen before – 2.5:1 proportion street photograph with all the detail of a large format negative. What was the success rate with this work? How many exposures did you make for every good one?
The success rate was pretty good, but there was a lot of waiting time – a lot of time *not* shooting, not seeing anything I wanted. Although I wasn't able to look through the camera while shooting, I had a good idea of the framing. I would mark off in my mind the area out there in the space before me that would be in focus.

Is that how you made the picture from *Uncommon Places* of the woman in green coming down the street?
Yes. As she was coming towards me, I knew I had to shoot when she reached the spot on the ground on which I had pre-focused. That wasn't such a technical challenge; she was not that close and the depth of field was small.

In New York, you were able to catch those figures just coming into or leaving the frame. I think of those New York street photos as your first shutter pictures. By that I mean the shutter is not just determining the correct exposure, it's producing the pictorial effect: arrested motion.
With colour film I always overexpose it. It's just essential. So, I'm working at 100 ISO. If I'm photographing baseball, there are only certain times I can take my shot. For a fraction of a second, Graig Nettles is poised, almost still, as he waits for the ball to be delivered. I can take a fifteenth of a second exposure right then, and it is absolutely crisp. Now, going to black and white, there's a two-stop difference, and when you're at the margins of what you can technically do, two stops is a lot. When I went to Italy, I found I could photograph people. And as long as they don't move forward and backward, out of the focus range, I can photograph much more freely. I wasn't freezing action in the Winogrand sense, but I felt that in Italy the shutter was, as you say, beginning to come into play in a different way. I was looking for real moments of expression, fleeting moments, and trying to capture them. I remember

while I was making one of the New York pictures, a policeman came up to me and said, "Are you a photographer?" I'm standing there with an 8-by-10! I said, "Yes". He said, "I'm a photographer, too. That's an 8-by-10; I use a 4-by-5". So, we start a conversation while I'm still keeping an eye out for people going by. I take a few pictures while we're talking. Eventually, he asks my name and I tell him. He says, "I know your work. I have one of your books. I show it to my family, and they think your pictures are boring. But I tell them they don't understand!" [laughs] In the frame there was a car illegally parked on 57th Street, but it was a structural part of the picture. The driver was just about to pull out, and the policeman said, "Do you want me to stop him?".

Oh, that's enough to restore one's faith in humanity. And in art, too! How civilized life would be if we all understood how photographs were made! [laughs]
So far, we haven't really discussed scale. The size of photographs seems to have become such a dominant way that people understand the medium now. Were the New York street pictures the first big ones that you made?
Yes, the final prints are about 3-by-8 feet. Eventually, digital silver printing was developed and I didn't have to use the inkjet printer. They are selenium toned and much sharper edge-to-edge than a print made with an enlarger. Really beautiful prints. Around the time I was making these, I was also showing my landscape work at 35-by-40, up to 46. They were large for me but not large by the standards of the Germans, for example! [Andreas Gursky and Thomas Ruff, among others].

Were the New York pictures conceived to be that 3-by-8 feet? What I mean by that is, were you envisioning a final size while shooting, knowing what it would be for a viewer to stand in front of them?
Yes.

It's interesting that, while a painter doesn't paint a painting and then decide what size it's going to be, a photographer can face the question of scale a long time after taking the photo. Scale is intrinsic to painting but not to photography in the same way. Several commentators, including Michael Fried and Jean-François

Chevrier, noted a change in the late 1970s, when some photographers really did begin to conceive their work at a particular large size. Think, for example, of Jeff Wall's interest in what he calls "life scale". Wall has suggested that classical street photographers like Cartier-Bresson, Robert Frank, and Winogrand had internalized the printed page as their preferred size and that their work often looks grotesque when it is blown up larger than that; the cutoff figures and the looming foregrounds don't work at a large scale. Certain photographers, for example, William Klein, have blown up their street photos for decades, but in order to invoke the public poster, not the fine art tableau. It's as if the whole pictorial adventure of classic street photography took place within a white border no larger than 16-by-20 inches and even with 8-by-10 inches. And, of course, most of those photographers either worked for magazines or wanted to make books; exhibiting on the gallery wall was often quite secondary. But this whole question is much more complicated in your work.
I'd agree with all that. I've never been happy with the reproductions of my New York street photographs precisely because they were conceived at a different scale. They become so different when they're reproduced. The prints of *American Surfaces* were at that small drugstore-print size.

There is an absolutely incomprehensible amount of detail in an 8-by-10 negative.
That's true. In fact, there is so much detail that it can't be seen in a contact print. The prints I've been making recently are 20-by-24. There's no loss of sharpness, and an expansion of detail. There is probably some point where the detail stops expanding and the sharpness begins to decrease. When I started doing landscapes in Montana, I'd see a row of cattle go by in the far distance. You can barely see this, even in a 20-by-24 print. It may be a size of roughly 36-by-48 where you can see all that detail with no loss of sharpness.

I presume you get more on an 8-by-10 negative that you could ever have seen at the time of shooting. It's a kind of hypervision. As a result, the photographs become worlds unto themselves. It's nobody's intention, but it just comes with the procedure. The photographer has organized the frame, but the wealth

of material goes beyond that, in what might be quite a radical and unsettling way, no?
There are different degrees, or different kinds, of conscious awareness. I could look at you now and see the pattern of books behind you; I could take a picture and not be surprised by the books. But if I were asked to draw what I see, I would have to look at each and every book individually. The same thing can happen if I look at a tree or a street.

But by the same token, you could be surprised or, more exactly, you could not rule out the possibility of being surprised by what you find in the negative or print.
I could not rule out that possibility, and occasionally I am surprised. But I think that attention is a faculty that can be exercised. I used to spend a while with an 8-by-10, just looking at the scene in front of me.

Trying to imagine how the camera will see it.
Yes, I'd be trying to make a mental note while looking through the scene. After a while, that process starts going faster as I'm developing that faculty of attention.

It can start to become kind of godlike – gargantuan feats of attention. Are there limits to this?
It's not godlike, and there are limits. As you feel your faculty of attention developing, you realize you can really notice a lot and maybe not in specific detail. I understood early on that the 8-by-10 camera bore a particularly strange relation to time. It was the time of a certain kind of experience, which is, I think, what you're getting at. I could stand in front of a scene, and for me to notice everything I'd be photographing could take several minutes. Then I see the pictures, and it's as if that time of experience has been compressed and I can take it all in, in a few seconds.

Do you think there are modes of attention that are appropriate to different cameras?
Absolutely.

Can they be transgressed?
Well, I don't know. "Trangressed" is a moral judgment.

I didn't mean it that way. If one says there is a mode of attention "appropriate" to a specific camera, it implies there might be inappropriate ones.
Oh, I see.

Arguably, your 8-by-10 New York street shots transgress the way an 8-by-10 camera is usually used; you were exploring a different mode of attention there and facilitating a different mode of attention for the viewer. At the other extreme, are we getting to a point now with digital cameras where the amount of capture – or perhaps the ability to shoot in low light with a very small and mobile camera – is breaking down those older distinctions between different modes of attention? What happens when a digital "snapshot" begins to have the amount of detail we associate with a 4-by-5 but with all the lightness and flexibility of a compact machine? It won't be long before that's possible.
Well, it's happening already to some extent. In terms of appropriate attention: when you said that, I thought about Garry Winogrand *World's Fair* of 1964 and the print of it I have hanging in my home. I've had that picture for maybe thirty-five years. It seems to me an Olympic feat to be able to pay attention to seven or eight people at once. I'm also convinced that he was not really paying attention to the background. If you look at the picture, there's a sense of collaging, in a way. There are people on the bench, and then there's an out-of-focus woman walking in the background. That sense of collaging, I believe, comes from one part of a picture resonating off all the decisions a photographer makes – the framing, the timing, the angle. It locks gears with it. And then another part of the picture is unconscious. Here, it's the background and it's not locking gears. So, Winogrand has a different kind of attention than an 8-by-10 photographer. With an 8-by-10, you generally have the time to exercise attention in a way Winogrand could not. So, if I was photographing that park bench, I would have noticed what was behind. But I wouldn't be able to have that extraordinary feat that Winogrand achieved of watching each of those people at once; that kind of attention is amazing but appropriate to his kind of photography. I believe he learned a way of speeding his mind up. You know when you're in an auto accident and everything seems to be going in slow motion?

Your senses are suddenly heightened.
Exactly, and there is also a sense of inevitability. You see what is happening and what is going to happen. Think about what it would be if you could put yourself in that frame of mind, photographing on the street. I think Winogrand could see like that when he was photographing; he could see in slow motion.

He had the time to see all those little micro-events coinciding.
And he lifts the camera and takes the picture.

There's chance, too.
Oh, there has to be a lot of chance! It's the being alert to chance that really matters. I guess my 8-by-10 street work was trying to get at a little of both modes of attention – the slowness and the quickness in one.

This way of thinking about photography interests me because it is very physiological; it hinges on not just eyes and brains but a whole musculature and nervous system. It's particularly heightened in Winogrand's street photography, but all photography and all modes of attention have a physiology. I wonder if this itself has a bearing on what we were saying about the short creative life of so many photographers. I remember seeing a documentary in which Robert Frank was asked what it was like shooting for his book *The Americans*. He sighed and said, "Well... I was in really good shape back then". So honest. It was a very physical understanding. That kind of work, that kind of attention, is heroic. It's exhausting, and few photographers manage to sustain it beyond a few years. We just can't see, and react to what we see, the way we did when we were young. Few people can. Do you feel that?
When you say "can't see the way we did", do you mean physiologically or conceptually?

I mean physiologically.
I find I can see more now than I could in my youth.

Your eye is just as "hungry"?
I'm not sure about hungry, but I think that years spent working out a

picture with an 8-by-10 – where if I want to see it from a different angle, I have to physically lift up the camera and put it down somewhere else – if you do this hundreds and hundreds of times for years, it starts coming faster. You get better at making mental notes of everything you are seeing.

Yes, but it's not reactive shutter photography; you have time to train your vision. It's interesting that many photographers extended their creative lives by moving from 35 mm shutter photography, rapid hunter photography, to the slower stalking of the 4-by-5 and 8-by-10.
I agree. As I get older, even the physical effort of using the 8-by-10 camera gets harder, but the decision making gets easier because I've been doing it for so long. In terms of the exercising of my attention, I feel no diminishment of my faculties – quite the opposite.

It seems that around 1990, with twenty years or so of work behind you, you began to move faster from one pictorial challenge to the next. The bodies of work since then have become more defined from the outset, they are made over shorter periods of time, and you move to the next challenge with more confident purpose. Has that been the case?
I would say that's true. It comes back a little to what we were discussing earlier: about coming into photography at a point where it has an established history and noticing how so many intense, creative lives in photography had been very short. I knew I wanted a long life in photography. I wasn't simply interested in documenting America; I was also interested in learning and understanding photography and perception.

A photographer may change as they get older, but so does the medium, either through technical innovation or through shifts in wider attitudes toward what is significant about it.
There are four things that are changing: the photographer is changing, the technology is changing, attitudes are changing, and the subject matter, the *world*, is changing. My students may not realize that, because they're only eighteen years old. But the world I knew forty, fifty years ago has changed enormously, in all four ways.

You seem quite acutely aware of all four of those factors, but it is possible for a photographer to be unaware of at least three of them. Back in Timothy O'Sullivan's day, the medium really had no history, and those factors were barely on the table yet.
Right, he couldn't think about his creative life span in the same context as us.

And he probably wouldn't have even understood "creativity" in the same way. When we get to Walker Evans' moment, he very much is a photographer who is aware of the rich history of his medium – maybe one of the first to really work with that knowledge. And he senses that what interests him are either the photographers who worked without creativity as a conscious motivation or those who tried to restrain their creativity, to not impose it too heavily upon what they were photographing – style-less-ness, or "the documentary style". But in that restraint, there is an attempt to let the dominant factor of change be the world itself. I know there were moments when he was at the edge of what was technically possible – for example, when he made his New York subway photos around 1938 with the fastest film and the fastest lens commonly available, and again at the other end of his career when he used the then-new Polaroid SX-70. But in general, and certainly in that creative hot streak, his equipment and approach were very straightforward and familiar; it's the subject matter, his world, that was not.
It's the photographer's temperament that keeps the four factors in whatever balance they are.

What is it that brings a body of work to a conclusion? Do you always know when you have finished and what was successful?
It varies with the project. I was interested in archaeology in the 1990s; it wasn't that I was interested in archaeological photography. For several years I subscribed to a number of archaeological magazines – read them cover to cover. I wanted to get on digs, which wasn't always easy, as I was not helping. They were doing me a favour, letting me wander around. I went on three digs and made some photographs. I didn't reach the point where I was repeating myself, and I didn't repeat myself in the New York street pictures.

So, do you find your interest now falls away as you are beginning to sense that you have met the challenge, rather than having to repeat in order to discover that you've done all you can?
I'd say so, yes.

Is there a sense in which successful photographs are often metaphors for photography, for the photographic procedure? Put another way, is there a sense in which one can be attracted to a subject matter because of its particular resonance with the medium? For example, a photographer might be interested in archaeology because the subject matter – digging in the ground and revealing a fragment – has some kind of affinity with photography itself, understood as a medium of fragmentary traces of the past, fragments that cannot explain themselves? Likewise, an intersection might be appealing because photography is always at an intersection, a situation in which not all directions can be taken and a choice has to be made.
Well, when I was on the archaeological digs, there was also a site photographer because photographs are all they have; as they dig, the archaeologists are destroying. There are certain artifacts they can keep, but the record they have is made up of precise drawings and photographs. I would watch the archaeological photographer take a picture, then pick up a 10-inch brush and back out of the site, wiping away his footprints as he went. When I was looking, I loved the way objects appeared to be emerging from the earth, but at the same time I could recognize this was an archeological dig and these things were not on their own emerging from the earth; they were being uncovered in a particular context.
What you say about intersections being consonant with photography is also interesting. I guess I didn't think about it like that. Maybe the fragmentary nature of photography is so inherent that it can be consonant with *any* motif in the experience of the modern world. But I would say that I have seen my interest in motifs and subject matter change. In the seventies, I wanted to explore American culture. I would even dress the part of an explorer with a jumpsuit, like an astronaut. One year I dressed at Abercrombie & Fitch [which was, back then, a safari outfitter]. It was my country, but I was an explorer in it.

And at that point, you start to feel you are exploring photography as much as exploring America. But once the formal takes over and subject matter is merely the means to an end, does the whole process become too dry and boring? When photography is only photography, it isn't even photography.
Right! That's the point at which those particular formal questions stop arising. But as a result of that experience, when I then began to explore other things – from the 1980s onwards – I did have a different relation to subject matter. From then on, subject and form were explored much more in unison.

You've been teaching for three decades, and you have been a very open-minded teacher.
To lead each student to find their own voice, it meant that I had to think like each of them. It wouldn't do them any good to get them all to make work the way I had been making work. So, teaching really involves imagining you are the student and thinking what might be the next thing they should do. This led me, in a class of ten people, to think like ten different photographers. I wound up seeing more photographic possibilities. I think that in some way this led me to begin to make print-on-demand books and – eventually to making eighty-three of those books. I would see something that I wouldn't be interested in devoting a year to but *would* be interested in devoting a day to. The books allowed me to do that.

You started with these in 2003.
Yes, and I made print-on-demand books over a period of five years. There were a number of different series of these books. Each is shot in a day and shot with a book in mind. I was shooting on a compact digital camera – although a couple at the beginning were on a more high-end camera, and there's a book using postcards of civic architecture I had collected in the late sixties and seventies, and there's one that's all text, called *Heavy Metal Alphabet*, with the names of heavy metal bands in alphabetical order, one page for each letter. But mostly the books are image sequences.

Although print-on-demand books are technologically new, did you feel this work was a return to a certain kind of thinking

you were doing in the sixties and seventies – a return to vernacular image forms and conceptual frameworks, but under new terms?
Yes, or at least some of them. Some were fairly rigid conceptual sequences – for example, walking along a path and taking a picture every ten meters. Two of the books combined pictures and text. Two series were based on trees. One was the marula tree: its leaves, its fruit, its bark. Marula is the favorite food of elephants, and it's believed they may even get high on it. There are pictures of elephants eating the marula, a page of text describing the tree, photos of a curd made from it called amarula. Another book is called *The Firewood Tree*. It's the favourite food of giraffes and has medicinal uses and burns for a long time. But this book is entirely fictional; there's no truth to it at all. The text is fabricated.

Your work before this seems to have been motivated by parameters. When you come to the print-on-demand books, although there are fewer parameters, it seems you're saying to yourself, "Okay, anything is possible with this book format?"
Well, since these are book-based projects, the limits are really various parameters of the sequence. For a while I would commit to making a book on each day that *The New York Times* had ran a six-column banner headline, which would be a major news day: George Bush re-elected President, Hurricane Katrina wipes out New Orleans. On those days I would do a book and it would be like a time capsule. Other books are based on places as I was traveling to. Some are connected visually. Some are cultural, like the one of a flea market in Vienna, where each picture contains an image that feels typically Austrian or Germanic-Austrian. There are all different kinds of ways of organizing pictures as sequences.

Can I ask you a broader question about how the world of photography has changed around you? You talked earlier about being just one of a few isolated individuals making colour work in the 1970s. Then, after a decade or so, there is a lot of wider interest in photography and in that work in particular. So, while you're moving forward – changing how you do things, exploring photography, meeting new challenges – there is a broader

discovery of your archive. I imagine you found yourself being a contemporary artist and also a "figure from the past".
Just this past week, I read somewhere a reference to the 1970s as a "golden age" of photography. I'd never thought of it like that.

To some extent, I feel it was. There has been more than one golden age, but I think that, artistically, a number of doors had opened for photography during the 1960s. Also today's art market did not exist, which overinflates not just prices but reputations and critical standings; determines the consensus; ignores what buyers don't like or understand; and forces a slow and incremental development that does not allow for the great leaps that photographers are able to make. So, it was a very free time for photography. Several photographers covered huge artistic ground in relative obscurity and in a short period of time: Robert Cumming, Robert Heinecken, John Divola, Les Krims, William Eggleston, John Baldessari, yourself. Even at the tail end of the 1970s – think of the ground covered by Cindy Sherman. She mapped out everything for herself in just a few years. Photography was available technically and artistically in ways that it hadn't been before. There is also a "golden era" understood in broader ways – simply to do with life in America then. I was showing the book of *Uncommon Places* to a friend, and he was fascinated by the period details. He named all the vehicles, looked at what was on at cinemas, looked at prices of things in shop windows. He wondered if you had a thing for MGB cars or whether there were a lot of them in America at that time.
They do recur in my pictures! By coincidence, in 1980 my wife bought one.

I'm sure there is an appeal of those pictures that is now to do with their social-historical content.
I do run into people who talk about those pictures as nostalgic. But at the time, they would have looked at them and thought, Why would he photograph all *this*? It's just what the world looks like!
But I would say there was a consciousness about how pictures change in time, which I had learned from Walker Evans. A car functions very specifically in a photograph because cars change faster than buildings.

A building can be five hundred years old, but a car isn't going to be more than five or ten years old. Although, occasionally, Evans would photograph a particularly old car. Still, if you have a line of cars on a street, it gives the photograph a particular time frame: cars are seeds of time.

I feel that way about your print-on-demand books. The self-imposed restriction of making each book in a day makes you acutely aware of time and the present.
One of my favourites of those books has my son holding an iPod in his hand. It has a gas station with a sign for the price of milk. It has a movie theatre, so you can see which movie is playing. I'm doing this because I'm thinking about how this cultural information is going to be viewed maybe fifty years hence.

That's funny. When I was a student about two decades ago, I got a computer floppy disk and on the paper label I wrote "Notes for Lasting World Peace and Understanding". I threw it onto the sidewalk, let people walk all over it, and then photographed it on 4-by-5.
[Laughs] World peace in format we can no longer read!

Right, but at the time I wasn't thinking that even the 4-by-5 film would also be an historical relic!
About three weeks ago, there was a very funny cover of *The New Yorker* that was a reference to the disastrous launch of Obama Care. Obama is holding a huge, early 1990s cell phone, standing next to a CRT computer monitor. An assistant is about to load a floppy disk of the Obama Care programme as they stand there with their fingers crossed!

What's next for you, Stephen?
I've no idea.

Has that always been the way?
No. I've just finished a project in the Ukraine. My wife had come across a foundation that helps give financial support to Holocaust survivors in Eastern Europe. She started making donations. I did, too. We got sent pictures of stories about these people who had escaped

execution by fleeing east. So, they had all done something to survive seventy years ago that was really heroic. Today, these people have fallen through the cracks because if they had been sent to Auschwitz or another camp, they'd be entitled to reparations from the German government. But because they were a little too far east, they live off what their own countries give them, which varies depending on the country. So, this foundation was set up to help them. These people are now in their mid-eighties to mid-nineties. My wife said this would be an interesting subject to photograph. So, I went. The foundation is in various countries – Moldova, Ukraine, Belarus, Lithuania – but I ended up photographing only in the Ukraine. My paternal grandfather emigrated from the Ukraine in the 1890s, and I knew which region he was from. So, there was some connection and I needed to start somewhere. I've been reading a lot about the region. I've found the people fascinating and admirable. And this is a life that in five years might not be possible to document. The foundation supports fifteen hundred people today, but in five years that might only be ten or twenty.

What have you been trying to do photographically?
A number of things. I was very aware that I'd never photographed anything that had a really strong emotional resonance. People have feelings about gas stations but not the way they have feelings about the Holocaust. I didn't get drawn into this project for aesthetic or formal reasons, obviously, but if there has been a formal problem on my mind, it is how to take a picture of a subject matter that is so emotionally charged but not have the pictures be illustrations – and not let them rest on that emotion. But not have the pictures avoid that content either. Can I communicate some of the emotional power I feel in that country without it simply being a connection to the label "Holocaust"?

I found being in Ukraine a very strong experience, but I didn't know if that was to do with family connections or the history of the place. I read Timothy Snyder's amazing book *Bloodlands*, which is a history of Poland and Eastern Europe from 1930 to around 1950, Stalin to Hitler to Stalin. What Ukraine went through was unbelievable. At the same time, part of the reason Ukraine has had problems is that it has such rich soil – the richest I've ever seen – almost black. Driving through parts of Ukraine is like driving through Iowa; cornfields, sunflower fields are far as you can see. Everyone wanted it. Stalin wanted it to feed all the Soviet Union; Hitler wanted to move the Ukrainians out and move German farmers in.

One can tell oneself why one is attracted to a place, but often it is very unconscious.
It's not easy to explain, this emotional connection to a place. I've had it in Yucatan, in Amarillo, in Scotland – very different places. Ukraine stirred something very different, and I'm hoping the pictures communicate something of that.

It's a brave way to work. In general, you've been attracted to the look and feel of the everyday, the familiar, which you try to render profound and compelling as a picture. In Ukraine, you're dealing not with the everyday but with an exceptional or atypical historical circumstance. The Greeks have two words for time: *chronos* is time as marked by, or organized by, historical events; *kairos* is all the unspecified, undefined bits in between. Generally you've been a photographer of *kairos*. Now you're coming into a relation to *chronos*. So, that's a big shift for you. It's a very different burden placed on the image.
Yes, it is.